Phillips / Polly

Cross Currents
in English Literature
of the 17th Century

By the same Author

THE BACKGROUND OF ENGLISH LITERATURE

ESSAYS AND ADDRESSES

CRITICISM AND CREATION

MILTON AND WORDSWORTH

*

In collaboration with J. C. Smith

A CRITICAL HISTORY OF ENGLISH POETRY

*

In collaboration with Sandys Wason

THE PERSONAL NOTE

*

Chatto & Windus

CROSS CURRENTS IN ENGLISH LITERATURE OF THE XVIITH CENTURY

OR

THE WORLD, THE FLESH & THE SPIRIT, THEIR ACTIONS & REACTIONS

BEING

The Messenger Lectures

ON THE EVOLUTION OF CIVILIZATION

Cornell University

1926–27

By

SIR HERBERT J. C. GRIERSON

LL.D., LITT.D., F.B.A.

Emeritus Professor of Rhetoric and English Literature in the University of Edinburgh

1951

CHATTO & WINDUS

LONDON

PUBLISHED BY
Chatto & Windus
LONDON

★

Clarke, Irwin & Co. Ltd.
TORONTO

FIRST PUBLISHED 1929
SECOND IMPRESSION 1948
THIRD IMPRESSION 1951
PRINTED IN GREAT BRITAIN
ALL RIGHTS RESERVED

IN MEMORIAM

A. O. et F. M. C.

Amabiles et decori in vita sua, in morte quoque non sunt divisi ; aquilis velociores, leonibus fortiores.

Contents

	PREFACE	ix
I.	RENAISSANCE & REFORMATION	1
II.	EDMUND SPENSER	29
III.	THE DRAMA: COMEDY	66
IV.	,, ,, TRAGEDY	96
V.	LOVE-POETRY	130
VI.	HUMANISM & THE CHURCHES	166
VII.	JOHN MILTON: THE MAN & THE POET	232
VIII.	COMMONWEALTH & RESTORATION	274
IX.	JOHN DRYDEN	311
	INDEX	341

PREFACE

A WORD of apology and explanation may be allowed for this book, not for its errors and shortcomings, which must accept the censure they merit, but for my choice of a subject which, it may well be said, lies somewhat outside my proper sphere, *ne sutor supra crepidam*. I am not a philosopher or theologian. The explanation is to be sought in the title of the foundation on which these lectures were delivered at Cornell University. The words 'On the Evolution of Civilization' are, I have learned, taken by the authorities of that University in the widest sense possible, and I might have chosen a more strictly literary theme. To me it seemed, when I received the kind invitation to deliver them, that I ought, if I could, to select for consideration some aspect of the contact between literature and the life and thought of the time, to discuss literature as reflecting the spiritual conflicts of an age, the growing pains (might one hope) of civilisation at a definite epoch: and so I was tempted to try to deal with a conflict which had often attracted my attention when studying the seventeenth century for more purely literary purposes. I thought I might venture to set forth to my sympathetic American audience what I had come to think, viz. that the conflict between the spirit or temper of the Renaissance and that of the Reformation, seen in its full power in the fanaticism of English Puritanism, had affected our literature in a deeper and more complex manner than our histories always made quite clear; that it had, as I thought, limited the range and fullness of Shakespeare's dramatic achievement, taking Shakespeare as the greatest of Elizabethan dramatists (if Ben Jonson is in intention the most serious artistically and morally), so that Shakespeare's tragedy is not quite such a serious and noble thing as Greek tragedy at its greatest, that he has left no play that strikes quite such a high ethical note as the *Ajax*, the *Antigone*, the *Philoctetes*. And if Shakespeare was thus, consciously or unconsciously, confined, limited by the character and ideals of his audience, another result of the same conflict was that the genius of Milton was narrowed, his temper embittered; he was to some extent soured and thwarted. He 'gave up to party what was meant for mankind', so that his great trilogy, epic and dramatic, have not, despite their wonderful art, taken quite the place in the literature of the Spirit of Man that has been by the ages assigned to Virgil and Dante, are not such classics of Humanism.

And that brings me to the second part of my preface. I should like to indicate as clearly as may be the exact sense in which I am using the words 'Humanism' and 'Puritanism', for both are current to-day in a looser and even misleading sense. There is much discussion at the moment of the nature and claims of Humanism as represented by Professor Babbitt, Mr. Paul Elmer More, Mr. Wyndham Lewis, and others. Now, in the controversial use of very general terms it is well to be sure what you and your antagonist have in mind as the opposite of the term you and he are using. When Pope and Wordsworth talk of 'following Nature' they do not mean quite the same thing, for the one is contrasting 'Nature' with the fantastic, the far-fetched,—True Wit with False or Mixed Wit; the other is thinking of the opposite of Nature as the conventional; he is contrasting language which is the 'spontaneous overflow of powerful feeling' with 'pseudo-poetic diction', contrasting personifications 'occasionally prompted by passion' with these used as 'a mechanical device of style, a family language which writers in metre seem to lay claim to by prescription'; and so with Humanism.

Setting aside the narrower meaning which the Oxford *English Dictionary* gives, viz. 'Literary culture: esp. the study of the Greek and Roman classics which came into vogue at the Renaissance', and taking it in the larger sense indicated by the same authority, 'any system of thought or action concerned with merely human interests (as distinguished from the divine)', it is still necessary to distinguish further, for the champions of Humanism I have named are not in the main contrasting Human with Divine things, but are championing the claims of the Human as opposed to the Natural. The opposite they have in view is Naturalism, the doctrine and art of those who, insisting on the animal nature of man, are ready to accept, in the fiction of Mr. T. F. Powys, of Mr. Dreiser and others, Swift's delineation of mankind in the *Voyage to the Houyhnhnms*. That is what Rousseau's return to nature seems to Mr. Babbitt and Mr. Paul Elmer More to have led to. But this is not, of course, the angle from which I am here concerned with Humanism. I am using it more in the sense of the Dictionary as given above. I mean by Humanism a due respect for human nature in all its fullness (therefore including our natural desires and instincts) as distinguished from the claims of the divine, of the other-worldly, religious inhibitions when the latter are exaggerated so as to overshadow the former unduly or entirely, the Humanism instinct in the saying: 'The Sabbath was made for man, and not man for the

PREFACE

Sabbath', which has a wide bearing. And this brings me to Puritanism.

Those who call themselves Puritans to-day are prone to sun themselves in the flattering light of the adjective 'pure', and to constitute themselves censors of sexual offences in life, literature, and art. But this is not, of course, the historical meaning of the word and, in fact, Puritan nations have not been notable for chastity and temperance. The 'purity' which gave its name to the historical Puritans referred not to life but to worship.[1] What distinguished them was an immovable conviction that all worship which had not Scriptural sanction, especially the use (and here the note of passion comes in) of any rite sanctioned by the Roman Catholic Church (*i.e.* by Anti-Christ), was Sin, Idolatry, a thing neither to be practised nor tolerated. This was the spirit which precipitated the Puritan Rebellion, is the root and source of the Protestant fanaticism which has left such an ugly trail through British History in Penal Laws, Popish Plots, Gordon Riots, and of which we hear the echoes still in street sermons and the eloquence of Home Secretaries. That Rome was Anti-Christ was, if not the cardinal doctrine, certainly the most animating conviction of historical Protestantism in Puritan England, Scotland, and New England. If the Anglican Divines, or the best of them, disputed this position, that was

---

[1] Primum et primarium eorum quae arcte tenent et accurate defendunt haec tam invisa capita est Verbum Dei, Prophetarum et Apostolorum scriptis comprehensum, numeris omnibus perfectum esse, eoque a Christo capite Ecclesiae suae traditum, ut eius canon sit et amussis unica in rebus omnibus quae ad religionem cultumve divinum quocunque modo spectant. Ac proinde illicitum esse quicquid in illo cultu eiusque administratione peragitur, nisi eodem nitatur verbo. Adeoque nefas esse Christianorum aliquem ad ullum religionis cultusve actum cogi cuius ratio ex Scripturis reddi nequit aperta.
WILLIAM AMES: *Puritanismus Anglicanus*, 1658.

PREFACE

just a proof that Prelacy and Popery were practically indistinguishable, were alike idolatrous and Anti-Christian, a thing not to be even tolerated. The more positive 'notes' of Puritanism, doctrinal and practical,[1] Salvation by Faith in the Imputed Righteousness of Christ, the condemnation of the drama as such, of all popular amusements, of dancing, of music, were coloured and intensified by this central hatred of Rome, of everything which the Mediaeval Church had sanctioned or condoned, the compromise which, it seemed to them, that Church had made with the World and the Flesh. This is the Puritanism with which I am concerned, a revival of the other-worldly spirit of the Early Church, animated by a hatred as intense as that felt by the Early Church for a persecuting idolatry, but directed now against a great branch of the Christian Church, a persecuting Church indeed, but which they also were persecuting and believed it their duty to persecute: 'Whatever was the cause, laws were made in many countries against Papists which are as bloody as any of those which have been enacted by the Popish Princes and States; and where these laws were not bloody, in my opinion they were worse; as they were slow, cruel outrages on our nature, and kept men alive only to insult in their persons every one of the rights and feelings of our nature' (Burke). It is this hatred which discolours the stream of Puritan poetry in its noblest representatives, in both Spenser and Milton. Of Puritanism in the looser, modern sense of the word the Protestant can boast no monopoly. The true

[1] Si etenim quispiam sit qui scenicis ludis adesse, qui in levioribus negotiis atque colloquiis juramenta fortiter spargere, qui alternando pocula vino semet ingurgitare, qui denique choris, aleae, luxui non audet indulgere, non aliter induitur ei nomen quam Puritani.
WILLIAM AMES: *Puritanismus Anglicanus*, Ad Lectorem, 1658.

PREFACE

Humanist will at times approve himself a Puritan, for he who endeavours to attain the mean must at times hold towards one extreme rather than the other. And the true Humanist will recognise the limits of human nature, recognise the need of some faith that transcends our vision. When in the *Republic* Socrates has finished his vindication of the central position of Humanism, viz. that the sanction of Justice is the constitution of our nature, that no external voice from Sinai has ethical authority if it finds no echo in the human heart, he has to recognise that the sanction of our nature needs some support in faith:

'And yet, I said, no mention has been made of the greatest prizes and rewards of virtue.

'If, he said, there are others greater than these, they must be of an inconceivable greatness.

'Why, I said, what was ever great in a short time? The whole period of three score years and ten is surely but a little thing in comparison with eternity?

'Say rather "nothing", he replied.

'And should an immortal being seriously think of this little space rather than of the whole?

'Yes, he said, I think he should. But what do you mean?

'Are you not aware, I said, that the soul is immortal and imperishable?'

—and so Socrates tells the story of 'Er the son of Armenius, a Pamphylian by birth' who returned to life and 'told what he had seen in the other world'.

H. J. C. Grierson.

CROSS CURRENTS IN ENGLISH LITERATURE OF THE XVIIth CENTURY

CHAPTER I

RENAISSANCE AND REFORMATION

John Foster on the spirit of 'polite literature'—The renewal of an old quarrel—The early Christian Church and Pagan literature—The Renaissance and the Reformation—Montaigne and the Humanist spirit—The revival of the more intransigent Christian temper—The conflict in Elizabethan and later literature.

IN an article written in 1805 John Foster, a sincere Christian of the Evangelical school, and a thoughtful and interesting essayist, surveying polite literature, ancient and modern, comes to the conclusion, and that in no fanatical, but rather a puzzled, deeply troubled, spirit, that 'what is denominated Polite Literature, the grand school in which taste acquires its laws and refined perceptions, and in which are formed, much more than under any higher austerer discipline, the moral sentiments, is, for the far greater part, hostile to the religion of Christ; partly by introducing insensibly a certain order of opinions unconsonant, or at least not identical, with the principles of that religion; and still more, by training the feelings to a habit alien from its spirit. And in this assertion I do not refer to writers palpably irreligious, who have laboured and intended to seduce the passions into vice, or the judgment into the rejection of Divine truth; but to the general community of those elegant and ingenious authors who are read and admired by the Christian world, held essential to a liberal education, and to the progressive accomplishment of the mind in subsequent life, and studied often without an apprehension, or even a thought, of their injuring the views and temper of spirits advancing, with the New Testament for their chief guide, into another world.'[1] It is thus that in the very middle of the second great period in the history of English poetry, the age of Wordsworth and Coleridge, Scott and Byron, Shelley and Keats, was renewed a protest and a quarrel as old as Christianity itself: 'What has Christ to do with Apollo?' What place in a religion, whose concern is not this life but that which lies beyond, is there for a literature or art whose theme is the mingled yarn of human nature, good and evil, wise and foolish, capable of astonishing heroism and of baseness that beggars description, presented at every moment with problems for which an other-worldly morality provides no obvious solution, intent on pleasures and pains, hopes and fears, whose sphere is strictly the world of the senses, here and now, or the future as we forecast it for ourselves or our children on the earth that we tread?

Foster writes as an Evangelical Protestant for whom the Roman Church lies outside the pale. 'I do not for a moment place among these causes' [*i.e.* of the aversion of men of taste to Evangelical Christianity] 'that continual dishonour which the religion of Christ has suffered through the corrupt institutions,

[1] *On the Aversion of Men of Taste to Evangelical Religion* in *Essays, in a Series of Letters*, London, 1823.

and the depraved character of individuals or communities, of what is called the Christian world. Such a man as I have supposed understands what the dictates and tendencies of that religion really are, so far at least that in contemplating the bigotry, persecution, hypocrisy, and worldly ambitions which have been formed as an opprobrious adjunct on Christianity during all ages of its occupancy on earth, his mind dissevers, by a decisive glance of thought, all these evils, and the pretended Christians who are accountable for them, from the religion which is as distinct from them as the Spirit that pervades all things is pure from matter and from sin. In his view these odious things and these wicked men, that have arrogated and defiled the Christian name, sink out of sight through a chasm like Korah, Dathan, and Abiram, and leave the camp and the cause holy, though they leave the numbers small.'[1] But it would be a mistake to treat Foster's condemnation of all polite literature which is not definitely Christian in sentiment as evidence of Protestant or Evangelical narrowness. Foster recognises and appreciates the worth of what he condemns. He admits that despite its non-Christian spirit 'Polite literature will necessarily continue to be a large department of the grand school of intellectual and moral cultivation'. 'It is indispensable to acquire the advantage; it is inevitable to incur the evil.' His own taste in literature was Augustan, an admiration of Pope's versification, and 'the smooth elegance, the gentle graces, the amusing, easy and not deep, current of sentiment of which Addison is our finest example', but he was sensible of the force and fire of the romantic literature of his own day, 'the inevitable accompaniment of the prodigious commotion in the state of the

[1] *Op. cit.*

world', *i.e.* the French Revolution. Nor does Foster's position differ radically from that of a great Catholic such as Cardinal Newman: 'Man's work will savour of man; in his elements and powers excellent and admirable, but prone to error and to sin. Such too will be his literature; it will have the beauty and the fierceness, the sweetness and the rankness of the natural man, and, with all its richness and greatness, will necessarily offend the senses of those who, in the Apostle's words, are really exercised between good and evil. "It is said of the holy Sturmer", says an Oxford writer, "that in passing a horde of unconverted Germans as they were bathing and gambolling in the stream, he was so overpowered by the intolerable scent which arose from them that he nearly fainted away." National literature is, in a parallel way, the untutored movement of the reason, imagination, passions and affections of the natural man, the leapings and friskings, the plungings and the snortings, the sportings and the buffoonings, the clumsy play and the aimless toil, of the noble, lawless savage of God's intellectual creation.'[1] So Newman defines the Christian attitude, if with more humour, also more broadly and discriminatingly, for Newman is thinking of the whole field of a national literature, including what is definitely immoral and irreligious, what is at least non-moral, and what he would admit is good so far as it is in the natural man to be good. He would not, I think, have disputed Foster's position that the spirit even of the best secular polite literature is non-Christian.

No; Foster is but repeating in the spirit of the second puritan movement in England a protest that is as old as Christianity itself, the protest of the early

[1] *The Idea of a University.*

Fathers and innumerable saints against the literature, the drama, and the art of a secular world, a protest which has been renewed at every great revival of the intenser, more intransigent spirit of Christianity. Face to face with the world of Paganism the early Church cut the secular almost clean away, and has never since found it easy to define accurately its relation to the secular, especially in its freer manifestations, the arts. The literature of no other religion, it has been pointed out, is so entirely religious in character as that of Christianity from its first appearance till the emergence of a secular poetry, romantic and erotic, at the end of the twelfth century, followed by the renaissance of the fifteenth century. It contrasts in this respect with the literature of the Old Testament, of India, of Persia, and of Islam. 'The cause is two-fold. On the one hand, the transcendent power of the central Christian truth, which set itself to transform the entire attitude of the human mind to knowledge; on the other hand, the inevitable reaction from the long and exclusive dominion of the secular intelligence.'[1] In the early Church the battle was joined along the whole line. A Christian's only interest in the secular world was the earning of his livelihood. St. Paul was a tentmaker, but no tent of his making has, so far as I know, been preserved as a relic by any branch of the Church. The work by which he earned his living had no religious significance. But the nature of the conflict and all that it involved was obscured by the apparent clearness of the issue as a conflict between Christianity and Paganism. Waging a war of life and death with the obscenity of the ancient panto-

[1] Charles Thomas Cruttwell: *A Literary History of Early Christianity.* Introduction. 1893.

mime and the cruelty of the arena it was not easy for the Christian Church to distinguish between the worse and the better elements in ancient literature, when almost all alike had their roots in that idolatry which it was their mission to replace by a purer, more ethical, spiritual religion. The cause of humanism, a finer humanism, was the cause which the Church was championing. The spirit which breathes in the Gospels, the Acts of the Apostles, and in the less dialectical or polemical portions of St. Paul's Epistles is not the spirit of fanaticism but of a finer humanity. 'So then, brethren, we are debtors, not to live after the flesh; for if ye live after the flesh ye must die; but if by the spirit ye mortify the deeds of the body, ye shall live.'[1] 'Owe no man anything save to love one another; for he that loveth his neighbour hath fulfilled the law. For this, thou shalt not commit adultery, thou shalt not kill, . . . thou shalt not covet, and if there be any other commandment it is summed up in this word, thou shalt love thy neighbour as thyself. Love worketh no ill to his neighbour; love therefore is the fulfilment of the law.'[2] The spirit of humanism in Aeschylus or Euripides or Plato has never spoken in finer accents than that; and it was this spirit, darkened at times by a fiercer fanaticism, which felt it could not afford to make any compromise with the literature and art of paganism. For its task of combating paganism, and penetrating every department of thought and conduct with the ethical influence of the new faith, two or three centuries were perhaps, as has been claimed, not too long; but the result was an attitude towards the free play of the human spirit in art, literature,

---

[1] Romans viii. 12-13, R.V.
[2] Romans xiii. 8-9, R.V.

and most of all the drama, which has produced at times unhappy effects. 'Idolatry', Cyprian declared, 'is the mother of all public amusements.' The puritan, whether Protestant, Anglican or Catholic, has always found it difficult to combat that conviction.

The Church conquered paganism. The deities of Greece and Rome, devils as the early Church came to describe them—and Milton follows the tradition,—faded into the background as symbolic or allegorical figures. The other pagan deities of Celtic or Germanic origin became fairies without losing all their hold on the imagination, forfeiting all faith in the reality of their power. But in conquering paganism the Church, as we know, made many concessions and compromises. Boissier, in *La fin du paganisme*, has shown how the Church found herself unable to dispense with the training of the schools of rhetoric in which ancient literature and pagan mythology were the chief models and sources. For the common people—and in things of the mind one must not exaggerate the difference between the classes—the Church had to make still greater concessions, to supply saints to take the place of local deities, and, above all, to make full allowance for that innate love of gaiety, revelry, and festival pageants which the masses will not for long allow to be baulked. Religion and the love of amusement are the two strongest passions of the human heart, one or other of which at times threatens to swallow the other entire, but the balance is sooner or later redressed. The early Christians, eagerly anticipating the advent of Christ and the end of all things, might be content to forgo even innocent amusements; but when that consummation was indefinitely delayed, the Church had to tolerate at least, and even in its own way, that, namely, of Church festivals and miracle plays, make concessions to the hunger for laughter and the joy of sympathetic tears. And so, if the middle ages are ages of faith, of monks and friars and hermits, there are also jugglers and tumblers and singers:

> Both iapers and ianglers . Iudas children
> Founden hem fantasyes . and fooles hem maden
> And habbeth wit at her wille . to worchen if hem luste:
> That Poule precheth of hem . I dar not preoven here
> *Qui loquitur turpiloquium* . he is Luciferes hyne.

It was a gorgeous and variegated world, with tournaments, guild ceremonials, fairs, Church festivals and processions, pilgrimages, the constant passage of the Host through the crowded streets. And as the eleventh century drew to an end the unquenchable secular spirit of man found a more artistic expression for itself in the lyric and epic of troubadour and trouvère. The background, the assumptions of mediaeval romance are Christian. The poets know nothing of any other religion than Christianity except it be a gross misreading of Mohammedanism. The Catholic faith and ritual, priests and monks and nuns and hermits, are all in the romances; and the Quest of the Holy Grail is an idealisation of mediaeval asceticism and aspiration. Yet the spirit of romance is secular, humanist, not Christian—as devout mediaeval Catholic or seventeenth-century protestant understood 'Christian'. Their splendid joy in life and love, their cult of personal prowess and the service of a mistress, the mediaeval dream of love and heroism, are at the opposite pole from Christian humility, distrust of passion, and contempt for temporal wealth or glory. The romancers know that it is not Lancelot

ROMANCE

the great lover who will achieve the vision of the Holy Grail:

    Far in the town of Sarras
        Red-rose the gloamings fall,
    For in her heart of wonder
        Flames the Sangreal.

    The gleaming fosses ring her,
        Haut dreams her turrets are,
    She riseth o'er the desert
        Like the great Magian star.

    Through the o'er-castled portals
        The knights ride out and in;
    Their tired sweet heads all drooping,
        They pray away their sin.

    Upon the carven causeway
        Pass damozels in vair
    And samite dropped with flamelets,
        Crowned on their ashen hair.

    Into the Town of Sarras,
        Most delicate and sad,
    Like a measure of rare music
        Came Lord Galahad.

    The Crown of Gold he beareth,
        A dream-king exquisite,
    Till the fair Lord of Heaven
        Yet closer needs his knight.

      ·   ·   ·   ·

    Dreams of the Town of Sarras,
        Ye ever give me dole,
    With dome and steeple staining
        Horizons of my soul!

> But where the Grail-Knight entered,
>   Ah! me! I enter not,
> For hard my spirit follows
>   The ways of Launcelot.
>
> By ruined cross and chapel
>   I lie in shameful trance.
> Within, the High Masque burneth,
>   The Saving Cup, the Lance.—
>
> Home to the Bower of Roses,
>   The viols calling clear,
> To Love's most perfect Lover!
>   Oh! Home to Guenevere.

So a modern poet[1] restates the problem, the conflict, which gives poignancy to the finest of the romances —the story of Lancelot and Guinevere, of Tristram and Isolt; the dualism inherent in mediaeval love poetry which makes his love of Laura at once the source of every virtue of which Petrarch can boast:

> Gentil mia donna, i' veggio
> Nel mover de' vostr' occhi un dolce lume
> Che mi mostra la via ch' al ciel conduce.[2]

and the great temptation which has made his life a long and weary aberration from its true goal, the love of God:

> E sento ad ora ad or venirmi al core
> Un leggiadro disdegno, aspro e severo,
> Ch' ogni occulto pensero
> Tira in mezzo la fronte, ov altro 'l vede;
> Chè mortal cosa amar con tanta fede,
> Quanta a Dio sol per debito convensi,
> Più si disdice a chi più pregio brama.

[1] Rachel Annand Taylor: *Poems*, 1904.
[2] *Sonetti e canzoni in vita di Madonna Laura*, ed. Carducci e Ferrari, lxxii.

> E questo ad alta voce anco richiama
> La ragione sviata a dietro ai sensi:
> Ma, per che ell' oda e pensi
> Tornare, il mal costume oltre la spigne
> E a gli occhi depigne
> Quella che sol per farmi morir nacque,
> Per ch' a me troppo et a se stessa piacque.[1]

> Leave me, O Love, which reachest but to dust,
> And thou my mind aspire to higher things,
> Grow rich in that which never taketh rust,
> Whatever fades but fading pleasure brings.[2]

But though this dualism is inherent in romance and becomes clear and acute when poet or saint or ascetic hears the higher call—Dante sees the saints of Love's Calendar all in Hell—the cleavage is not consciously realised by the romancers. There is no definitely anti-religious strain in mediaeval romance; and the Church placed no ban upon romance or song or drama. As Troeltsch says, 'The Catholic Church always regarded the sphere of the natural as a relatively independent sub-structure of the Kingdom of Grace; and, conditionally upon its readiness to submit, had allowed to the natural life a rich freedom of movement. It could, through the institution of confession and penance, be directed; and its excesses, through the same agency, could always be atoned for.'[3] Lancelot and Guinevere die exemplary penitents.

Then came the Renaissance and the Reformation; and though both of these originated in a movement, an aspiration after a new birth (*renascentia*), religious rather than secular in origin, and although both found in Humanism, in the narrower sense of the

---
[1] *Ibid.* cclxiv.   [2] Sidney: *Astrophel and Stella*, cx.
[3] Ernst Troeltsch: *Renaissance und Reformation*. Gesammelte Werke, iv. 19.

word, the armoury from which they drew, yet in Italy and the fifteenth century the Renaissance quickly revealed itself as a thoroughgoing secular, if not necessarily irreligious, movement; and when the Reformation followed there stood face to face a reasserted, self-conscious secularism and the re-awakened temper of early Christianity, other-worldly, intransigent in its attitude towards any acceptance of the world as an end in itself, as something to be enjoyed. Amusement is the bugbear of the severer spirit of Protestantism, especially the Calvinistic Protestantism of nonconforming England, Scotland, and New England. 'Nor have I ever', says Richard Baxter, 'been much tempted to any of the sins which go under the name of pastime.'[1] That spirit, unsupported by a dogmatic creed, is the soul of Carlyle's Gospel of Work. 'Work and be unhappy', for 'there is in man a Higher than Love of Happiness. He can do without happiness, and instead thereof find Blessedness. Was it not to preach forth this same higher that sages and martyrs, the poet and the priest, in all times have spoken and suffered; bearing testimony, through life and through death, of the Godlike that is in man, and how in the Godlike only has he strength and freedom.' 'Love not Pleasure; love God.' 'This is the Everlasting Yea, wherein all contradiction is solved: wherein whoso walks and works, it is well with him.'[2] But the love of pleasure springs for ever in the human breast, and from it have flowed some of the loveliest manifestations of the human spirit. The Muses are the ministers of man's pleasure. In the arts the spirit of man is at play even as the spirit of God, Milton tells us, was at play when he built the universe:

---

[1] *Reliquiae Baxterianae*, 1696.   [2] *Sartor Resartus*.

RENAISSANCE

> Thou with Eternal Wisdom didst converse,
> Wisdom thy sister, and with her didst play
> In presence of the Almighty Father, pleas'd
> With thy celestial song.[1]

Puritanism in England destroyed two native and flourishing arts—the drama and music. 'Music', says Fuller, 'in some sort sung her own dirge (as to the general use thereof) at the dissolution of the Abbeys.'[2]

In speaking of the Renaissance I shall not take as typical such extreme manifestations as the Italian tyrants, or even such characters as Benvenuto Cellini or Machiavelli or Aretino. What I wish to consider is rather the saner spirit of a secularism which no longer feels it necessary to apologise for itself, but has awakened to a curious and serious interest in nature, and especially in human nature. For this purpose I will take Montaigne as representative. He, with perhaps Erasmus and, in his own sphere and manner, Shakespeare, seems to me an ideal representative of the new humanism, nurtured by the thought and literature of antiquity. He is untouched by the pedantry of his age. Like Erasmus he has only contempt for the Ciceronian cult of style of the Italian scholars. His own style is at the opposite pole from that of the Italians as described by Bacon in *The Advancement of Learning*. Nor is Montaigne a devout disciple of any revived school of philosophy—Platonism or Stoicism or Epicureanism. What Montaigne learned from the ancients was not a dogmatic, philosophical scepticism, but a new interest in and understanding of human nature. The scepticism of the *Apology for Raymond Sébond* is a scepticism about human nature rather than concerning dogmatic Christianity. Indeed Montaigne

---
[1] *Paradise Lost*, VII. 9-12.
[2] Fuller: *The Church History of Britain*, 1655.

accepts Catholic Christianity on trust, seeing that ultimate things transcend human reason. He studied human nature by introspection, for, before Coleridge,[1] Montaigne emphasised the fact that we understand others only in so far as they are revealed in ourselves, in what we feel we might ourselves be. The better a man knows himself, the more he knows of human nature. 'Chacque homme porte la forme entière de l'humaine condition.' 'Ce n'est pas dans Montaigne', says Pascal, 'mais dans moi que je trouve tout ce que j'y vois.' This is what Montaigne learned, not so much from the ancient philosophers, as from the moralists, biographers, historians, and poets—Seneca, Plutarch, Livy, Tacitus, Lucretius, Virgil. These it was that

[1] 'Now I appeal confidently to my hearers whether the closest observation of the manners of one or two old nurses would have enabled Shakespeare to draw this character of admirable generalisations? Surely not. Let any man conjure up in his mind all the qualities and peculiarities that can possibly belong to a nurse, and he will find them in Shakespeare's picture of the old woman: nothing is omitted. This effect is not produced by mere observation. The great prerogative of genius (and Shakespeare felt and availed himself of it) is now to swell itself to the dignity of a God and now to subdue and keep dormant some part of that lofty nature and to descend even to the lowest characters—to become everything in fact but the vicious.' 'Where from observation could he have learned such lines as these which are put into the mouth of Othello when he is talking to Iago of Brabantio?

> Let him do his spite:
> My services which I have done the signiory
> Shall out-tongue his complaints. 'Tis yet to know,—
> Which, when I know that boasting is an honour,
> I shall promulgate—I fetch my life and being
> From men of royal siege, and my demerits
> May speak unbonneted to as proud a fortune
> As this that I have reached: for know, Iago,
> But that I love the gentle Desdemona,
> I would not my unhoused, free condition
> Put into circumscription and confine
> For the sea's worth.

I ask where was Shakespeare to observe such language as this? If he did not observe it, it was with the inward eye of meditation upon his own nature: for the time he became Othello and spoke as Othello in such circumstances must have spoken.'—*Lectures on Shakespeare*.

quickened his interest in that 'sujet merveilleusement vain, divers et ondoyant, que l'homme'; and he learned to check their comments by his own introspection. Montaigne was the first of modern psychologists. The field of physical inquiry was not for him; but in his own field he had no rival. He anticipated much on which we dilate to-day—the small part played by reason in the life of most men, the enormous potency of the imagination.

The significance of all this, as Pascal saw, was that in Montaigne the natural man reasserted, rediscovered himself, in all his weakness and variableness, but capable also of amazing *élans* of endurance and of achievement, prone to *paresse* (the sin of *paresse*, sloth, is what Pascal lays to the charge of Montaigne, *orgueil*, pride, to that of Epictetus, for both have reckoned without the Fall and its consequences) and demanding pleasure as an essential element of the Good.[1] 'For my part I love life and cultivate it as it has pleased God to grant it to me . . . I accept cheerfully and gratefully what nature has done for me, and am pleased with it and proud of it. . . . Of philosophical opinions I more willingly embrace those which are the more solid, that is to say, the most human and the most our own. . . . Nature is a gentle guide, yet not more gentle than she is prudent and just. I hunt everywhere for her trail. . . . These transcendental humours terrify me, like lofty and inaccessible places, and nothing I find so hard to digest in the life of Socrates as his ecstasies and his intercourse with daemons. . . . The fairest lives, to my mind, are those which are regulated after the ordinary human pattern, without miracle, without extravagance.'[2] Thus sanely and luminously Montaigne ex-

[1] 'Poetry which produces delight, the parent of so many virtues.'— COLERIDGE. [2] *Les Essais*, III. 13, *De l'Experience*.

presses one thing which the revival of learning was bringing back, a fairer estimate of man's nature, his natural capacities and virtues, the legitimate instinct of enjoyment. 'You will never convince me that the marriage of pleasure with necessity is not a most suitable one, with which, saith an ancient writer, the gods even conspire.' In the Middle Ages—ages of great saints, great sinners, and great penitents—average human nature had been distorted under the sense of sin and judgement, and overstrained by the ideals of asceticism. 'Man at that time', says Huizinga, 'was convinced that right is absolutely fixed and certain. Justice should prosecute the unjust everywhere and to the end. Reparation and retribution have to be extreme, and assume the character of revenge. In this exaggerated need of justice primitive barbarism, pagan at bottom, blends with the Christian conception of society. The Church, on the one hand, had inculcated gentleness and clemency, and tried in that way to soften judicial morals. On the other hand, in adding to the primitive need of retribution the horror of sin, it had to a certain extent stimulated the sense of justice. . . . The barbarous idea of retaliation was reinforced by fanaticism . . . crime came to be regarded as a menace to order and society, an insult to divine majesty. Thus it was natural that the late Middle Ages should become the period of special cruelty.'[1] To one who has come to think of human nature as less wicked than 'divers et ondoyant' such rigour is repellent; and there is no vice against which Montaigne protests more warmly than cruelty: 'Cowardice is the mother of cruelty. . . . All that goes beyond simple death seems to me pure cruelty; our justice cannot hope that he whom the fear of death and of being beheaded

[1] Huizinga: *The Waning of the Middle Ages*.

or hanged will not keep from wrong-doing will be deterred therefrom by the apprehension of a slow fire, or of pincers, or of the wheel. And it may be that we thus drive them to despair; for what can be the state of a man's mind awaiting death for twenty-four hours broken on the wheel, or, after the old manner, nailed to a cross.' . . . 'Even the execution of the law, however just it be, I cannot view with steadiness.'[1]

So speaks the spirit of humanism in Montaigne, and not in Montaigne alone, but in Rabelais and Erasmus and others. It was Erasmus' dream to unite the spirit of humanism with that of Christianity, and to substitute for a scholastic, dogmatic, monastic, ascetic Christianity what he called the philosophy of Christ. But the temper of the age was too warlike for compromise or philosophy. Luther and Calvin and Ignatius Loyola were more to its taste than Erasmus or Montaigne, Milton than Shakespeare. But of that later. What I wish for the moment to emphasise is that Humanism was not a reawakening of man's interest in his own life on earth. *That* he never has lost and never will lose, by whatever means he may attempt to reconcile his interest in love and war and the game of life with the more transcendent claims to which he does obeisance. In the ages of faith men played that game passionately and fantastically enough,

> Le Donne, i Cavallier, l' arme, gli amori,
> Le cortesie, l' audaci imprese

—these were the interests of life and poetry in the centuries of romance, shaping the ideals and dreams of men and women. The difficulty was to justify them on Christian grounds. To slay Saracens was doubtless always a Christian's duty, and to defend women

[1] *Les Essais*, II. xi., *De la Cruauté*.

and succour the helpless a humane task. But life and romance were filled with many other things, and these, if more exciting, less easy to sanctify, and accordingly life and literature abound in great conversions and repentances. For warrior and lover alike the hour comes when one must repent in sackcloth and ashes, or run the risk of losing one's way, like the Templars, in perversions of passion and unbelief. Humanism was an acceptance of human life and values as right and reasonable, and, if controlled by a sense of measure, needing not in themselves to be repented of, a revival of values and ideals on which the best thought of antiquity had set the seal of its approval; and among these values is pleasure, the enjoyment of life and its good things, and chief among them the arts—the great decorators of man's life, the fullest and finest expression of his sense of the joy of life, the beauty inherent in all that is.

Now the Church in the Middle Ages had taken the arts under her wing. Sculpture, music, painting, poetry, the drama—there is none of them that does not owe more to the Church than to any other institution, even the Court; it could hardly be otherwise in an age when the Church intellectually dominated civilisation, and felt the need of responding, so far as she might, to every instinct of human nature, of compromising where she could not control. Yet it may be doubted if she was ever quite at ease and of one mind as to their place and function. At times the more consistent, puritan temper of an other-worldly religion, of early Christianity, made itself felt. The Cistercians forbade decorative churches, elaborate services, illuminated manuscripts. The counter-reformation of a later date had a puritan aspect as well as that which was manifested in baroque art and the sentimentalities of Jesuit art and poetry and ritual.[1] When put on her mettle, the Christian Church has always distrusted and must always distrust the arts, for in them the free spirit of man will endeavour to express itself uncurbed and in its entirety. Foster's indictment is justifiable; Newman's description true and vivid.

The Renaissance witnessed such an emancipation of the imagination that produced many extravagances in poetry and art, in ethical and political speculation. Bruno, Marlowe, Machiavelli, Aretino are only a few of the names which one recalls as typically renaissance. But my concern is not with these but with what went with it, and has given to the renaissance its true place as an epoch in the history of human thought and feeling, the reassertion, as in Montaigne, of a sane secularity of mind, not prejudiced by anti-religious feeling, contemplating with delighted interest the world without and the world within, shaping to itself ideals of life and conduct, for men and women, but shaping them from experience and history, not accepting them—except now and then conventionally—from tradition and authority. It is this which I wish to study in its reactions on our literature, but not alone and by itself, rather as it comes in conflict with its antithesis, a revival in the most extreme form of the other-worldly spirit of early Christianity, intolerant of the secular accepted as an end in itself, as something to be enjoyed, and of the arts which minister to this acceptance of life— dance and song and drama. The renaissance produced the reformation and that the counter-reformation.

[1] Bellarmine hated nude statues and pictures as much as any Puritan, English or American. See Brodrick, *Blessed Robert Bellarmine*, II. 410. For the other strain in baroque art see M. Praz on the artistic cult of the Magdalen, *op. cit.* p. 178 note.

Christianity was not dead, far from it; and the dominant note of the seventeenth century was to be the conflict of the secular and the spiritual, the world, the flesh, and the spirit, a conflict which troubled every sphere of life. I put it, for the moment, thus crudely as a conflict in which the spirit is on one side, the world and the flesh on the other—leaving the devil out of account at present. It was, of course, a more complex affair. The professed champions of the spirit were too often ranged in deadly battle against one another—Catholic and Protestant, Anglican and Puritan, Lutheran and Calvinist; and to us, looking back, it appears as if at times the deepest concerns of the spirit were left to the protection of the world and the flesh, of the moderate, reasonable spirit which gradually made it impossible, because absurd, for Catholic or Protestant, to burn old women and torture those who thought differently from themselves.

There are many reasons why the humanist spirit should not have won at the Renaissance an immediate or complete victory. It was a spirit which appealed mainly to the cultured few. Moreover, a reflective humanism is quickly aware of its own limitations. Montaigne will illustrate what I mean. In no one, as I have said, does one find the human spirit awakened to a more delighted and curious interest in human nature and human life, more sympathetic with human inconsistencies and frailties, more averse to cruelty, and ready to include under the head of cruelty any too exorbitant demands made on our nature in the name of church or state or philosophy. 'Nature is a gentle guide, yet not more gentle than she is prudent and just.' But he is the unsparing critic of human presumption, and as well aware as Pascal of the parlous plight of human nature left to itself. The *Apology for*

Raymond Sébond is a sustained indictment of the presumption of human reason, and exposure of its frailty, from which Montaigne deduces the justification of his acceptance, on grounds of faith and faith only, of the authority of the Catholic Church. It was from the contemplation of his own nature in the pages of Montaigne that Pascal attained to the passionate conviction which was to form the basis of his defence of the Christian faith:

> Misère de l'homme sans dieu.
> Félicité de l'homme avec dieu.
> Autrement:
> Que la nature est corrompue. Par la nature même.
> Qu'il y a un réparateur. Par l'Écriture.[1]

And in proving the corruption of human nature from a survey of that nature Montaigne is his guide. 'Let us now consider man by himself, without external aid, armed only with his own weapons, and deprived of divine favour and recognition, in which consists all his honours, his strength, and the foundation of his existence. Let us see how much support he has in that fine equipment. Let him make me understand by the force of his reasoning upon what foundations he has set up the great advantages that he believes himself to have over all other creatures. . . . Is it possible to imagine anything so ridiculous as this paltry, wretched creature who not being even his own master, exposed to injuries from everything, calls himself master of the universe of which it is not in his power to understand the smallest fragment, far less to govern it?'[2] . . . 'Presumption is our natural and original malady. The most unfortunate and frail of all creatures is man, and at the same time

[1] *Les Pensées*, ed. Brunschvig, 1900, Section ii. 60.
[2] *Les Essais*, II. 12, Apologie de Raymond Sébond.

the most vainglorious. This creature feels and sees that it is lodged here amid the mire and filth ... and it establishes itself in imagination above the circle of the moon and brings heaven under its feet. It is through the vanity of the same imagination that he equals himself to God, that he attributes to himself divine conditions, that he selects and separates himself from the crowd of other creatures, assigns their shares to other animals his companions, and distributes among them such powers and faculties as seem good to him.'[1] 'Man is a reed, but a reed which thinks', cries Pascal. This double aspect of human nature, its grandeur and its smallness, haunts the greatest minds of the Renaissance. 'What a piece of work is man! How noble in reason! How infinite in faculty! In form and moving how express and admirable! In action how like an angel! In apprehension how like a God! The beauty of the world! The paragon of animals!' So Shakespeare puts one side, but he presents the other with equal force:

> Reason thus with life:
> If I do lose thee I do lose a thing
> That none but fools would keep: a breath thou art
> Servile to all the skyey influences,
> That dost this habitation where thou keep'st
> Hourly afflict; merely thou art death's fool;
> For him thou labour'st by thy flight to shun,
> And yet runn'st towards him still ...
> ... Thou hast nor youth nor age,
> But as it were an after-dinner sleep,
> Dreaming on both; for all thy blessed youth
> Becomes as aged, and doth beg the alms
> Of palsied eld; and when thou art old and rich
> Thou hast neither heat, affection, limb, nor beauty
> To make thy riches pleasant.[2]

[1] *Les Essais*, II. 12, Apologie de Raymond Sébond.
[2] *Measure for Measure*, III. 1. 5 ff.

ENGLISH HUMANISM

So long as men must die there will be those who will wish to know where the bird betakes itself when it quits the warm precincts of the day. And if after Erasmus and Montaigne and Shakespeare one recalls Luther and Pascal one realises that there was another spirit at work besides that which they represent, the spirit of the Reformation, for Pascal was a Jansenist, and Jansenism was closely akin to Protestantism and Calvinism. The English Humanists, the revivers of classical studies in this country, were all men of ardent religious feeling—Linacre, Grocyn, Latimer, and others. 'English Humanism', says a recent German writer, 'was closely akin to Puritanism, the first stage in the Puritan revolution.'[1] Colet returned from Italy not to found a Platonic Academy, but to lecture on the epistles of Saint Paul. When English literature, after a period of tentative and unequal flights, revived in full force in the last twenty years of the sixteenth century, Protestantism hardening, if one may so speak, into Puritanism was rapidly becoming the dominant force in English life.

With the theological and political aspects of the movement I am not concerned, but only with its reaction upon literature, especially poetry and the drama, which were springing into life inspired in part by the tradition of Chaucer and mediaeval allegory, but in the main by the influence of the Italian Renaissance, a literature penetrated with the free imaginative spirit of humanism, its joy in life and art. How would this free spirit, this delight in the high pleasure which is the gift of the Muses, accommodate itself to the other spirit which was agitating a much wider circle—the desire for a closer walk

[1] Schirmer, *Antike, Renaissance und Puritanismus*, 1924, p. 75 ff.

23

Philip Sidney says that pleasure is justified if it is used to persuade men to virtue. Thus he unites the two positions.

with God, a purer and more spiritual religion, with certain social implications too, though these did not always manifest themselves at once. The puritan spirit was a democratic spirit. Now a great spiritual religion will affect literature and art as it affects life, that is, as a rule of life controlling man's conduct towards himself and his fellow-men; and as a revelation, a scheme of salvation, requiring belief in certain dogmas and specific duties towards God as well as men; and in historic Christianity the latter have always taken the first place. Human virtues have been reckoned virtues only in so far as they were inspired by religious motives. The first requirement is faith. Without faith human virtues are only splendid vices. Protestantism and Puritanism show both these aspects. It was a moral movement, demanding a higher code of conduct, personal and social, and a stricter observance. But it was also and principally a new theology, a new reading of the conditions of salvation. Faith and specifically religious duties were more imperative than mere human and social virtues, which were regarded rather as a necessary consequence of the former. Salvation by faith was the watchword of Lutheranism and Calvinism. Colonel Hutchinson, according to his wife, attained at last to full Christian fellowship when he came to 'a right belief in that great point of predestination', 'laying a foundation of sound and necessary principles, among which he gave the first place to this of God's absolute decrees'. This was the line of cleavage between Erasmus and Luther. 'To Erasmus' temperament', says Professor Preserved Smith, 'the all-important matter in religion was the life; beliefs were interesting, even rather important, but they were subordinate to the moral issue.' 'It was natural that the battle should be joined on precisely the issue taken, that of the free will, for both to the dogmatic and ethical mind this question is fundamental. To talk of morality without freedom of choice is absurd, said Erasmus; to speak of our own powers to attain grace and merit apart from God's "eternal decree" is impious, pontificated Luther.'[1] Doctrine—election, effectual calling, free grace, imputed righteousness, perseverance, and religious duties, as hearing sermons and observing the Sabbath, these are the principal themes of Puritan sermons.

Thus if a poet is moved by the religious thought and feeling of his time, it may be by the ethical and human, more often it will be by the doctrinal and transcendent element; and if it is by the ethical, it may be the more positive. The poet may be interested in the positive beauty of the Christian character, the new colour Christianity gives to some human values, the purifying and heightening of the mediaeval dream of love and chivalry, the new worth that is given to charity and mercy. Or, like most of the preachers, he may concentrate on the negative aspect of Christian ethics, the 'thou shalt not!' to which a sterner sanction has been given.

The different tendencies might be illustrated by a comparison of *The Faerie Queene* and Milton's *Paradise Lost* and *Paradise Regained*, as ethical and religious poems. Whether successfully worked out or not—that I shall consider later—*The Faerie Queene* is a poem inspired in its inception by the spirit of Christian Humanism, 'the philosophy of Christ', by the desire to illustrate the beauty of the Christian virtues—a Christian Holiness, Temperance, Chastity, Friendship, Justice, and Courtesy. It is on ethical

[1] Preserved Smith, *Erasmus*, 1923, p. 337.

rather than doctrinal grounds that Rome, symbolically personified in Archimago, Duessa, and Orgoglio, is condemned. Of definite theological doctrine there is little, though I suspect that Arthur in the first books represents not only the Aristotelian virtue of Magnificence or Magnanimity, whichever it be that Spenser intended, but even more the prevenient grace of God without which all human aspiration or effort is fruitless. But so far as he achieves his first serious purpose, Spenser's joy is in the positive and humanist aspect of Christian virtues, not comprehended in any one of his characters, but dispersed through the meekness, patience and purity of Una, the active philanthropy of Arthur and Britomart, the invincible temperance of Guyon. Even in the House of Holiness Spenser is not content to close the education of the Christian knight with faith and repentance, the acceptance of the imputed righteousness of Christ which is the end of Bunyan's troubles. From Faith and Repentance he proceeds to the fruits thereof, deeds of Charity and finally spiritual Contemplation.

Paradise Lost and *Paradise Regained* are also, in conception, religious and ethical poems, 'doctrinal to a nation', how far successfully so I will consider again; but there is a great difference between the spirit of Spenser's work and of Milton's. Milton's chief interest was also ethical, his conception of Christianity fundamentally humanist, *i.e.* was less immediately concerned with how to gain Heaven than with the making of a new earth by the spirit of the philosophy of Christ,—a new Church, a new State, a new Family, a new School and University, a new Theatre, and a right use of Pastime, though to prove and illustrate this would need a survey of his prose works. But his first duty in *Paradise Lost*, he feels, is to state clearly his theological position, to justify the ways of God to men by a speech put into the mouth of God himself—stark, naked reasoning. Man was created free, and therefore is solely responsible for the consequences of his Fall. But Mercy shall temper Justice; and, with important modifications of his own, Milton sets forth the Protestant doctrine of salvation by imputed righteousness:

> Thy merit
> Imputed shall absolve them who renounce
> Their own both righteous and unrighteous deeds,
> And live in thee transplanted, and from thee
> Receive new life.[1]

Paradise Lost is thus at the core a theological poem, and Milton's ethical ideal, as it emerges less in *Paradise Lost* than in *Paradise Regained*, in Christ himself, presented as entirely human, is a more negative one than Spenser dreamt of. Milton is, as Emerson said, the poet of the restrictive virtues. He draws a noble picture of the Christian scorn of worldly values—sense and pomp, power and wealth,—his obedience to God and God only, God who is reason,—but the effect is somewhat chilling. But more of this anon. My immediate purpose has been to de-

---

[1] *Paradise Lost*, III. 290-294. Milton's position as stated in ll. 183 ff.:

> Some I have chosen of peculiar grace
> Elect above the rest; so is my will;
> The rest shall hear me call, and oft be warn'd
> Their sinful state, and to appease betimes
> Th' incensed Deity while offer'd grace
> Invites; for I will clear their senses dark
> What may suffice, etc.

seems to approach closer to the Molinist and Jesuit doctrine of 'sufficient' and 'efficacious' grace than that of any Protestant doctrine, except it be that of the Quakers. See Brodrick, *Blessed Robert Bellarmine*, 1928, II. p. 25 ff.

lineate the forces at work in life and literature in the period between the accession of Elizabeth and the Restoration, between Spenser and Dryden—the humanist, secular spirit which the study of antiquity had revived, interested in man as a child of nature, a complex being, half angel and half beast, as Montaigne sees him, set in a world that is full of all kinds of attractions, gifted with a keen love of pleasure physical, intellectual, and imaginative, and so a lover of the arts; and, on the other hand, the revived spirit of early Christianity, intent upon the world to come, the escape from the City of Destruction, mightily exercised about certain great doctrines, sin and death, effectual calling, free grace, the imputed righteousness of Christ, in morals tending to the ascetic, the 'thou shalt not', and so distrustful of pleasure, of pastime, and their great minister the arts.

In my next lecture I propose, after reviewing some of the general aspects of the conflict between these two tendencies of the time, to reconsider the significance of *The Faerie Queene*.

CHAPTER II

EDMUND SPENSER

*The Conflict more closely defined—Protestant and Evangelical Doctrines of the complete Corruption of Human Nature and the Imputed Righteousness of Christ—The type of Christian which this view has tended to produce does not readily appeal to the Humanist mind—But there is a type of Christian which has appealed—Chaucer's 'Povre Persoun of a Toune'—An attempt at reconciliation—Edmund Spenser—The influences literary and spiritual which shaped his work—*The Faerie Queene—*Value of allegory—Religion and ethics in the poem —The 'mediaeval dream of chivalry and love'— Rejection of the romantic tradition by Spenser's disciples.*

BEFORE I proceed to study the effect on Elizabethan and seventeenth-century literature of the sharp antagonism between the humanist, secular spirit of the Renaissance and the revived spirit of early Christianity, puritan if not ascetic, other-worldly, unyielding in its attitude towards all that savoured of the world and the flesh, especially the latter, it might be well to consider a little more closely the ground of the quarrel and, in a somewhat *a priori* fashion, what were likely to be the results of the antagonism. John Foster states clearly and succinctly the essential nature of the difference. Christianity and the spirit of polite literature are divided, as by a gulf, because of a radical difference in their estimate of human nature. 'Christianity, taken in this view' (that is the Evangelical, Calvinist, Augustinian), 'contains a humiliating estimate of the moral condition of man, as a being radically corrupt —the doctrine of redemption from that condition by the merit and sufferings of Christ—the doctrine of a divine influence being necessary to transform the character of the human mind in order to prepare it for a higher station in the universe—and a grand moral peculiarity by which it insists on humility, penitence, and a separation from the spirit and habits of the world.'[1] In that statement are comprised the main tenets of evangelical doctrine—complete corruption of human nature, redemption by the death and merits of Christ, God's free grace enabling the individual to appropriate the effects of that sacrifice, a complete breach with the world and its ways. 'My religious education', says Baxter, 'made the world seem to me as a carkass that had neither Life nor Loveliness: and it destroyed those Ambitious desires after Literate Fame which was the sin of my Childhood. I had a desire before to have attained the highest Academical Degrees and Reputation of Learning, and to have chosen out my studies accordingly; but Sicknesse and Solicitousness for my doubting Soul did shame away all these thoughts as Fooleries and Children's Plays.'[2]

The humanist, Montaigne or Shakespeare, will not dispute the weakness or corruption of human nature; and polite letters from Aristophanes to Bernard Shaw, if they have not indulged in such sweeping denunciations as the preacher, have presented the vices and frailties of humanity in more varied, vivid, and poignant detail. Yet humanism rests ultimately on a conviction of the good as well as the

[1] Foster, *op. cit.*, 'Letter I.'   [2] *Reliquiae Baxterianae*, 1696, p. 5.

evil that is in man: 'What a piece of work is man! How noble in reason! How infinite in faculty!... The beauty of the world! The paragon of animals!' It is the consciousness of splendid possibilities condemned to futility that has given resonance to the greater literature of satire and pessimism. 'I returned and saw that the race is not to the swift, nor the battle to the strong, neither yet bread to the wise, nor yet riches to men of understanding, nor yet favour to men of skill; but time and chance happeneth to them all.' It is of course in this consciousness of what human nature and life are and what they might be that the deeper humanist and religious feeling meet. But literature, it must be confessed, has not dealt sympathetically with the type of Christian which the theoretic doctrine of the complete corruption of human nature has tended to produce—doctrinal, intent upon his personal salvation and experience of assurance and sanctification, distrustful of pleasure in any form and stressing what Emerson calls the 'restrictive virtues' rather than the more positive and outgoing spirit of 'Thou shalt love thy neighbour as thyself'. He has figured as the eccentric, at times a sublime eccentric in virtue of his passionate inner conflicts (*e.g.* Scott's Balfour of Burleigh), more often a subject of satire, comic or hateful, Jonson's Zeal-of-the-land-busy, Dickens's Chadband, Trollope's Mr. Slope. In our own day he has been drawn without satire, with the vividness that comes from a rare combination of sympathy and antipathy, sympathy with the individual, antipathy to the type, in *Father and Son*. But the practical Christian, the Christian whose faith is not, or not *only*, a doctrine of salvation for himself, but a new spirit, a new orientation of life, the inspiration of which is his passionate love of

Christ and his fellow-men—to that type of Christian the humanist spirit *has* done justice in literature more than a few times from Chaucer's 'Povre persoun of a toune' and his brother the plowman, to Fielding's Parson Adams, Goldsmith's Preacher, and Mr. Vachel Lindsay's *General Booth enters Heaven*. If there are few of them in Elizabethan literature, it is partly because the Renaissance was not sympathetic even to this type. The self-assertive egotism which was a reaction from extreme self-depreciation made Renaissance thinkers, like Nietzsche in our day, inclined to depreciate Christian ethics as slavish. But the chief reason is the passionate interest in doctrine, the overwhelming stress laid on orthodoxy, Catholic, Lutheran, Calvinist. It is difficult for us to conceive the mind of men who saw all around them the evidences of God's anger directed against errors of doctrine. You could in the Middle Ages detect an heretic by his smell. Baxter, one of the most enlightened and charitable of Puritans, was convinced of the errors of Sir Henry Vane on learning from a New-England pastor that a woman who had professed his views brought forth a monster under shocking and horrifying circumstances. King James's bishops —and the Anglicans were the least fanatical of the contending parties—burned an Arian and a crazy Anabaptist; and James was much more merciful than his Parliaments. It is easy to understand that with such enormous importance attached to beliefs, and with fear made always the dominant motive, the lovelier, and to the humanist more sympathetic, aspects of Christian ethics will not be greatly in evidence. It is in some of the Anglican poets and in some of the Quakers, that the more winning aspect of Christianity is most evident. It was in the second

Puritan movement, the Evangelical Revival of the eighteenth century, that puritan piety and humanitarian feeling united themselves more closely; and even the Evangelicals failed a little when brought face to face with the cruelties of industrialism; and the spirit of industrialism is itself a by-product of the puritan temper, of its inclination to sanctify work, its distrust of pastime, of pleasure in any form.[1]

A little reflection will show, I think, what are likely to be some of the effects on literature of such a conflict as that in which the age was involved. One is a sharp distinction between the secular and the religious. Secular verse is a pastime which one forgoes or even condemns when one grows more serious. The writing of Latin verse is indeed a recreation which even a pious man may allow himself, with perhaps some apology. Beza[2] and Buchanan wrote and printed elegies and epigrams which might surprise some of those who know them only as great figures in the history of Protestantism. Milton in his Latin verses gives free play to thoughts and moods which he did not give expression to in English. To one of his elegies, indeed, he thought it necessary to affix, in printing it, an *apologia* pleading his youth. Latin verses of this kind were sports of wit, on recognised models, not to be taken too seriously. But the same is true, I suspect, of a good deal of English lyrical poetry of the sixteenth and seventeenth centuries. It is probable that we take Elizabethan sonnets, and even the songs and elegies of Donne

---

[1] 'In breaking down the motive of ease and enjoyment asceticism lays the foundation of the tyranny of work over men.'—MAX WEBER.

[2] 'Your bishop, Beza, to whom we are indebted for so many love-songs, some of them to Candida and the boy Audebert being vile enough in all conscience.'—BELLARMINE.

and his followers, more seriously than their authors intended they should be taken. I am not subscribing to the late Sir Sidney Lee's thesis that Shakespeare's sonnets were mere imitations or perhaps translations, or wishing, with some of his clerical admirers, to deny the licence of Donne's youth; but I suspect that Shakespeare could exploit experience poetically and dramatically without strict adherence to fact; and that Donne allowed his songs and elegies to circulate among his friends because he regarded them not as autobiography but as brilliant flights of wit. It is Blake and the romantics who weighted the lyric, the song, which we no longer sing, with intimate personal feeling and profound mystical thought. In earlier days a song was a song; and the writing of songs, elegies, epigrams was a vain and idle pursuit which you abandoned when you grew serious. Serious thought you might put into a poem of more elaborate construction, a *Nosce Teipsum* or an Epistle, or a Funeral Elegy like *Lycidas*, and to grow serious was generally to grow religious. But not always, or not always in an orthodox way; and another result of the sharp antagonism between Renaissance and Reformation might be that if you felt and wished to write seriously, as, for example, did Jonson or Chapman or Lord Herbert, you sought inspiration not in the orthodox religious thought of the day but in the revived thought of antiquity, Stoical, Epicurean, Platonic, and you might or might not be conscious of opposition between philosophy and faith. Chapman wrote some devout poems, notably *A Hymn to Christ upon the Cross*, but the general tenour of his thought is not Christian. But lastly, a poet might not be willing to accept a definite schism between Renaissance and Reformation, feeling acutely the power

RECONCILIATION

and beauty of both. The greater men of the Renaissance from the outset had not been irreligious or anti-Christian. They had sought rather, as Dillthey has emphasised, to attain by the help of ancient philosophy a profounder interpretation of Christianity. And to men like Sidney, Spenser, Daniel, Ben Jonson—and to Sir Thomas More earlier—the new thought, the new poetry, were not idle vanities, but things of high and serious interest. Might it not be possible to harmonise these two great forces, to unite the charm of this new and splendid poetry with the profound appeal of this new summons to a more spiritual religion, a closer walk with God? That was what a young English poet, fresh from Cambridge, set himself to achieve —to write a poem which should at once delight the courtier, enamoured of the new poetry, and satisfy the disciple of Cartwright. That Spenser failed, we know from his own admission, in the opinion of one important judge with Puritan sympathies, to whom, as to Ascham, the mediaeval dream of love and chivalry, which it was Spenser's ambition to reanimate and reorient, seemed but a tale of manslaughter and bawdry:

> The rugged forehead that with grave foresight
> Welds kingdoms, causes, and affaires of state,
> My looser rimes (I wote) doth sharply wite,
> For praising loue, as I haue done of late,
> And magnifying louers deare debate;
> By which fraile youth is oft to folly led,
> Through false allurement of that pleasing baite,
> That better were in vertues discipled,
> Than with vaine poemes weeds to haue their fancies fed.
>
> Such ones ill judge of loue that cannot loue,
> Ne in theire frosen hearts feele kindly flame;

For thy they ought not thing unknowne reproue,
Ne naturall affection faultlesse blame,
For fault of few that haue abusd the same,
For it of honour and all vertue is
The roote, and brings forth glorious flowres of fame,
That crowne true lovers with immortal blis,
The meed of them that loue and do not liue amisse.[1]

So Spenser restates the contention of Petrarch and Dante touching the ennobling power of love,—that love is the passion which quickens every virtue in the noble heart as the sun turns clay into diamonds. But Spenser is more akin to Petrarch than to Dante. For Dante carried through the doctrine of the ennobling power of love to its transcendental conclusion, when the Beatrice of his youthful adoration became divine theology, his guide through all the ardours and splendours of heaven. His doctrine is summed up in the lines in which he describes his last sight of her after St. Bernard has taken her place:

Answering not, mine eyes I raised
And saw her where aloof she sat, her brow
A wreath reflecting of eternal beams,
Not from the centre of the sea so far
Unto the regions of the highest thunder,
As was my ken from hers; and yet the form
Came through that medium down, unmixed and pure.
' O lady! thou in whom my hopes have rest;
Who for my safety hast not scorned in hell
To leave the traces of thy footsteps marked,
For all mine eyes have seen I to thy power
And goodness virtue owe and grace. Of slave
Thou hast to freedom brought me; and no means
For my deliverance apt hast left untried.
Thy liberal bounty still toward me keep:
That when my spirit, which thou madest whole,

[1] Spenser, *Faerie Queene*, Book IV. Introduction.

Is loosened from this body, it may find
Favour with thee.' So I my suit preferred:
And she so distant, as appeared, looked down
And smiled; then towards the eternal fountain turned.[1]

    sorrise e riguardommi;
  poi si tornò a l' eterna fontana.

In that sublime passage earthly passion is fused and sublimated into religious devotion. Beatrice smiles, but then turns back to God from Whom came, and in Whom is made perfect, her love for Dante. One may keep the lines in mind to use, in the way Arnold suggested, as a touchstone with which to test Spenser's religious verse, and so to realise the difference between a poet who has accesses of pious feeling and a great religious poet. For Spenser is more akin to Petrarch than to Dante. For him too love is at once an ennobling inspiration and a stumbling-block in the heavenward journey. For all his protest against Burleigh's condemnation, in the end he cries *peccavi*:

> Many loose lays (Ah, woe is me the more)
> In praise of that mad fit, which fools call loue,
> I haue in the heat of youth made heretofore
> That in light wits did loose affection moue.[2]

The primary reference may be to the *Hymne of Love*, but it must also be to the large place given to the theme of love in *The Faerie Queene*, and imply an admission that he had not quite achieved the great Christian poem of which he had dreamed in setting out. But I am anticipating. What I wish to do is to try to examine candidly *The Faerie Queene* as a

---

[1] Dante: *Paradiso*; xxxi. 70-93, Cary's translation.
[2] *An Hymne of heavenly Loue*, v. 2.

serious poem, entitling Spenser to the high praise which Milton bestowed upon him,[1] to consider with what degree of success he carried out his intention and reconciled the Poet and the Puritan. Much work on Spenser has been done of recent years, and no small part of it by American scholars. We have got a good deal away from the Victorian view which was fully and clearly stated by the late Professor Dowden in the essay he contributed to Grosart's edition in 1882, *Spenser the Poet and Teacher*. Indeed, in the criticism of Yeats and Jusserand and Legouis, the balance has been tipped so much against the teacher that American scholars, with whom the puritan tradition still lingers, have endeavoured to redress the balance and defend the view of Spenser as the 'sage and serious' ethical poet. With what success I am to consider.

As a result of the work of the scholars named, and of others such as Professor Renwick, we can survey more clearly the purpose which he had in view, the forces by which he was influenced, and the development of the poem so far as it went. Before he left St. Paul's school he had become interested in the new poetry as represented by the work of Du Bellay. At Cambridge he became a leading member of a group of young men gathered round Gabriel Harvey, who, whatever time they may or may not have given to their academic studies, were eager readers of the same new literature, French and Italian. Harvey's letter on the earthquake, after Spenser had gone down, describes what was, and had been, the literary atmosphere of the university: 'Matchiavel a great man; Castilio of no small reputation; Petrarch and

---

[1] 'Our sage and serious poet Spenser, whom I dare be known to think a better teacher than Scotus or Aquinas' (*Areopagitica*).

Bocace in every man's mouth; Galateo and Guazzo never so happy; over many acquainted with Unico Aretino; the French and Italians when so highly regarded of scholars? The Latine and Greeke when so lightly?' Spenser himself was probably no great classical scholar. There are things which suggest that his knowledge of Plato came through Cicero, and Mr. Merritt Hughes has shown that he had no first-hand knowledge of Theocritus's pastorals. Italian and French poets were his models in *The Shepheardes Calender*, and the other early experiments which he describes to Harvey or which have survived, they and such English poets as there were, Chaucer and Gascoigne and Sackville and some contemporaries. It is from the same Italian and French sources that he derived the theory of poetry which was to direct him in giving England a new poetry. The different kinds of poetry, the style, and the language—the poet's right and duty to enrich the tongue by borrowings and coinings—his experiments in metre and stanza, his studied picturesque effects, his imitation of and translation from other poets, his use of allegory—in all these Professor Renwick has shown Spenser accepted as his guide French and Italian criticism.

That is one side of Spenser's Cambridge career—the eager study of his art with a growing consciousness that it was in him to create a new English poetry, the first justification of which was *The Shepheardes Calender*. Once set in motion, Spenser's fluency never failed. No poet is so copious. 'He brought into the world with him', says Legouis, 'the gift of a sovereign ease. It seems indeed that his thought flows into verse in perfect order and without the least effort. Always clear, always ample, indefatigable, it follows its course like a river whatever be the subject, whatever the form adopted. It never checks, never grows obscure, and never is the harmony interrupted.'[1] But the theory and practice of the art of poetry was not Spenser's sole interest at Cambridge during the years 1569 to 1576. For there were subjects about which the world of Cambridge was more deeply agitated than quantitative or accentual metres, whether one should write pastorals, romances, or classical comedies. Thomas Cartwright returned from Ireland to Cambridge in 1567 and was appointed one of the preachers for the year, and 'when his turn came to preach at St. Mary's the sexton was fain to take down the windows by reason of the multitude that came to hear him'. In 1569, the year that Spenser went up, Cartwright was appointed Lady Margaret Professor of Divinity, and began by his lectures the movement out of which came the Puritan party in the strict sense of the word, the party which was determined to remodel the Church of England on Presbyterian and Genevan lines. In the following June a complaint was lodged with Cecil (who had Puritan sympathies himself, but was responsible for the Queen's government), as Chancellor of the University, which states the position very clearly: 'One, Mr. Cartwright, latelie chosen into my place reader of the divinity lector founded by Lady Margaret, who hath alwaies stubbornlie refusd the cappe and such like ornaments agreeable to Gods law, and the Queenes Majesties Injunctions, doth now in his daily lectors teache such doctrine as is pernitious and not tollerable in a Christian commonwealth: That is, that in the Churche of England there is no lawful and ordynarie calling and choosinge or admittinge of ministers, neither anie minesterie: and that the election of ministers and

[1] *Spenser*, par Émile Legouis, 1923, p. 219.

bishoppes at this daye is tyrranous: and Archiepiscopi, decani, Archidiaconi be officia et nomina Impietatis.'[1] Grindal, Archbishop of Canterbury, was compelled to take action, and Cartwright was restrained, and by December deprived of his lectureship. But he had many supporters and it is clear that the University was deeply moved, and not least its younger members. It is not necessary to retrace the history of the movement, including the suspension of Grindal for his gentle dealing with the Puritans, Grindal who appears as Algrind in *The Shepheardes Calender*. That poem shows clearly how Spenser had felt the influence of the religious revival. The Evangelical, Puritan note is clearly sounded in several of the poems, as the July *Aeglogue*:

> Such one he was (as I have heard
>   Old Algrind often sayne)
> That whilome was the first shepheard
>   And liued with little gayne,
> And meeke he was as meeke mought be,
>   Simple, as simple sheepe;
> Humble, and like in each degree
>   The flock which he did keepe.
> Often he used of hys sheepe
>   A sacrifice to bring,
> Now with a Kidde now with a sheepe
>   The Altars hallowing.
> So louted he unto hys lord,
>   Such fauour could he fynd
> That neuer sithens was abhorrd
>   The simple shepheards kynd.[2]

Spenser left the University in 1576 apparently with the intention of entering the ministry. In 1578 he became secretary to Young, Bishop of Rochester (Roffie),

---

[1] Scott Pearson, *Thomas Cartwright and Elizabethan Puritanism*, 1925, p. 28.
[2] *Shepheardes Calender*, July.

but this does not, I think, imply, as Legouis infers, that he had already recanted his allegiance to Cartwright. Not everyone who thought that the Church of England needed reform was prepared at once to abandon it or to refuse orders. It was while secretary to Young that he wrote some of his severest satires on the bishops and clergy. But before *The Shepheardes Calender* was finished Spenser had come under another potent influence that was to colour his life and work ever afterwards in hues radiant and sombre—<u>the influence of the Court</u>. Of the flesh and the spirit he had felt the pull, and now came the world. Up to the September *Aeglogue* we hear of no patron except the Bishop of Rochester. His themes, in writing to his friends, had been his unhappy love, his disappointed hopes as an aspirant to the ministry, his religious sympathies. The only great person he had flattered was she whom every poet must flatter—Queen Elizabeth. But the October *Aeglogue* sounds a new note. He has found a patron and, though his tone is still despondent, it is to the Court that he will sing:

> Abandon thou the vile and baser clowne;
> Lift up thyself out of the lowly dust
> And sing of bloody Mars, of wars, of giusts;
> Turne thee to those that weld the awful crowne,
> To doubted knights whose woundless armour rusts,
> And helmes unbruized waxen daily browne.
>
> There may thy Muse display her fluttering wing,
> And stretch herself at large from east to west;
> Whether thou list in fair Eliza rest,
> Or if thee please in bigger notes to sing,
> Advaunce the worthy whom she loueth best,
> That first the white Bear to the stake did bring.

But Cuddie replies despondently, and Spenser soon found that, even with the favour of Leicester, promotion at Court was slow and uncertain. Yet his ambitions had been quickened. The October and November eclogues are the finest of the collection, and *November* is inspired by the death of some lady of Leicester's circle. Moreover, the correspondence with Harvey shows that his mood was not always one of despondence, that all his interest in the theory and practice of his art had revived, and that encouraged by Sir Philip Sidney he was experimenting on various themes in various styles. And then, in the midst of other poems projected or composed (for many of the *Complaints* of 1591 were written at this earlier date), appears a mention of *The Faerie Queene* and the declared purpose of 'overgoing' the prince of Italian courtly poets, Ariosto. I need not retell the story of Spenser's indiscretions and disappointments, his transference from Leicester to Lord Grey of Wilton and from the Court to Ireland, land of lakes and bogs and rivers and forests that are reflected in the stanzas of *The Faerie Queene*, but also the land of an unhappy, turbulent people, a 'rabble rout' with whom the protestant and patriotic poet has no sympathy and whom Lord Grey, like Sir Artegall, will endeavour to subdue with an iron hand. One of the unhappy results of the Protestant Reformation was to turn the hearts of Englishmen towards Ireland into stone. But my purpose has been to show what successive experiences led up to the composition of *The Faerie Queene* and what were the different aims which he set himself to harmonise in that poem. It was to be a work of art embodying all the new beauties of diction, verse, and elaborate ornament of the poetry of the Renaissance in Italy and France, yet preserving also the tradition of English poetry from Chaucer to Sackville. It was to 'overgo' even the *Orlando Furioso* in its revival and embellishment of romance, the dream of love and chivalry. It was to be a courtly poem, like its model, more courtly even than Chaucer's poems had been, a poem reflecting the brilliant revival of courtly life which was a feature of the Renaissance. Spenser would not write of millers and reeves and maunciples, but only of men and women of noble birth:

> In braue pursuit of honorable deed,
> There is I know not what great difference
> Betweene the vulgar and the noble seed,
> Which unto things of valorous pretence
> Seemes to be borne by natiue influence;
> As feates of armes and loue to entertaine.
> But chiefly skill to ride, seemes a science
> Proper to gentle bloud.[1]
>
> O what an easie thing is to descry
> The gentle bloud, however it be wrapt
> In sad misfortunes foul deformity,
> And wretched sorrowes, which haue often hapt?
> For howsoeuer it may grow mis-shapt,
> Like this wyld man, being undisciplynd,
> That to all vertue it may seeme unapt,
> Yet will it shew some sparkes of gentle mynd,
> And at the last breake forth in his owne proper kynd.[2]

Spenser's poem, even more than Ariosto's, is lavish of flattery to the Queen and her courtiers; and it reflects vividly the pomp and glitter of courtly life, the pageantry of Court masques and entertainments, the beauty of knightly armour and well-born ladies. But the other side of court life would assert itself too, if more fully in *Mother Hubberds Tale* and *Colin Clouts Come Home Again*, yet in *The Faerie Queene* also; and Spenser will seek escape in dreams of a golden age in the past:

---

[1] *Faerie Queene*, II. iv. 1.   [2] *Ibid.* VI. v. 1.

> So oft as I with state of present time,
> The image of the antique world compare,
> Whenas mans age was in its freshest prime,
> And the first blossome of faire vertue bare,
> Such oddes I finde twixt those and these which are,
> As that through long continuance of his course,
> Me seemes the world is run quite out of square,
> From the first point of his appointed sourse,
> And being once amisse, growes daily wourse and wourse.[1]

And then he forgets that he is writing of this earlier and greater age, and Sir Calidore is fain to forsake even the ideal court of Gloriana and live the shepherd's simple life:

> How much (sayd he) more happie is the state,
> In which ye father here doe dwell at ease,
> Leading a life so free and fortunate,
> From all the tempests of these worldly seas,
> Which tosse the rest in daungerous disease;
> Where warres and wreckes and wicked enmitie
> Doe them afflict, which no man can appease,
> That certes I your happiness enuie,
> And wish my lot were plast in such felicitie.[2]

But pastoralism is itself a courtly pose, an aspect of the dream of love. Calidore is only echoing, often translating, the refined and sensuous stanzas of Tasso. Spenser never speaks of the court with Milton's scorn. But the young poet and courtier is also a Puritan whose heart has responded to the appeal of Cartwright, if his first ardour has a little slackened, and he is anxious that his poem should justify itself to those whose supreme interest is a purer religion, a closer walk with God. How is he to reconcile the serious spirit of Protestant Evangelical religion with the vanities of chivalrous romance, the extravagant cult

---

[1] *Faerie Queene*, v., Proem 1.   [2] *Ibid*. vi. ix. 19.

of love, the egoistic conception of personal prowess, the endless absurdities of romantic fiction, a medley of pagan superstitions, Greek gods and goddesses, hermits and monks, the asceticisms and mysteries of mediaeval Catholicism; and running through it all a strain of subtle and elaborate flattery of the Queen and her courtiers? These things and 'the Gospel' go not easily together.

For some of these elements of the older romances Spenser had no use. Of the mysticism and sacramentalism of the Quest of the Holy Grail there is nothing in *The Faerie Queene*, not so much as in the *Idylls of the King*. Spenser knew the *Morte d'Arthur* and borrowed incidents from it, but his models were Ariosto and Tasso, and in these, even the pious Tasso, a poet of the Counter-Reformation, there is none of the mystical atmosphere of the Quest and adventures of Galahad and Lancelot; and Spenser is a Protestant full of scorn for friars and hermits and relics. The religious atmosphere of the House of Holiness is very different from that of the vision at the Castle of Narbonek. But after the first book there is not much religious atmosphere investing the story. Spenser's justification of his dallying with romance is the allegory, the hidden meaning of the poem, and to estimate aright his claim to be a 'better teacher than Aquinas' one must consider the imaginative, emotional value of allegory.

Dickens, you may remember, describing Mr. Tulkinghorn's rooms, mentions 'its painted ceilings, where Allegory in Roman helmet and celestial linen sprawls among balustrades and pillars, flowers, clouds and big-legged boys, and makes the head ache—as would seem to be Allegory's object more or less'. That is Dickens's intuitive statement of what Croce elaborates more philosophically, that allegory from which we have to detach the secondary meaning by a purely intellectual process has no imaginative, no aesthetic value. So long as the allegory is what the old works on rhetoric used to define it, an extended metaphor, and so long as we can feel the full force of the original image unweakened by the accumulation of detail, the effect is imaginative and emotional. A simple example is Arnold's fine poem, 'The Future':

> A wanderer is man from his birth,
> He was born in a ship
> On the breast of the river of Time;
> Brimming with wonder and joy
> He spreads out his arms to the light,
> Rivets his gaze on the banks of the stream.
>
> As what he sees is, so have his thoughts been, etc.

All the details of the successive pictures serve only to strengthen the emotional effect of the comparison. But so soon as you have to ask what this and that detail means,—and it has taken us two centuries and much research, English and American, to find out what Spenser did mean by this and that person or episode,—the allegory ceases to have value for the imagination. If a poem is to deserve the name of a great religious or ethical poem it must be in virtue of the impression it makes on the imagination and feelings, not because you can with sufficient ingenuity pick out of it a moral or religious lesson. Marino read a moral allegory into his sensual poem the *Adone*.

Now for his purpose Spenser was as unfortunate in the choice of his main image as Bunyan was happy. For if there is one thing truer than another about the Christian life, as a life of high spiritual aspiration, it is that it is a life of arduous yet inspiring endeavour and encounter with difficulties, relieved by moments of unspeakable joy and refreshment in which the struggler looks back with mingled thankfulness and awe upon what is past, and forward with confidence and hope to what has yet to be faced; and what better image of such an experience could there be than a journey on foot beset by perils such as Bunyan describes? Or even in our days, when such perils are fewer, is there any better image by which to suggest the interchange of toil and refreshment, are there any happier moments than those which a pedestrian enjoys in the evening after a day of toil not without peril, or in the morning as he looks from the door on the country he has yet to travel? We can readily enter into the feelings of Christian as we see him go up the hill: 'When I perceived he fell from running to going, and from going to clambering upon his hands and knees, because of the steepness of the place'; or retrace his steps to recover his lost roll: 'How far might I have been on my way by this time! I am made to trace these steps thrice over which I needed not to have trod but once: yea, now also I am like to be benighted, for the day is almost spent. O that I had not slept!' And it is easy to share his feelings when entertained at the House Beautiful: 'Then I saw in my dream that on the morrow he got up to go forwards, but they desired him to stay till the next day also: and then said they, we will (if the day be clear) shew you the delectable Mountains; which they said, would yet further add to his comfort; because they were nearer the desired Haven. . . . So he consented and staid. When the morning was up, they had him to the top of the house, and bid him look

South; so he did: and behold at a great distance he saw a most pleasant, Mountainous Country, beautified with Woods, Vineyards, Fruits of all sorts; Flowers also with Springs and Fountains, very delectable to behold. Then he asked the name of the Country; they said it was *Immanuel's Land* and it is as Common, say they, as this Hill is, to and for all the Pilgrims. And when thou comest there, from thence thou mayst see to the gate of the Cœlestial City; as the Shepherds that live there will make appear.' In such allegory the physical and the spiritual are but two sides of the same shield. Spenser's main image, that of romantic warfare, allows of no such vivid and convincing symbolism, for if an arduous journey on foot through dangerous country is a readily realisable experience, nothing is more unreal than the jousting and warfare of chivalrous romance, in which victory seems to depend on none of the factors that determine the result in real warfare, except it be courage. The weak may vanquish the strong, the few the many; and the unreality is only heightened when we know that the one set of combatants are vices who must of necessity be overcome by the opposing virtues. Spenser's tourneys are intolerably tedious.

Only once to my mind has Spenser achieved the kind of symbolism in which Bunyan excels, an image the moral, emotional symbolism of which is immediately significant, needs no intellectual disentanglement, and that is in the episode of Guyon's visit to the subterranean caverns of Mammon:

> At length they came into a larger space,
> That stretcht it selfe into an ample plaine,
> Through which a beaten broad high way did trace,
> That streight did lead to *Plutoes* griesly raine:

> By that wayes side, there sate infernall Payne,
> And fast beside him sat tumultuous Strife:
> The one in hand an yron whip did straine,
> The other brandished a bloudy knife,
> And both did gnash their teeth, and both did threaten life.[1]

The sensation which this and the stanzas that follow convey (discounting some fantastic but beautiful details) of darkness, temptation, danger, strain, does to me suggest the dark and crooked ways, the peril of losing one's soul indeed, to which no passion conduces so powerfully as covetousness and ambition, the lust of wealth and power: 'What shall it profit a man if he gain the whole world and lose his own soul?' If Spenser elsewhere strikes the same ethical and spiritual note, it is not in allegoric passages but where he speaks straightforwardly, as in the speech of Despaire (i. 9. 38), the speech of Belphoebe (ii. 3. 11-12) or in some of his personal digressions.

But it is not in the books in which the religious and ethical purpose predominates that Spenser is most successful in suggesting a deeper significance. In these, the first and second books, the finest passages, apart from the Despaire and Mammon episodes, are just those in which the ethical purpose is overshadowed by the musical and sensuous beauty of the poetry. His poem gains in symbolical significance when its main theme becomes love and all its contrarieties. For what is the burden of Spenser's religious allegory, the story of Una and the Red Cross knight? Hatred of the Church of Rome. There it begins and there it ends. The knight is a sixteenth-century Lothair, led astray by the blandishments of Duessa or Rome, and delivered, like Disraeli's hero, by a beautiful young lady who brings

[1] *Faerie Queene*, II. vii. 21.

ALLEGORY

to his rescue Prince Arthur, a knight who, Spenser tells us, stands for the complete embodiment of all virtue, but who in his first conception represented rather the Protestant conception of that prevenient grace of God without which no human virtue can achieve anything. Only with the tenth canto does one enter the region of religion as a personal experience—the experience, as Catholic as it is Protestant, of repentance, faith, penance, charity, and the contemplation of God. The tone of the poem is sincere and pious, but far enough removed from the passionate devotion, the flame of aspiration which makes great religious poetry of the *Paradiso*, the *Dark Night of the Soul*, the *Pilgrim's Progress*, *The Temple*, or even the allegoric poem of Spenser's disciple Giles Fletcher. For Spenser, religion is not a passionate aspiration after a richer, intenser experience than any that earth has to offer. It is an insurance, and it is an escape, a refuge from the fever and fret of a world full of jars and disappointments. His imagination is in love with the world of the senses, its splendour and beauty, and with love. In his happier moods he could say with William Morris:

> How can I have enough of life and love?

Think of the beautiful verse, afterwards (1596) cut out of the third book:

> Lightly he clipt her twixt his armes twaine,
> And streightly did embrace her body bright,
> Her body, late the prison of sad paine,
> Now the sweet lodge of loue and deare delight;
> But she faire Lady ouercommen quight
> Of huge affection, did in pleasure melt,
> And in sweete rauishment pourd out her spright:
> No word they spake, nor earthly thing they felt,
> But like two senceles stocks in long embracement dwelt.

His *Epithalamion* overflows with the joy of life. But from the earliest days Spenser's spirit was easily jarred and fretted, by the failure to find a patron, by the disappointment of hopes too easily kindled, by the contrast between his ideal of Court life and the reality, by the wear and tear of official life in an unhappy country in whose conflicts with English government he could see nothing but evidences of a double dose of original sin. Poetry was one refuge, the other religion. Christianity is the promise of an ultimate escape from the ills that flesh is heir to:

> the fretful stir
> Unprofitable, and the fever of the world.

from the endless mutability of all things earthly:

> When I bethinke me on that speech whyleare
> Of Mutability, and well it way;
> Me seemes that though she all unworthy were
> Of the Heav'ns Rule; yet very sooth to say,
> In all things else she beares the greatest sway.
> Which makes me loath this state of life so tickle,
> And loue of things so vaine to cast away;
> Whose flowring pride, so fading and so fickle,
> Short *Time* shall soon cut down with his consuming sickle.
>
> Then gin I thinke on that which Nature sayd,
> Of that same time when no more *Change* shall be,
> But stedfast rest of all things firmely stayd
> Upon the pillours of Eternity,
> That is contrayr to *Mutabilitie*:
> For, all that moveth, doth in *Change* delight:
> But henceforth all shall rest eternally
> With Him that is the God of Sabbaoth hight:
> O that great Sabbaoth God, graunt me that Sabaoths sight.[1]

That comes from Spenser's heart; but it is a different sentiment from Dante's aspiration, even from the

[1] *Faerie Queene*, VII. viii. 1-2.

ALLEGORY

tone of Milton's lines *On Time*, or the blended fear and love of Bunyan. Religion is for Spenser a pillow on which he would fain lay down his head and forget the endless disappointments of this life whose splendour and beauty and ambitions he had so keenly anticipated and appreciated. Paradise is not for Dante a place of rest, but of that activity, the contemplation of God, which takes up into itself every other activity, raising it to the power of infinity. Beatrice looks once downward toward Dante to encourage him, and then turns back to God, in Whom her love of Dante with every other rightly ordered desire is made perfect:

> The good which in created things
>   Exists in part is here complete
> In beauty, power, and majesty,
>   One ocean where all rivers meet.

as another Catholic of the same epoch writes.[1]

And what of the moral allegory of the second book? The babe with the bloody hands, the House of Medina and her sisters, Pyrochles and Furor and Occasion; does any one of these leave an impression on the imagination to counterbalance the sensuous beauty of the Bower of Immodest Mirth, or the Bower of Bliss, or the Song of the Rose, which Spenser translated from Tasso:

> The whiles some one did chaunt this louely lay;
> Ah see, who so faire thing doest faine to see,
> In springing flowre the image of thy day;
> Ah see the Virgin Rose, how sweetly shee
> Doth first peepe forth with bashful modestee,
> That fairer seemes, the lesse ye see her may;

[1] Vondel: *Nitvaart van Maria van den Vondel*, 1668.

> Loe see soone after, how more bold and free
> Her bared bosome she doth broad display;
> Lo see soone after, how she fades, and falles away.
>
> So passeth, in the passing of a day,
> Of mortal life the leafe, the bud, the flowre,
> Ne more doth flourish after first decay,
> That earst was sought to decke both bed and bowre,
> Of many a Ladie, and many a Paramowre:
> Gather therefore the Rose whilest yet is prime,
> For soone comes age, that will her pride deflowre:
> Gather the Rose of loue, whilest yet is time,
> Whilest louing thou mayst loued be with equall crime.[1]

It is not only Guyon but the reader whose moral alertness is lulled by stanzas such as these, and their tone is that which predominates in one's memory of *The Faerie Queene*. I know that Milton and Professor de Selincourt assure us that in the description of the Bower of Bliss the poet displays the charm of the sensuous in order to emphasise the stern morality which destroys the Bower. But this is not quite relevant. The senses have their legitimate claims. There is no virtue in the mere destruction of the beautiful. The moralist must convince us that the sacrifice is required in the interest of what is a higher and more enduring good, that the sensuous yields place to the spiritual. It is this Spenser fails to do imaginatively, whatever doctrine one may extract intellectually from the allegory.

To my mind the spirit and the form of Spenser's poem become most harmonious, his symbolism most significant, when, retaining moral allegory as a shield, a series of enigmas for Professors de Selincourt and Padelford to interpret, he reverts in spirit to the allegory from which his own ultimately derives, the

[1] *Faerie Queene*, II. xii. 74-75.

Romance of the Rose, and his theme is love, in the third and fourth books and again in the sixth, for the political fifth is the dullest of all. Chastity, Friendship, Courtesy—these are the labels, and one may with the help of critics disentangle Spenser's treatment of different types of friendship and find a deep moral significance in Marinell's overthrow by Britomart or the sufferings of Amoret. But the real theme of the whole is love, and persons and pageants derive hence their effect. Here is his gallery of women types— Florimell the lovely, whom all that see her must love; the maiden Belphoebe, who, though she will not wed, yet, like Queen Elizabeth, jealously demands fidelity in her lovers; Amoret, the loyal wife of Scudamore, who yet suffers from the solicitations and agitations of illicit passion; Britomart, who combines the rôles of Belphoebe and Amoret, maiden and wife, but whose chief appeal is her beauty as we catch sight of her in one or two scenes:

> And eke that straunger knight among the rest
> Was for like need enforst to disarray:
> Then whenas vailed was her lofty crest
> Her golden locks that were in trammels gay
> Upbounden, did themselves adown display,
> And raught unto her heels; like sunny beams
> That in a cloud their light did long time stay,
> Their vapour vaded, shew their golden gleames,
> And through the persant aire shoot forth their azure streames.[1]

It is in these books too that we encounter the best of what have always seemed to me the most individual features of the poem, Spenser's picturesque and symbolic pageants. As a story-teller Spenser is hopeless; Ariosto's story of the faithless squire could hardly be worse told than it is by Spenser, and he

[1] *Faerie Queene*, III. ix. 20.

made a poor job of adding to Chaucer's tale of Cambell and Canacee. Chaucer is as much his superior in the art of telling a story as Shakespeare in dramatic range and insight, Milton in seriousness and sublimity, Dante in depth and vision. But when he describes a pageant of symbolic figures, then Spenser is a poet *sui generis*. The music of his verse becomes an enchanter's pipe to the sound of which there rises before our eyes a succession of mysterious and beautiful figures either delightfully meaningless or charged with a significance that is neither moral nor Christian. Indeed the less relevant to his main purpose, moral or religious, the theme of his song, the more Spenser becomes an emancipated and delightful poet, like a schoolboy set free from his task, and singing for the pure delight of song. What could be more irrelevant in the middle of his first serious allegory than the description of Duessa's descent to the underworld to seek aid for the quite unimportant person Sansjoy? But nothing else in the first book is more delightful and nothing so entirely Spenserian. What is more delightful or more irrelevant than the procession in which Marinell, of whom we know and for whom we care nothing, is conveyed by his mother to the depths of the sea to be healed by Tryphon, whoever he may be:

> A teme of Dolphins raunged in aray,
> Drew the smooth charet of sad *Cymoent*;
> They were all taught by *Triton*, to obay
> To the long raynes, at her commaundement:
> As swift as swallowes, on the waues they went,
> That their broad flaggie finnes no fome did reare,
> No bubbling roundell they behind them sent;
> The rest of other fishes drawen weare,
> Which with their finny oars the swelling sea did sheare.

> Soone as they bene arriu'd vpon the brim
> Of the *Rich strond*, their charets they forlore,
> And let their temed fishes softly swim
> Along the margent of the fomy shore,
> Least they their finnes should bruze, and surbate sore
> Their tender feet vpon the stony ground.[1]

Of the same irrelevant and delightful kind are the episodes of Belphoebe and Timias (iii. 5. 27 ff., and iv. 7. 29, to 8. 18), the strange incident of the sacrifice of Serena (vi. 8. 31 ff.), and, loveliest of all, the pictures of the Graces dancing round Colin's love to the music of Colin's pipe (vi. 10. 1-18):

> All they without were raunged in a ring,
> And daunced round; but in the midst of them
> Three other Ladies did both daunce and sing,
> The whilest the rest them round about did hemme,
> And like a girlond did in compasse stemme:
> And in the middest of those same three, was placed
> Another Damzell, as a precious gemme,
> Amidst a ring most richly well enchaced,
> That with her goodly presence all the rest much graced.
>
> . . . . . .
>
> These were the Graces, daughters of delight,
> Handmaides of Venus, which are wont to haunt
> Vppon this hill, and daunce there day and night:
> Those three to men all gifts of grace do graunt,
> And all, that *Venus* in her selfe doth vaunt,
> Is borrowed of them. But that faire one,
> That in the midst was placed parauant,
> Was she to whom that shepheard pypt alone,
> That made him pipe so merrily, as never none.

Among these pageants are some less obviously irrelevant, which strike a deeper, more philosophical note, even if the philosophy is not very profound and certainly not what a Puritan would have accepted as

[1] *Faerie Queene*, III. iv. 33-34.

either moral or Christian. They are those whose theme is the old mystery of sex, love as a power in nature and an all-subduing, essentially lawless force in the heart of man and woman. Spenser's poetry of love has more than one source, but the most immediate is the *Romance of the Rose*, that fountainhead, as Huizinga declares, of paganism in the later Middle Ages, the allegoric elaboration of *amour courtois*, the free love of the romances of which Guillaume de Lorris presents the decorative, Jean de Meung the seamy side. In the House of Busyrane and the Maske of Cupid (III. 11 and 12) he elaborates in a symbolic pageant the power of love as a great natural passion in which the most contradictory elements are blended, and which recognises no law. What inner meaning Spenser intended the enslavement of Amoret and her release by Britomart to bear I must leave to the interpreters. It is conceivable, if at all, only as a notion. In some way or other Chastity delivers married love from the thraldom of passion. The impression left on the imagination is something different; it is the old theme of the *Romance of the Rose*, and later of Donne's *Songs and Sonnets* and witty, sensual *Elegies*, the power and complexity of love, its power to ennoble and to degrade, to attract and to repel:

> Behinde him was *Reproch, Repentance, Shame*;
> *Reproch* the first, *Shame* next, *Repent* behind:
> *Repentance* feeble, sorrowfull, and lame:
> *Reproch* despightful, carelesse, and vnkind;
> *Shame* most ill fauourd, bestiall, and blind:
> *Shame* lowrd, *Repentance* sigh'd, *Reproch* did scould;
> *Reproch* sharpe stings, *Repentance* whips entwind,
> *Shame* burning brond-yrons in her hand did hold:
> All three to each vnlike, yet all made in one mould.[1]

[1] *Faerie Queene*, III. xii. 24.

'ROMANCE OF THE ROSE'

Here as in Jean de Meung's part of the older poem and in Donne's Songs or Elegies it is the darker aspect of the passion which is emphasised. The other side, that of Guillaume de Lorris, is seen in the description of Scudamore's ordeal as a lover making his way to the capture of Amoret. It is the same passion, beset by the same perils and pains, but purified, because the passion is now directed, as Plato might say, to the Good and Beautiful, a harmony of souls:

> Concord she cleeped was in common reed,
> Mother of blessed Pease and Friendship trew.

And Spenser is doctrinally a Puritan because, like Wither and Milton, as we shall see in a later lecture, he seeks the realisation of the Good in love, not with Plato in the love of the abstract Idea of Beauty, but in a perfect wife, anticipating Milton's invocation:

> Hail wedded Love, mysterious Law, true source
> Of human offspring. . . .
> Here Love his golden shafts imploys, here lights
> His constant Lamp, and waves his purple wings,
> Reigns here and revels; not in the bought smile
> Of Harlots loveless, joyless, unindear'd,
> Casual fruition, nor in Court Amours,
> Mixt Dance, or wanton Mask, or Midnight Ball,
> Or Serenate, which the starv'd Lover sings
> To his proud fair, best quitted with disdain.[1]

But for Spenser, at least in *The Faerie Queene*, it is more a doctrine than a conviction. His treatment of love is essentially that of his predecessors Guillaume de Lorris and Froissart and Chaucer. He lingers in the garden of the Rose from which the more puritan

[1] *Paradise Lost*, IV. 750 ff.

Milton turns away as dangerous precincts for one who would be captain of his own soul:

> For what admir'st thou, what transports thee so,
> An outside? Fair no doubt, and worthy well
> Thy cherishing, thy honouring, and thy love,
> Not thy subjection: weigh with her thyself;
> Then value.[1]

For Spenser, no more than any other poet or philosopher, can quite moralise the free passion of love, which in the last resort, as he tells us in the canto of the Garden of Adonis, is the irrational, unfettered procreative power of nature pouring forth in endless forms of life (III. 6, 29 ff.), troubled only by the great destroyer Time:

> But were it not that Time their troubler is
> All that in this delightful garden grows
> Should happie be and have immortal bliss:
> For here all plenty and all pleasure flows.

Spenser's own poetry, one feels, flows with most freedom and joy when his theme enables him to escape from the inhibitions of puritan ethics and piety and expatiate over flowery meadows of irrelevance—pageants and processions and the marriage of rivers and Colins piping to their naked loves. He is no rebel like Marlowe or Donne, or satyr like Marino and some other Italian poets; he is an Ariel set free by the spirit of the Renaissance to wing his way from flower to flower like Clarion in his charming poem *Muiopotamos*:

> What more felicitie can fall to creature
> Then to enjoy delight with liberty,
> And to be Lord of all the world of Nature,
> To raine in the aire from earth to highest skie,

[1] *Paradise Lost*, VIII. 567-571.

> To feed on flowres and weeds of glorious feature,
> To take whatever thing doth please the eye?
> Who rests not pleased with such happinesse
> Well worthy he to taste of wretchednesse.

But he could not quite rest 'pleased with such happinesse', or let himself for long 'enjoy delight with liberty'. The spider of Cartwright's Puritanism had fixed him with her glittering eye and he was never quite to escape from her, though the high seriousness at which the first book aimed was not long maintained. He must moralise his song and make the romance of lovers and knights a vehicle for the inculcation of the Calvinist doctrine of salvation by divine grace, and of puritan ethics condemnatory or distrustful of the sensuous in every form and of the free play of the imagination in fiction of every kind: 'Poetry is a lie'. It was not to be done; and when we come upon tedious episodes like the House of Medina and her sisters Perissa and Elissa, or the dreadful allegory of the human body which Phineas Fletcher was to elaborate still further, we feel that Clarion has been snared in the dusty web of the didactic, and can only rejoice when he escapes again to his favourite theme of love, or to expatiate in picturesque and musical irrelevancies.

So far from succeeding in harmonising the spirit of the Renaissance and the Reformation, Spenser's poetry is not most deeply affected by either the one or the other. With the art of the Renaissance he is in love, the new beauty of diction and harmony which he found in the French poetry of the Pléiade and the stanzas of Ariosto and Tasso. That he has made his own and enriched with—to our ears at least—a fuller, sweeter music. But neither the thought nor the temper of his poetry is quite that of the Renaissance as we meet it in Marlowe and Chapman, nor of the Puritan Reformation as it sounds in Milton. The spirit of his poetry is that of the age which was passing away, the age of romance and allegory and the cult of courtly love, the religion of love. *The Faerie Queene* is the last poem whose direct descent is from the *Romance of the Rose*, through Tasso and Ariosto. I speak, of course, of the effect of the poem on the imagination, not of its express purpose. The allegory is there to remind us from time to time that, as Dowden says, 'the end of the whole is virtuous action'. Nor do I wish to deny that in his own way Spenser does homage to ideals of holiness and purity and loyalty as well as courage and love. So does Ariosto; so does Tasso. We are apt to be a little self-righteous about the superior piety and purity of Protestant poetry; to think, both Americans and English, that seriousness is the first of virtues, and to misjudge a flippant and humorous poet like Ariosto. Mr. R. Neil Dodge, an American critic, quotes examples of borrowings by Spenser where what is comic or ironical in Ariosto's poem is by the Englishman taken quite seriously; and he adds: 'When Spenser read the *Orlando Furioso* for suggestions he read it in the light of his own serene idealism.' It might with equal justice be said that the English poet is deficient in a sense of humour. For it is not fair to judge Ariosto only by the cynical, ironical, humorous strain in his work. Mr. Edmund Gardner contends that Ariosto is a far more serious poet than his predecessor Boiardo, that his whole attitude towards women is far higher, that 'Bradamante is a maiden warrior though no mere virago, as pure and steadfast as our Spenser's own Britomart, but incomparably more human and loveable'. The worst canto in the *Orlando* is not more disgusting than Spenser's story of Malbecco and Hellenore or more frankly sensuous than the sacrifice of Serena. But Gardner's criticism goes deeper. It would not be unjust to contend that both the *Morte d'Arthur* and the *Orlando Furioso* are more impressive ethical poems than the *Faerie Queene* because they are more human, deal with more realisable characters, their temptations and sins and repentance. Arthur and Artegal are no more than names; Belphoebe and Florimel and Britomart but charming shadows. No one of them is either an individual for whose fate we feel deeply concerned, or, as an abstraction, assumes the proportions of Everyman face to face with one of the great, elemental temptations or experiences of men.

But the allegory after all served its purpose by allowing Spenser to write his poem and serious Protestants to read it. Giles Fletcher in justifying his writing of a religious poem, after citing Gregory Nazianzen, Juvencus, Prosper, Prudentius, Sedulius, continues: 'all which were followed by the choicest wits of Christendome: Nennius translating all Saint John's Gospel into Greek verse, Sanazar, the late living image and happy imitator of Virgil, bestowing ten years upon a song only to celebrate that one day when Christ was born unto us on earth and we (a happie change) unto God in heaven: thrice honour'd Bartas and our (I know no other more glorious name than his own) Mr. Edmund Spencer (two blessed Soules) not thinking ten years inough, layeing out their whole lives upon this one studie', and lastly 'the Princely Father of our Countrey', *i.e.* James the First. It is a strange assembly, but one can imagine what a relief it was to be able to defend one's enjoyment of *The Faerie Queene* by being able to class it with such edifying if tedious authors. Henry More tells us that his father, a strict Calvinist, 'from my childhood tuned mine ears to Spenser's rhymes, entertaining us on winter nights with that incomparable piece of his *Faerie Queene*, a poem as richly fraught with divine morality as Phansy'. And to Milton's encomium I have already referred. We may forgive allegory some headaches inasmuch as it has enabled serious Christians and Protestants to enjoy the *Song of Solomon* without a scruple of conscience, indeed with a sense of positive edification.

Yet that Spenser failed in his attempt to revive and purify mediaeval romance is clear from the line which his admirers and followers take in their own poems. The Fletchers retained the allegory; they dropped the romance. The day of courtly romance was over; and the popular romances which circulated in chap-books, and are probably one of the sources of *The Pilgrim's Progress*, were reckoned with Maypoles, dancing and drinking healths as things which a regenerate man repudiates. Among his early sins Baxter includes that 'I was extremely bewitched with a Love of Romances, Fables and Old Tales, which corrupted my affections and lost my time'.[1] I do not know if *The Faerie Queene* was included in this list, but when Prynne makes a list of allowable or commendable authors—du Bartas, Beza, Scaliger, Buchanan, Heinsius, Withers, Hall, Quarles, James I.—he does not include Spenser. There were but two forms of poetry which a severe Puritan was disposed to regard as legitimate, Scriptural paraphrase and definitely religious allegory. Quarles and Milton may be taken as very different representatives of the one tendency; Bunyan of the other. It was not possible

[1] *Reliquiae Baxterianae*, 1696, p. 2.

to effect a real compromise between the courtly sensuous chivalrous poetry of the Renaissance, the dream of love and chivalry, revived with less of conviction but a more elaborate embellishment of presentation, and the intenser spirit of Protestant, Puritan, or Catholic Christianity intent on otherworldly values. The values of *The Faerie Queene*, and there are such, are not Christian as Bunyan and Foster understood Christian, but Humanist.

CHAPTER III

THE DRAMA: COMEDY

The dramatic tradition, its character and strength—The Puritans and the drama—Prynne's Histriomastix—*The religious and ethical element in the Elizabethan drama—Shakespeare's comedies and Roman plays.*

IN Spenser's *Faerie Queene,* and to some extent in all his poetry, one can study the meeting of the stream of tradition, romantic and allegoric, with new currents humanistic and religious, with which the poet feels himself in sympathy and yet does not fully comprehend, does not quite realise the entire breach they involve with the past, with the mediaeval tradition of romance and love poetry which has still so much charm for him. Spenser is an eclectic. None of the Elizabethans looks so much backwards and forwards. His chief work is in the direct line of descent from the *Romance of the Rose* and Chaucer's *Prologue to the Legend of Good Women* and *Parliament of Foules* through *The Kinges Quair, The Golden Targe, The Palice of Honour, King Hart, The Pastime of Pleasure, The Bowge of Court, The Spider and the Fly,* and Sackville's *Induction.* In later allegory the thread of connection with the Rose is broken, not in *The Faerie Queene.* And yet Spenser's art in theory and practice is that of the new poetry, the poetry of France and Italy, Ariosto and Ronsard; and spiritually his poem is a product of the Reformation, breathing hatred of Rome, and exalting theoretically and allegorically, if it cannot assimilate them to the tradition of romantic love, the moral ideals of puritanism.

It is this eclectic combination of the traditions of the later Middle Ages, of the fifteenth century, with the new inspirations blowing in from Italy and Geneva, that makes Spenser's poetry so different from that of his contemporaries and immediate successors, great as was the influence of his diction and verse on Elizabethan poetry of every kind. Daniel, Drayton, Lodge, Marlowe, Shakespeare (the poet), Davies, Donne—they have all broken much more completely with the Mediaeval tradition of chivalry and romantic, courtly love. Even Spenser's sonnets are not quite like those of the other poets in form or spirit. *He* takes the Petrarchan, chivalrous strain more seriously. *They* are more Italianate, more of *virtuosi* experimenting in new fashions, more interested in the style than the subject-matter, whereas Spenser's interest in chivalrous ideals is obviously sincere even if, to justify it to himself and serious Protestants, he must draw over it the veil of allegory. In the poetry of the last ten years of the century all is experiment—'passionating' legends, overwrought Ovidian idylls, historical poems, classical satires, pastorals in various forms, philosophical poems or verse letters reflecting fashionable poses, sceptical, Stoical, Epicurean. But the whole trend is away from the chivalrous romance which Spenser loved. The next great English poem will be Classical in form and more sternly Puritan in tone.

There was, however, another tradition, besides that of chivalrous and erotic romance and allegory, which had come down from the Middle Ages and was strong enough to take up into itself the influence of the new humanist spirit and, fertilised thereby, to produce a body of literary work of the most unequal value, but including, in the work of one man, the fullest and sanest expression of that spirit which we possess—and that was the drama.

The vitality of the dramatic tradition in England did not lie in the excellence of any dramatic work this country had produced either in religious or secular drama. We have no great religious plays, and the secular plays of the early sixteenth century are banal in style and the versification is unmusical doggerel. Its strength lay in the taste of the English people of all classes and in the organisation which had grown up to gratify that taste. For three centuries dramatic entertainments had been becoming an increasingly important element in the amusement of the Court, the Nobility, and the people; and, in the course of the last two, companies of professional actors had established themselves among and not noticeably superior to the jugglers, bear-baiters, dancers, singers, and entertainers of all kinds who formed so important, if also despised, a section of mediaeval society. The question which the last twenty years of the sixteenth century had to decide was whether this kind of entertainment would or would not, under the influence of the great revival of learning and letters, acquire a higher worth and beauty, whether the English drama which Sir Philip Sidney in 1580 condemned as artistically and morally worthless should, by 1600, be a drama comparable at its best with that of Greece. But before this question was answered a second had been raised in an ominous tone—had the drama as such any right to exist at all? Religion and the desire to be amused are, I have said, two of the strongest passions of the human mind, each at times threatening to displace the other altogether. They never perhaps flowed more strongly side by side, like the clear and the discoloured streams which constitute the Rhone as it issues from the Lake of Geneva, than during the years from the accession of Elizabeth. The nation was growing wealthy and luxury was on the increase. The Court loved to be amused and so did the people, and with both the drama had become the favourite source of amusement. To turn over the records of dramatic activity at Court, as these have been made available by the work of scholars from Malone and Collier to Feuillerat and Murray and Chambers, is to realise the strength with which the current was flowing. The output of plays was enormous, for those which have survived are but a few of those produced. Look at the list of plays from Henslowe's diary and other sources, printed by Mr. Greg and Sir Edmund Chambers, as having been acted by the Admiral's men alone; and consider how few of them have survived.

That is one side of the picture. The other is a continuous stream of protest against drama and the stage, gathering in strength till when the Long Parliament meets one of its earliest acts is to close the public theatres. In an appendix under the heading *Documents of Criticism* Chambers has illustrated the trend of this criticism from about 1565 onwards. The artistic improvement of the drama in the eighties and nineties begot no alteration in the Puritan attitude. It rather hardened and expressed itself more bitterly as, under James, the Court gave itself up more recklessly to the pursuit of amusement. 'The honour, wealth and glory of the nation', says Mrs. Hutchinson, 'wherein Queen Elizabeth left it were soon prodigally wasted by this thriftless heir; and the nobility of the land were utterly debased by setting honours to public sale. . . . The generality of the land soon learned the Court fashion, and every great house in the country became a sty of nastiness. To keep the people in their deplorable security, till vengeance overtook them, they were entertained with masks, stage-plays, and sorts of ruder sports.'[1] This is the language of political and religious prejudice, but there is a measure of truth in it. The Court of Charles was purer, the same witness admits, but in his reign the attack upon the stage culminated in the *Histriomastix* of William Prynne in 1633, and it will be interesting to examine it in order to see that the attack was not really inspired so much by hatred of the actual immorality of the stage as by religious fanaticism, the conviction that play-acting was in itself a sin the toleration of which must bring down the wrath of God. Prynne's attack is not directed against the abuses of the stage but against the drama as such. His is a root and branch policy; and if his tone is bitterer than that of his predecessors (and he is not much bitterer than Stubbes) the arguments he uses are the same. He shows no such first-hand knowledge of the contemporary drama as Collier at a later period does. He makes no exceptions, no comparison of later dramatists as Beaumont and Fletcher with Shakespeare or Jonson, as Collier and as Coleridge do. Indeed he defends the length of his book by citing the scandalous fact that 'Ben Jonson's, Shackspeer's, and others' published plays 'are growne from Quarto into Folio; which yet beare so good a price and sale that I cannot but with griefe relate it, they are now printed in farre better paper than most Octavo or Quarto Bibles, which hardly find such vent as they'; and a

[1] *Memoirs of the Life of Colonel Hutchinson*, ed. C. H. Firth, 1906, p. 64.

marginal note adds 'Shackspeer's plays are printed in the best Crowne paper, far better than most Bibles'. This must refer to the second Folio of 1631 containing Milton's eulogistic lines, for which he in part apologised later.

What Prynne undertakes is no less than to prove 'that all popular and common plays, whether Comicall, Satyricall, Mimicall or mixt of either especially as they are now compiled and personated among us are such sinful, hurtful, pernitious recreations as are altogether unseemly, and unlawful unto Christians'. When one comes, however, to study his elaborately classified and syllogistically stated arguments most of them seem to us to-day singularly irrelevant. For whenever he touches on 'plays as they are now compiled and personated among us', he advances nothing from his own experience but falls back on the instances cited by his predecessors Gosson, Stubbes, and other controversialists whose judgments Sir Edmund Chambers has collected. The weight of his own argument is supplied by citations from the early Christian writers and Fathers. It does not seem to have entered his head that there was an essential difference between the position of the early Christians combating the paganism and obscenities of the later Roman theatre and that of Christians dealing with a theatre which took its rise within the Church itself, and which, whatever its faults, was as ignorant and innocent of pagan beliefs and cults as Prynne himself. Whatever is said of the ancient theatre by Chrysostom or other early Christian preacher or father is applied immediately and without modification, or change of perspective, to the stage of his own day. 'Peruse, I say, these generall fathers and Councells (whose words if I should at large describe them would amount unto an ample volume) and you shall find them all concurre in this: that Stage-Plays are wholly composed of or at least fraught with Ribaldrie, Scurrilitie; unchaste and amorous Streines and passages; Obscene and filthie jests which inquinate the mindes, corrupt the manners, and defile the Soules of men, yea pollute the very places and common ayre where they are but acted. Whence they all condemne these Theatricall Enterludes, as unseemly, pernicious, abominable, and utterly displeasing unto God; stiling them the very sinkes of all uncleanesse, the Lectures of Obscenitie, the Meditations of Adulterie,' etc. etc. (pp. 66 ff.). That is the strain in which Prynne flows on from chapter to chapter of endless repetition. Each of his indictments (which he entitles Acts and Scenes of his Tragedy) is set out in the form of a syllogism whose major and minor he is to make good, *e.g.*:

That whose style and subject-matter is Bloody and Tyrannical, breathing out Malice, Anger, Fury, Crueltie, Tyrannie, Fierceness, Treason, Violent Opposition, Murther, and Revenge, must needs be Odious, Unseemely, and Unlawful unto Christians. But such is the stile and subject-matter of most, but especially of our Tragicall, Stage-Playes. Therefore they must needes be, &c. &c.

Clearly everything will depend on the proofs which Prynne advances in support of his minor premiss, and it would have been both valuable and interesting to have had a thoughtful description of Elizabethan tragedy as it struck a contemporary, to have seen the plays of Shakespeare, Jonson, Massinger, and Ford through the eyes of a Puritan of the type, say, of Milton, of Milton before he had become committed to the cause of a party, the Milton who wrote *Comus* at this very time. There is much in these plays

'HISTRIOMASTIX'

which would have met with his censure on both artistic and moral grounds, though even of the worst it would be difficult to argue that the tragedies breathe forth or seek to inspire the audience with murder, cruelty, tyranny, and treachery. They portray such evils with at times to our minds a certain callousness and brutality, which is more naïve than decadent, but they seldom fail to show us, with something of the same naivety, the nemesis which overtakes crime. Fletcher's levity and florid rhetoric go ill with his tragic horrors; but only Ford, I think, a more serious spirit, can be charged with decadence, in that he set forth deliberately the thesis that a great passion is its own justification, condones any crime. Of Shakespeare's tragedies the most that such a critic might, with Dr. Johnson, have complained is that he 'sacrifices virtue to convenience, and is so much more careful to please than to instruct that he seems to write without any moral purpose'. But Prynne attempts no such survey. For the proof of his minor, he appeals to early Christian writers who were dealing with an entirely different drama, and adds a few references to his predecessors Gosson and Stubbes. In a note he brings all tragedies without exception within the scope of his condemnation: 'read Sophocles, Euripides, Seneca his Tragedies, with all our Moderne Tragedies which confirme it'. The bulk of the section on tragedy is then given up to the proof of the major premiss, which nobody would dream of denying, and he proceeds to identify the motive and effect of tragedy Greek and English with those of 'swordplayes, Duels and suchlike cruell and bloody spectacles which Constantine and Nerva suppressed'.

This elaborate *ignoratio elenchi* runs through the whole of Prynne's long and furious tirade, and I dwell on it only because, as events prove, it expressed the mind of a powerful minority in the country, to which the civil war gave for a time the upper hand. I will select three of his arguments to illustrate the fanatical rather than moral spirit of the anti-humanistic current the interactions of which with the spirit of the Renaissance in our literature I wish to investigate. One long section is devoted to an indictment of the stage because of its choice of pagan themes, presumably such stories from Ovid as Lyly chose for his flimsy comedies, or Shakespeare used in *A Midsummer Night's Dream*, and other dramatists occasionally. This opens a sluice through which Prynne floods the reader with early Christian denunciations of ancient mythology and rites. Whether the early Church was justified in its root and branch condemnation of the ancient stage is a question I need not here discuss; but surely the arguments and denunciations of the Fathers fighting a life and death battle (as they believed) with a still living paganism have little relevance to such Elizabethan plays as those in which Lyly and Peele and Shakespeare sport with the shadows of ancient mythology reflected from the pages of the *Metamorphoses*. The thought which the power exercised by the ancient drama might have suggested to a serious but open-minded Christian is rather whether so potent an instrument as the stage might not be enlisted in the service of a purer religion and ethics. To create a Christian drama on the model of the ancient had been the dream of many of the early Humanists, and on the Continent had produced Latin plays for school performance of real and varied excellence, from Reuchlin's *Henno* (1498) to the *Jepthes* and *Baptistes* of Buchanan and the dramas of Grotius. Classical subjects, historical and mythical, had competed with Biblical, and become the more popular as the secular spirit gained the upper hand; but in Holland in the seventeenth century Vondel preferred to the classical and patriotic themes of Hooft stories from the Bible or the legends of the saints, presented with the utmost seriousness and all the wealth of poetry, declamatory and lyrical, of which he had command. But the furious Puritanism which speaks in Prynne's treatise would have none of it. If there is anything worse than a drama which revives pagan deities and legends, it is that which profanes things Christian by bringing them upon the stage. 'As the historicall passages of the Old Testament, so the historie of Christ's death, and the celebration of His blessed Sacraments are often prophaned in theatricall enterludes, especially by Popish Priests and Jesuites in foraigne parts: Who as they have turned the Sacrament of Christ's body and blood into a Masse-play; so they have likewise transformed their Masse itself, together with the whole story of Christ's birth, his life, his Passion, and all other parts of their Ecclesiastical service into Stage-Playes. . . . Ludovicus Vives complains that it was the custome of the Priests and Papists in his age, when as the solemnity of Christs death was celebrated, to exhibit plays unto the people, not much different from those ancient Pagan Enterludes. . . . There Judas is derided, uttering the most foolish things he can devise, whiles he betrayes Christ. There the Disciples flie, the souldiers pursuing them, and that not without the derision and laughter, both of the actors and spectators. There Peter cuts off the ear of Malchus, the ignorant multitude applauding him, as if by this means the captivity of Christ were sufficiently revenged. And a little after he who had fought so valiantly, being affrighted with the questions of one little Girle, denies his Master, the multitude deriding in the meantime the Maide that questions him, and hissing at Peter who denies him. Among so many Players, among so many shoutes and ridiculous fooleries, Christ only is serious and grave.... Loe here their own Author declaiming against Popish Priests for their frequent acting of Christs Passion, in the very self-same manner as the Pagans of old did use to act the lives and practises of their Devill-gods. A sufficient testimony how little Papists really esteem the bitter passion of our blessed Saviour since they make a common play or pastime of it.' After admitting that the Roman Church had itself disapproved of abuses attending the plays, he proceeds in the same scornful tone: 'But yet to quit the credit of their Church which might justly be taxed for approving this ungodly practise they put this fair glosse upon this so execrable villainy: that the acting of Christs Passion, however it came to be abused, was a custom religiously practised and brought in at first. A most irreligious evasion.... But hath his provincial Councell or Synodus Carnotensis ... abolished this abuse out of the Antichristian Church of Rome? No verily, for the Jesuites themselves are not ashamed to publish to the world, that instead of preaching the word of God, the fall of Adam and Eve, with their exile out of Paradise, and the history of our Saviour, they acted and playd them among their Indian Proselites. A true Jesuitical practise beseeming well this histrionicall infernall Society who have turned the very truth of God into a lie, and the whole service of God into an Enterlude.'[1]

In these denunciations we feel the whole soul

[1] *Histriomastix*, pp. 112 ff.

'HISTRIOMASTIX'

of Puritanism, its hatred of idolatry and paganism, but still bitterer hatred of the Church of Rome, its question-begging condemnation of acting as acting. Yet surely a little reflection on the description which Prynne cites from Ludovicus Vives might have suggested the question: was that an entirely evil thing which awakened such an eager sympathy in the hearts of simple onlookers, making them applaud the boldness of Peter at one moment and explode his cowardice at another, the same sympathy as that with which a pious Mohammedan contemplates the sufferings of Hassan and Hussein?[1] Was it a wise thing to relegate religion to the Church, or to Church and family worship, supposing we had more of us the leisure and patience to sit out two sermons a day as Prynne recommends? What is associated only with seriousness is apt to become associated also with boredom. But on that I need not dwell, nor on two of the arguments which recur again and again in the tirades of Prynne and like-minded writers, first, that all acting is in the nature of a lie, an argument with which Sidney deals in the *Defence of Poesie*, and secondly, that it is a sin because expressly forbidden by God for a man to wear woman's apparel, an argument based on Deuteronomy xxii. 5: 'Women shall not wear that which pertaineth unto a man, nor shall a man put on a woman's garment: for all that do so are abomination to the Lord thy God.' To do so is, Prynne declares, a direct breach of the moral law, 'having a relation to the 7th commandment and to severall Scriptures in the New Testament concerning modesty and decency in apparell'. And on these grounds he justifies the execution of Joan of Arc,

[1] See M. Arnold's *Essays in Criticism*, 1865, 'A Persian Passion Play'; Ridgeway: *Dramas and Dramatic Dances*, 1915, pp. 65-85.

the 'Pucelle de Dieu, that notable French virago, who arrayed herself like a man, and turned a great commander in the wars, till at length she was taken prisoner by the English in the field, attired as like a man; for which unnatural act of hers she was condemned and burnt at Roan'. Selden prided himself on having shown the irrelevancy of the text: 'I never converted but two: the one was Mr. Crashaw' (*i.e.* the father of the poet) 'from writing against plays by telling him a way to understand that place of putting on woman's apparel, which has nothing to do in the business, as neither has it that the Fathers speak against plays in their time, with reason enough for they had real idolatries mixed with their plays having three altars perpetually upon the stage'.[1]

More significant are two other of Prynne's arguments because they reveal the full scope of Puritan antagonism to art and the Humanities and indicate the source of that antagonism. The first is the condemnation of plays not alone for their own sake but because they are accompanied by other evil things such as dancing, singing, and music. Each of these nouns is, indeed, qualified: 'lascivious, mixt, effeminate, amorous dancing', 'amorous Pastoralls, lascivious, ribaldrous Songs and Ditties', 'effeminate, delicate, lust-provoking musick as S. Basil phraseth it, which Christians ought to flie as a most filthy thing'. But Prynne throws the epithet 'lascivious' about with a reckless hand, and the reader finds it difficult to discover what kinds of dancing (if any) or music are excepted. 'If David danced it was not by couples or in measure but with a modest, grave, and

---

[1] *Table Talk of John Selden: Poetry*. In a letter to Ben Jonson (Selden's *Works*, ii., 1690) Selden develops his exposition of the text as directed against rites in which men personated a female and women a male deity. See the edition of the *Table Talk* by Sir Frederick Pollock, London, 1927.

sober motion, much like to walking or the grave old measures, free from all amorous gestures, gropings, kisses, compliments, love-tricks, and wanton embracement which abound in all our modern dances. If Solomon said, "There is a time to dance", he meant merely an inward cheerfulness.' Whence he derived this information, Prynne does not tell us. One may more safely assume that David would have thought himself a poor worshipper if there had been no abandonment in his dance (unless Micah laughed because David was performing the goose-step) and that Solomon was no enemy of kisses and compliments. Of song and music Prynne will tolerate only Psalms and spiritual songs, and the section on music is a sustained indictment of music generally, and especially instrumental music and choir-singing in Church. The history of the Protestant churches in Scotland and New England will show how representative of serious religious feeling Prynne was in this condemnation of church-music. Puritanism was fatal to the two great arts in which the English people had delighted, vocal music and the drama, both of which require for their support a regular and organised system of supply and demand. English music was dealt its first blow with the closing of the Abbeys, and the revival in the seventeenth century was killed by Puritanism.

Prynne's argument culminates in the indictment of plays because they provoke laughter, 'excessive cachinnations in the public view of dissolute graceless persons'. Here again the laughter is qualified as 'lascivious', but it is evident that to provoke laughter is itself a proof of lasciviousness in the cause. It is the spirit of laughter which he mistrusts. 'Our Saviour whose doctrine no Christian dares controll hath denounced woe to all those that laugh, that live in ease, jollity, and carnall pleasures now, because they shall mourne and suffer eternall torments. ... For Christians therefore to make this world a paradise of all earthly pleasures, to spend their days in Epicurism, mirth, and jollity, glutting themselves with sinfull Spectacles and mirth-provoking Enterludes, as, alas, too many doe ... is to be most unlike their Saviour who was oft-times weeping, never smiling that we read of. *Quem flevisse legimus, risisse non legimus*, how can it but be sinfull yea abominable.'

However extravagantly or even absurdly stated, the thought of this section contains the very essence of the Puritan protest against the drama and much else that they saw around them, survivals of the 'Merry England' of the Middle Ages, in origin probably pagan,—wakes, fairs, maypoles, pageants, Church-ales, music, and dancing. They encountered the world and its ways with the unsparing sternness and reproval of the early Christians, renewed with (one must think) an imperfect sense of proportion, a faulty perspective, the protest of the early Fathers against institutions and forms of amusement which in the days when the Fathers wrote were inseparably bound up with superstition, cruelty, and lubricity. A soberer witness than Prynne may be cited to show what it was which to a Puritan seemed to divide him from the world around him—a deeper seriousness, a view of this world as but a gallery conducting to eternal life, so that every form of pastime was in the nature of sin, tempting Christian to linger by the wayside when the shades of night were already falling. It was not this or that doctrine which made one a Puritan. Baxter, Bunyan, Cromwell, Milton, were far from seeing eye to eye on all points of doctrine or church-government. What united them was a spirit of intense seriousness, an ever-present awareness of the 'Eternal Verities'. 'There is an universall and radical enmity', writes Baxter, 'between the Carnall and the Spirituall, the Serpents and the Womans seed, the fleshly Mind and the spiritual Law of God through all the world, in all generations. This Enmity is found in England as well as in other Countries, between the Godly and the Worldly minds; as he that was born after the Flesh did persecute him that was born after the Spirit, even so it was here: The Vulgar rabble of the carnal and prophane, the Fornicators, Drunkards, Swearers, etc., did ever hate them that reproved their Sin, and condemned them by a holy Life.... So that everywhere serious, Godly people that would not run with others to excess of Riot were spoken against or derided by the names of Precisians, Zealots, Over-strict, the holy Brethren, and other terms of scorn.'[1]

If Prynne, thus summing up the argument of Rainolds, Gosson, Stubbes, Crashaw, and others, may be taken as an index to the ever-strengthening current of religious protest, the question I wish to consider is how this reacted upon the drama, how did the consciousness of religious and moral disapproval, of being as it were without the pale of serious respect, affect the work of the better dramatists, those whom it would be manifestly unjust to describe as pandering to the coarser taste of the populace or the corrupter taste of the Court. Here are two powerful currents flowing counter to one another, the deep, swift stream of the passion for amusement which had gathered strength in the later Middle Ages and was further stimulated by the

[1] *Reliquiae Baxterianae*, pp. 31-32.

Renaissance, and had found in the drama probably its fullest and most promising expression; and, on the other hand, the rising tide of religious feeling, breaking into the waves of a fiercer fanaticism, almost as passionately hostile to the stage as to the Anti-Christian Church of Rome. One may dream, but it is only a dream, that if the temper of Erasmus rather than that of Luther and Calvin had prevailed, Christian feeling might have set itself to capture and control the drama, to enlist in its service this potent moulder of popular feeling, either by the creation of a definitely religious drama, as in Spain, or by making the Christian view of life the background, as it had been in mediaeval romance, of a varied picture of the foibles and frolics, the passions and aberrations of human nature. The Elizabethan drama might not then have been what a recent German critic calls it, and what in the main it is, an 'areligiös drama', not irreligious but non-religious. It was not to be. What did happen, it seems to me, was broadly one of three things: the greatest of the dramatists, and his most direct inheritors, Shakespeare and Beaumont and Fletcher, and their school, avoided the raising of moral and religious issues in any definite or dogmatic fashion, were content to accept the rôle of purveyors of amusement for Court and City. If, on the other hand, a thinker and poet was impelled to make the drama a vehicle for the explicit formulation of his thought about life, that thought is not distinctively Christian, but derives from Seneca and Cicero and Plutarch and Epictetus. I have in view to some extent Marlowe and Jonson, but more especially that strange and interesting character Chapman. But the final result was undoubtedly the rapid decline of the drama after the first decade of the seventeenth century. Encouraged neither by Court nor people to strike its roots deep into life and the problems of life, it sprung up quickly and soon withered away. The transition from Shakespeare to Beaumont and Fletcher is a significant one, from the portrayal of life with no definite didactic intention, no attempt at a dogmatic interpretation of life, but with a wide sympathy and a deep insight to a drama superficial, sentimental, flippant. The later Jacobean drama, if it evades Prynne's reckless and irrelevant charges, cannot escape the sentence of a better instructed critic such as Milton who, if also with some political prejudice, speaks of 'the writings and interludes of libidinous and ignorant Poetasters, who having scarce ever heard of that which is the main consistence of a true poem, the choice of such Persons as they ought to introduce, and what is moral and decent to each one, do for the most part lay up vicious Principles in sweet Pills to be swallowed down, and make the taste of virtuous documents harsh and sour'.[1] But Milton diverges from his political and religious friends in recognising the need of 'some recreating intermission of labour', and pleads the cause of drama in a well-ordered state.

But there were advantages as well as disadvantages in the fact that the stage was regarded as lying outside the pale of serious approval, as something not to be reformed but abolished. It might have fared worse with Shakespeare had the stage been not condemned but controlled by the serious temper of the age, not abused by a Prynne but censored by a Milton; for in that case the drama could not have escaped from the didactic purpose which serious people, by no means only Puritans, believed to be

[1] Milton: *The Reason of Church-Government*, Book II. Introduction.

the ultimate justification of both poetry and the drama. Had the drama come too much under the control of serious thought, critical and moral, as expressed in Sidney's *Defence* or represented by the earlier Senecan and other school plays, the result would have been a drama both pedantic and didactic. Jonson's Herculean effort to 'correct' the English drama, though the work of one who had to cater for a popular audience, is, with all its force and merit, pedantic, didactic, and very definitely dated. It was after all just because the stage was an amusement, like bear-baiting or tumbling, the players a somewhat despised when not detested class of vagabonds, that Shakespeare was left free to draw his varied picture of life, restrained by few rules or conventions—politics are most safely eschewed, as you may find yourself in prison or lose your ears, and after James's Act, strong language and anything savouring of blasphemy or unbelief must be eliminated. But apart from these few and, except as regards politics, rather uncertainly enforced restrictions, there does not seem to have been much which the censor would not let pass.

A landmark in the history of the Elizabethan drama is the formation in 1594 of the company which we know as Lord Hunsdon's, the Lord Chamberlain's, and ultimately the King's. In that year Kyd died; Marlowe had been murdered the year before, and Greene was dead two years earlier; Lyly's work as a dramatist was over, and so apparently was Peele's. These had been the pioneers who had given to the banal, doggerel, story-telling drama of the sixties and seventies, examples of which survive in *Cambyses*, *Damon and Pythias*, and a few others, a becoming vesture of style and verse. Lyly had created what may be called a comedy of manners, and Marlowe had done something greater. He had discovered and revealed where the centre of serious drama lay, neither in the incident and bustle of the popular plays nor in the declamation and 'sentences' of Senecan plays like *Gorboduc*, but in the passionate soul of man and its conflicts with circumstance and fate. *Tamburlaine* is not only our first great piece of blank-verse, but it is the first serious English play in which the germ-plasm of drama has been vitalised, because the interest of the play is neither incident nor thought but what Tamburlaine is, and what he does, and how he affects others just because he is Tamburlaine.

In 1593 plague had driven the players from London. In the following year there emerged from various fluctuating combinations of companies of the previous years two notable and stable companies, the Admiral's and the Chamberlain's, with Edward Alleyn as the principal actor in the first, and Richard Burbage in the second. Alleyn and Burbage have gone the way of all actors and become names that signify nothing, but with Burbage was William Shakespeare. 'An upstart crow beautified with our feathers,' Greene had called him while he was still oscillating in a way very dim to us between various shadowy companies, and the description is, in a truer way than Greene dreamt of, an accurate description. Revising old plays, and the number of his plays that were thus constructed seems to grow with every close investigation, or composing new ones alone or in collaboration with others, he had absorbed and assimilated all that proved most attractive in the work of his predecessors—the passionate eloquence of Marlowe, the winning pathos and greenwood note of Greene, the patterned elegance and fanciful filagree work of Lyly, the sweetness of mellifluous Peele. To Marlowe Shakespeare's debt in his earlier serious plays, histories, and tragedies, is greater and more obvious, and yet in the dramas of Marlowe there is something which Shakespeare's work never manifests, a passionate spirit of resistance to accepted conventions and beliefs.

There is no resistance to accepted standards in Shakespeare's work. When his spirit does grow rebellious, in plays like *Troilus and Cressida* or *Measure for Measure*, the quarrel is not with social conventions but with human nature, with man's ingratitude and the lightness of woman. 'Shakespeare', says Mr. Mackail, 'is not a moral teacher. He lets morality take care of itself; what he sets before us is life. Cruelty, falsehood, lust, treachery, are represented by him, as are heroism, truth, self-sacrifice: but they are only displayed, they are neither approved nor condemned, as causes with their effects, or it may be with their strange apparent effectlessness. . . . The lesson, if it can be called a lesson, of Shakespeare, as of Sophocles, is that we should not draw lessons, but see and feel and understand.'[1] What all this means is not very clear. To see and feel and understand is to draw lessons. Nor is it possible for any poet to represent life without letting us learn what he thinks about it one way or another. What puzzles one in Shakespeare's plays is that not infrequently while presenting the story and characters so faithfully and vividly that it is difficult for the reader to avoid passing moral judgment on it, Shakespeare himself seems willing not only to omit comment, but to acquiesce in a view that to us is repellent, to accept standards of

[1] Mackail, *Studies of English Poets*, 1926, p. 25.

which his own vivid telling of the story affords the most effective condemnation. What a strange moral confusion is suggested to our minds by that brilliant comedy, as rich in figure and colour as a picture by Paolo Veronese, *The Merchant of Venice*. Whatever may have been the didactic intention, the moral tone of the old play on which it was based and which Stephen Gosson commended as 'representing the greediness of worldly choosers and bloody minds of usurers', Shakespeare seems to have got rid of it fairly completely. For of all the suitors who come to Belmont, Bassanio best deserves the title of a 'worldly chooser'. The others have apparently as much to give as to receive, but Bassanio, like Lord Byron when he proposed to marry Miss Milbanke, was a suitor in order to be able to pay his debts and generally settle himself, *se régler*. And as for the second moral, it is hard to say that the Christians are a whit less 'bloody minded' than Shylock. At least to modern feeling to rob a man of all his wealth and compel him to change his religion seems even worse than to deprive him of a pound of flesh. As Sir Arthur Quiller-Couch says: 'Shakespeare misses more than half the point when he makes the intended victims, as a class and by habit, just as heartless as Shylock without any of Shylock's passionate excuse.'[1] He attributes the failure to the immaturity of his art, but it lies deeper than that. It was not Shakespeare's business to correct or even to criticise the moral standard of his audience, but to amuse them.[2] He was neither an Ibsen nor a Shaw, not

[1] *Works of Shakespeare*, ed. Sir Arthur Quiller-Couch and John Dover Wilson. The *M. of V.* Introduction.
[2] But Schücking has wisely distinguished between such plays as may and others that may *not* be used to reconstruct the moral and social ideals of his time. The *Merchant of Venice* is a fairy-tale to which we might apply, more justly than to the comedies of Wycherley and his contem-

even a Jonson or a Molière. But his imagination was so truthful a recorder that in part he transcended his own purpose and the prejudices which he shared with his audience. The Jew came alive in his hands, and in the greatest speech in the play struck a note which modern critics and actors would like to regard as the keynote of the whole. It was not so for Shakespeare or his audience; and he endeavours to redress the balance by Portia's declamation upon mercy. Unfortunately neither Portia nor anyone else lives up to the fine sentiments to which she gives utterance. The best proof which an Elizabethan could give of his being a good Christian was a readiness to persecute Jews, Turks, Infidels, and Heretics. *The Merchant* is a sparkling comedy adapted to the moral level of its auditors, glorified by delightful poetry, and deepened at moments by the penetrating imagination of its creator, deepened but also troubled. Nor is it very different with *Much Ado about Nothing*. The question is not what do we think of Claudio's behaviour in and after the scene in the Church, but what does Shakespeare think of him? Here again modern critics have been fain to detect a satiric purpose or at least to contend that the poet shows us in a fine spirit of detachment what these young gallants really were when brought to the test, as Jane Austen does with the manners and character of the young gentlemen of her day. No, Shakespeare seems to think him an excellent young fellow, excusably misled by the scoundrel Don John, behaving then in a perfectly justifiable fashion, and in the end making honourable amends:

---

poraries, the words of Lamb: 'The whole is a passing pageant, where we should sit as unconcerned at the issues for life or death, as at a battle of the frogs and mice.' Would that actors would revert to this tradition!

PROBLEM PLAYS

I know not how to pray your patience;
Yet I must speak. Choose your revenge yourself;
Impose me to what penance your invention
Can lay upon my sin: yet sinn'd I not
But in mistaking.[1]

What, again, is one to think of the handling of the moral problems raised in those difficult plays *All's Well* and *Measure for Measure*? These are, or should be, quite definitely problem plays. They raise definite moral issues. What shall a young woman do who, loving a 'bright particular star' more than is discreet, is tempted to take the bold step of securing him for her husband by the authority of his guardian? To us any solution seems inconceivable; certainly Shakespeare's is not satisfactory, rather makes matters worse. What, again, is a young woman to do who is called upon to sacrifice her brother's life or her own chastity? One may admire a great deal in the play and yet feel that Shakespeare has not really faced the problem even as Scott did a somewhat similar one in *The Heart of Midlothian*. I am not concerned to blame Shakespeare for not transcending the moral standards of his age, but wish merely to suggest that he did not, even to the extent of Jonson in his own day and Molière a little later, think that it was the business of comedy to deal with moral problems at all. Its business was to amuse a courtly or a popular audience.

Is it very different if we turn from the comedies to the historical plays? The English Histories have for motive, besides their dramatic and poetic interest, a patriotic appeal, and I need not dwell upon them. I will just say in passing that a candid reader will not find it easy to accept Shakespeare's apparent approval of Prince Hal or the King that he becomes. The

[1] *Much Ado*, Act v. sc. i. 184-287.

THE DRAMA: COMEDY

Prince's declared motive for amusing himself with low companions, that he hoped thereby to dazzle the more when he should choose to break through the clouds and appear in the popular rôle of the reformed rake and virtuous, patriotic monarch, is more politic than admirable:

> And like bright metal on a sullen ground,
> My reformation, glittering o'er my fault,
> Shall show more goodly and attract more eyes
> Than that which hath no foil to set it off.[1]

His treatment of Falstaff leaves one feeling uncomfortable; and his acceptance of the reasons given for forcing a war upon France is exactly on a par with the pious and lofty statements with which every government preludes the commission of some exceptionally atrocious crime:

> But this lies all within the will of God,
> To whom I do appeal; and in whose name
> Tell you the Dauphin I am coming on,
> To venge me as I may and to put forth
> My rightful hand in a well-hallow'd cause.[2]

It is a brilliant portrait of a politician of whom one must not ask too high standards. But Shakespeare's Roman plays illustrate even better Shakespeare's indifference to the ethical or political problem raised by his story, his interest in men as they are, not as they ought to be. For plays on Roman subjects, especially on themes from the later history of the republic and the early days of the empire, presented an interesting challenge to the dramatists of the Renaissance as, far more than national subjects, they raised the question of political liberty, of freedom against tyranny, of Brutus and Cassius against Caesar; and nothing could

[1] *Henry IV.* Part I. Act I. sc. ii. 234-237.
[2] *Henry V.* Act I. sc. ii. 289-293.

be more striking than Shakespeare's apparent indifference to the theme. The feeling which had placed Brutus and Cassius in the deepest pit of Dante's Hell had passed. Hobbes describes what had taken its place: 'And as Aristotle; so Cicero and other writers have grounded their civill doctrine on the opinions of the Romans, who were taught to hate Monarchy at first, by them that having deposed their Sovereigns, shared amongst them the Sovereignty of Rome; and afterwards by their successors. And by reading of these Greek and Latin authors men from their childhood have gotten a habitude (under a false show of liberty) of favouring tumults and of licentious controlling the actions of their Sovereigns and again of controlling those controllers, with the effusion of so much blood, as I think I may truly say that never was anything so dearly bought as these Western parts have bought the learning of the Greek and Latin tongues.'[1] If a dramatist like Muret or Grévin or Sir William Alexander or Ben Jonson took up a Roman subject it was impossible for them to do so without becoming to a greater or less extent champions of political liberty; and if that presented difficulties to a courtly dramatist, the difficulties could be evaded by pleading the distinction between a legitimate monarch and a tyrant:

> If Caesar had been born, or chus'd our Prince,
> Then those who durst attempt to take his life
> The world of treason justly might convince.
> Let still the States which flourish for the time,
> By subjects be inviolable thought,
> And those (no doubt) commit a monstrous crime,
> Who lawful Sovereignty prophane in aught.[2]

[1] Hobbes: *Leviathan*, Part II. chap. xxi. *Of the Liberty of Subjects.*
[2] Sir William Alexander's *The Tragedy of Julius Caesar*, Act III. sc. i.

Shakespeare, in his Roman plays, shows no clear interest in the political or moral principles which the story raises. For joining the conspirators Brutus can give no reason except the rather far-fetched one that, given absolute power, Caesar *may* commit crimes of which, so far, he has been entirely guiltless:

> He would be crown'd:
> How that might change his nature, there's the question.
> It is the bright day that brings forth the adder,
> And that craves wary walking. Crown him? That!
> And then, I grant, we put a sting in him,
> That at his will he may do danger with.
> The abuse of greatness is when it disjoins
> Remorse from power; and to speak truth of Caesar,
> I have not known when his affections sway'd
> More than his reason. But 'tis a common proof
> That lowliness is young ambition's ladder, etc.[1]

It is a very speculative ground on which to commit murder. No wonder that Coleridge says: 'Surely nothing can seem more discordant with our historical preconceptions of Brutus, or more lowering to the intellect of the Stoico-Platonic tyrannicide, than the tenets here attributed to him—to him, the stern Roman republican.'[2] Compare Shakespeare's conception with Jonson's:

> Where is now the soul
> Of God-like Cato? He that durst be good
> When Caesar durst be evil: and had power,
> As not to live his slave, to die his master?
> Or where the constant Brutus, that being proof
> Against all charm of benefits, did strike
> So brave a blow into the monster's heart
> That sought unkindly to captive his country?
> O they are fled the light! Those mighty spirits
> Lie rak'd up with their ashes in their urn,

---

[1] *Julius Caesar*, Act II. sc. i. 12-22 *et seq.*
[2] Coleridge's *Lectures on Shakespeare*, Bohn's Libraries, 1897, p. 313.

And not a spark of their eternal fire
Glows in a present bosom!
       . . . nothing good,
Gallant or great: 'tis true that Cordus says
'Brave Cassius was the last of all that race.'[1]

Ben Jonson's interest in his theme is a moral or, at least, a politico-moral interest; Shakespeare's is purely dramatic. In the *Sejanus* Jonson is on the side of liberty against tyranny, in the *Catiline* he is on the side of established government against political *enragés*, what we should call Bolshevists; and the same is true of Chapman in his *Tragedy of Caesar and Pompey* as well as in his other political, though not Roman plays, the two Biron plays and the *Tragedy of Chabot, Admiral of France*. They are ethical plays, whatever we may think of their dramatic merits. The characters are less interesting to Jonson and Chapman than the principles for which they stand, the virtues, in Chapman's case, which they illustrate. It is never so with Shakespeare. For him the interest begins and ends in the story and the characters which the story throws into relief—Brutus, the conscientious man, as we know him in our own experience, scrupulously anxious to do the right thing and for the purest of motives, more of an egotist than he suspects, fatally wanting in judgment and involved by his virtues as well as his weakness in the tangled web of politics where purity of motive cannot condone for blindness and error—a prototype of President Wilson, and like him a noble being. Shakespeare's sympathies are with him in the end, not with Caesar or Antony, but the sympathy is personal, not political, for he has no political sympathies:

This was the noblest Roman of them all.

[1] Jonson: *Sejanus*, i. 1.

THE DRAMA: COMEDY

And Cassius—the honest republican as he sincerely believes and poses to his friends:

> I know where I will wear this dagger then;
> Cassius from bondage will deliver Cassius,

and yet quite human, the kind of person who cannot understand why someone whom he knew at school and could beat at swimming or Latin verses should now be held so remarkable a person. Mr. J. M. Robertson maintains [1] that the speech in which Cassius claims to have saved Caesar's life (for which there is no authority in Plutarch) must be an insertion by Jonson, an expression of his anti-Caesarian prejudices:

> And this man
> Is now become a god, and Cassius is
> A wretched creature, and must bend his body
> If Caesar carelessly but nod on him. [2]

To my mind there is nothing in the play so Shakespearean because so human, except it be—what the same learned critic would also attribute to Jonson and his dislike of Pompey—Portia's failure to live up to her rôle as the Stoical wife:

> I grant I am a woman, but, withal,
> A woman that Lord Brutus took to wife;
> I grant I am a woman, but, withal,
> A woman well-reputed, Cato's daughter. [3]

Such are the ways of human beings, and they are more interesting to Shakespeare than political principles or abstract virtues. No, *Julius Caesar* is just the kind of Roman play Jonson could not have written, for its interest is purely human. On the moral and

---

[1] J. M. Robertson: *The Shakespeare Canon*, 1922, pp. 66-154.
[2] *Julius Caesar*, Act I. sc. ii. 115-118.
[3] Ibid. Act II. sc. i. 292-295.

political principles at stake Shakespeare has not a word to say; and the same is true of *Antony and Cleopatra* and *Coriolanus*. Are Shakespeare's sympathies so entirely with Coriolanus and the nobles as Hazlitt thinks? To some extent they are. Shakespeare, like Chaucer, is a courtly poet, but Professor Bradley has well pointed out that for once he comes near to being fair to the many-headed multitude:

> *First Citizen.* You must think, if we give you anything, we hope to gain by you.
> *Coriolanus.* Well then, I pray, your price o' the consulship?
> *First Citizen.* The price is to ask it kindly.[1]

It is not the aristocratic principle that interests Shakespeare, but the man himself, proud, hot-headed, wrong-headed, abrupt, and withal, susceptible and affectionate. And what to Shakespeare is the battle of Actium, the moral and political issues of which were to Virgil so tremendous? Merely an episode in the story of the loves of Antony and his Egyptian Queen, an episode in the rivalry between the great soldier and lover and the thin-blooded politician Octavius:

> He at Philippi kept
> His sword e'en like a dancer, while I struck
> The lean and wrinkled Cassius.[2]

Shakespeare's interest in character is unlimited; in principles is what Carlyle would call 'a frightful minus quantity'.

Is it very different in the tragedies?

---

[1] *Cor.* Act II. sc. iii. 77-80.
[2] *Antony and Cleopatra*, Act III. sc. ix. 35-37.

CHAPTER IV

THE DRAMA: TRAGEDY

The religious and ethical element in tragedy—Greek and mediaeval tragedy—Seneca and Elizabethan tragedy—Shakespeare's tragedy—His contemporaries and successors—Shakespeare's last plays.

'THE very foundations of tragedy', says the classical scholar van Leeuwen, 'rest on religion.'[1] In tragedy, says a countryman of van Leeuwen, when writing on the Dutch dramatist and poet Vondel, there are always two protagonists—the hero of the play, Agamemnon, Orestes, Antigone, Lear, and on the other hand the divine, inscrutable power which controls man's destiny:

> Zeus, whosoe'er he be—if such the name
> That most delights his ear.[2]

If a miracle be, as Professor Taylor suggests, 'an event in which the character of a divine purpose underlying the whole course of events becomes exceptionally transparent; a sign of the mercy, the justice, the power of God',[3] then a tragic happening is of the very opposite kind, one in which such a purpose is exceptionally obscure, in which there is, on the face of it, no sign of justice, mercy, benevolence, whatever there may be of power:

---

[1] J. van Leeuwen: *De Aristophane, Euripidis censore*, Amst., 1876.
[2] Jan Te Winkel: *Bladzijden uit de Geschiedenis der Nederlandsche Letterkunde*, 1882.
[3] Gifford Lectures at St. Andrews, as reported in the Press.

TRAGEDY

> In tragic hints here see what evermore
> Moves dark as yonder midnight ocean's force,
> Thundering like ramping hosts of warrior horse,
> To throw that faint thin line upon the shore!

'Requital, redemption, amends, equity, explanation, pity, mercy, are words without a meaning here:

> As flies to wanton boys are we to the gods;
> They kill us for their sport.

Here is no need of the Eumenides, children of night everlasting; for here is Night itself.' That is the modern conception of tragedy, and it comes down to us from Shakespeare himself. For it is not quite the conception of the Greek tragedians, at least of the greatest of them, Aeschylus and Sophocles. To them the power of the gods is evident enough in the tragic incident. It is no chance that dooms a whole house like that of Pelops or Laius; as to the Jewish prophets it is no chance that has brought the Assyrian hosts upon Israel. The question for both is the motive, the purpose underlying the course of events. Does the tragic story reveal the justice and mercy as well as the power of God? If Aeschylus' answer is less clear and authoritative than that of the prophets, it is of the same kind, a vindication of the ways of God to men. Like them he is a rebel against, a critic of, the explicit or latent ethics of the myths which he dramatises, the ethics of popular religion. He will not accept the creed, if it can be called a creed, of the average man of his day, that the gods are powerful but not necessarily good, that they are envious of human excellence and prosperity, that the gods must be conciliated by sacrifices and due rites. Aeschylus, like the prophets, believes that God is just, Zeus at least is so, whatever his predecessors may have been; and the purpose of his tragedies is to 'justify the ways of God to man', to effect a reconciliation of our feelings with the mysterious workings of Providence:

> One there was who reigned of old,
> Big with wrath to brave and blast,
> Lo! his name is no more told!
> And who followed met at last
> His third thrower and is gone.
> Only they whose hearts have known
> Zeus the conqueror and the friend,
> They shall win their vision's end:
>
> Zeus the guide, who made man turn
> Thoughtward; Zeus who did ordain
> Man by suffering shall learn.
> So the heart of him again
> Aching with remembered pain,
> Bleeds and sleepeth not until
> Wisdom comes against his will.
> 'Tis the gift of One by strife
> Lifted to the throne of life.[1]

Sophocles accepted the stories more entirely in the spirit of the artist, but he too acknowledges the essential if mysterious justice of Zeus, the inviolability of divine law, 'the unwritten and unfailing statutes of heaven'. Euripides criticised the myths more in the temper of a rationalist, realist, and sceptic, at least a humanist, but in doing so he disintegrated tragedy and prepared the way for tragi-comedy.

How do Shakespeare and the Elizabethans stand? How did they conceive of tragedy? In this age of a great revival of Christian thought and sentiment does Christianity offer them any solution of the tragic problem? Christianity has its root in one great

[1] Aeschylus' *Agamemnon*, translated by Gilbert Murray. The last two lines translate a notably difficult passage.

tragedy, the story of One who staked everything on 'the mercy, the justice, and the power of God', accepted voluntarily the humiliation and agony of death upon the Cross that He might hasten the advent of the Kingdom of Heaven, and in His dying anguish 'cried with a loud voice saying . . . My God, My God, why hast thou forsaken me?' That history, conceived as the death of God himself, and as ending not in death and silence but in victory—'O grave where is thy victory? O death where is thy sting?'—had been dramatised, if rudely enough, in the Middle Ages, a great tragi-comedy in the largest sense of the word, rather than a tragedy, as we have come to think of tragedy. Might not the Renaissance have made possible a deeper and more adequate treatment of that great theme? To ask the question is, I suppose, to misapprehend the nature both of Renaissance and Reformation. Certainly the English dramatists were cut off from any thought of such an attempt by the change in religion and the temper of Protestantism. Calvinistic Protestantism was positively averse to any dwelling upon the recorded incidents in the life and death of Christ in preaching or ritual. These things savoured of Rome and idolatry. For the Protestant, as perhaps for St. Paul, the earthly life of Christ was subsumed and transcended by the great truths of the Eternal Decrees of God and man's salvation through the imputed righteousness of Christ.[1] The dramatists might, and some of them did, choose Biblical subjects, as Vondel in Holland and Milton in England at a later date. But such Biblical plays as Peele's

---

[1] The Evangelical movement revived the same distinction of emphasis. My father has told me how, when to his pious Free Kirk mother's house came wandering ministers, a test of their godliness was that they read at family prayers from the Epistles of St. Paul. One who chose the Gospels was reckoned a mere Moderate.

David and Bethsabe or Lodge's *Looking-Glass for London* are few and worthless. Almost equally few are the serious plays that are Christian in spirit or implication, that imply a Christian view of life. There is Massinger's and Dekker's *Virgin Martyr* and Massinger's *Renegade* and *The Roman Actor*, and even these have suggested to critics that Massinger was a Roman Catholic.

Moreover, the Biblical plays reveal a difficulty which, even had other circumstances allowed, might have cramped and limited the development of a Christian type of tragedy—that is the necessity of being rigidly orthodox. One feels it in the Biblical plays of the Dutch dramatist, for example in the *Gebroeders*, in which the slaughter, at David's command, of the sons or grandsons of Saul has to be accepted by the poet as a pious deed done on the direct injunction of God. It almost seems as though great tragedy can never be quite orthodox, that there is always in the tragic happening something that seems to arraign the justice of God, if it be only that the penalty appears to outweigh the wrong-doing of which it is accepted as the penalty. Aeschylus believes that Zeus is just, that evil-doing is punished—*drasanti pathein*—but that there is an element of mystery in the penalty which pursues a family from generation to generation:

Nay, nay, this is the house that God hateth.

Be that as it may, it was neither from Mediaeval Mystery and Morality, nor from Greek Tragedy, that the Elizabethan dramatists derived the formula for tragedy as they composed it, nor the spirit which inspired it. Both derive from Seneca. But that formula has a religious significance, if not a Christian one. It is a superficial and melodramatic version of Aeschylus' conception of retribution which has been crudely expressed by Cyril Tourneur in the line:

When the bad bleed, then is the tragedy good.

The proper theme of tragedy is, they learned from Seneca, crime and the Nemesis which overtakes it; and in Elizabethan hands this became too often simply a tragedy of revenge. This is the formula underlying such tragedies as *The Spanish Tragedy*, *The Jew of Malta*, *Hamlet* (as originally dramatised), *Antonio and Mellida*, *The Duchess of Malfi*, *The White Devil*, *The Revenger's Tragedy*, *The Changeling*, *Women beware Women*, *The Maid's Tragedy*, *The Duke of Milan*, *'Tis Pity she's a Whore*, *The Broken Heart*, and many more. But probably there is no worse receipt for tragedy than this of crime and vengeance abstractly conceived, for in none is it so difficult to secure that sympathy with, and respect for, the hero which is surely essential if the drama is to evoke the emotion proper to tragedy—the feeling with which we contemplate the fate of Antigone, Hercules, Lear, Cordelia, Othello, Desdemona, Clarissa, The Master of Ravenswood, Tess of the D'Urbervilles. The Elizabethan dramatist more often evokes horror than pity and awe.[1] He conducts us

[1] In making horror the dominant effect of tragedy the dramatist was more in harmony with the critical and classical taste of his day than we are apt to suspect. Scholars also looked at Greek tragedy through the medium of Seneca. As late as 1641 in Holland Jan Vos produced a tragedy on the story of Titus Andronicus, viz. *Titus en Aran, of Wraeck en Weerwraeck* ('Titus and Aran, or Revenge and Counter-Revenge'), a hideous and bombastic version of the story. It was not only hugely popular, but received the highest critical sanction from the classical scholar, Casper Barlaeus. He witnessed the performance seven times, and declared that in tragic significance this play equalled or surpassed all that antiquity had achieved, that not even Sophocles would have had reason to be ashamed of such a work. An utterance which, as a German critic suggests, gives to think. We see the antique with other eyes than a classically educated man

through a welter of crime, murder, and vengeance, through the mists of which it is difficult to contemplate with any degree of pure and ennobling sympathy the sombre figures of Vittoria and her brother, or many others in the long procession of villains that troop across the stage. Dramatic and poetic scenes there are, and the freshness and colour of Elizabethan English compensates for much; but I confess that, after many years' study, I find it difficult to think of one tragedy of Shakespeare's contemporaries which is a great and impressive drama. Two men, and two only, seem to me to have escaped from the disastrous effect of the Senecan formula, to have seen that the proper theme of tragedy is the defeat of a great soul, the undeserved ruin of one who, whatever his faults, establishes a claim upon the heart and the imagination. Of these, Chapman[1] was no dramatist, though

---

of the seventeenth century. I have long suspected that the Hecuba speeches in *Hamlet*, which have rather worried modern readers, represent Shakespeare's conception of classical tragedy, something that moved on loftier buskins than would suit a play at the Globe Theatre or his own taste for life and reality.

[1] I do not mean to assert that Chapman conveys more of tragic feeling than Webster or Ford. Both Webster and Ford have outlined tragic characters and situations and invested them with more of tragic atmosphere than Chapman could do, for his interest is philosophical and rhetorical rather than dramatic. But Chapman has got a sounder idea of what a tragedy should deal with. Both Webster and Ford are hampered by the conception of crime and Nemesis, with the result that we get only glimpses of the finer strains of soul in their heroes and heroines. The stage is too often filled with subordinate villains and villainies. Vittoria, the best of Webster's characters, is finely presented in the opening scenes, suggesting murder to her lover, baffling her accusers, but thereafter she falls into the background to allow the evolution of the Nemesis that is to befall her and her lover. She emerges again only at the close:

> My soul, like to a ship in a black storm,
> Is driven I know not whither.

A fine speech, but by the time it comes we have almost forgotten the Vittoria of the first scenes. Chapman, like Shakespeare, knows that his hero must dominate the play throughout, that the interest begins and ends in the conflict of his passionate soul with destiny.

a genuine if pedantic poet. The other is Shakespeare.

Now if it be true that great tragedy has always, explicitly or implicitly, a religious significance, concerns not only men's relations to one another, but to the power that overrules all things, call it what we may, God or the gods or the Eternal Verities, is Shakespeare's tragedy explicitly or implicitly religious in spirit like that of Aeschylus or Sophocles? On the face of it, Shakespeare's tragedy seems to me less religious than that of his contemporaries. For if there is nothing in his tragedies of the definitely anti-religious temper of Marlowe's, the veiled or outspoken defiance of the gods, there is a strangely unbroken silence, a strange abstention from any pronouncement upon the ethical or religious significance of the dire events which the poet presents with so much of dramatic insight and vividness. For if one considers it, one will recognise a certain both ethical and religious significance, a didactic purpose, in the Senecan type of tragedy. It is rooted in the essentially religious conception of wrong-doing as sin, as not only an offence against an accepted rule of conduct, not only a wrong done to our fellow-men, but a wrong done to God, and sure, therefore, to bring in its train retribution. The plays may not treat of sin and retribution quite after the manner that Prynne and Baxter would approve, but the conception is essentially the same as theirs. As it seemed to Prynne and others quite in the nature of things that the acting of a play should be punished by the fall of the room where the performance was taking place, so to these dramatists it is an accepted formula that in the end the bad will bleed. There is a power which exacts the penalty of transgression. In a play like Cyril Tourneur's *The Revenger's Tragedy*, one is almost back in the earlier Morality. The characters are types—Lussurioso, Ambitioso, Supervacuo, Vendice, Castiza, abstractions of lust, ambition, revenge, and chastity. Webster even disturbs the dramatic effectiveness of his two carefully constructed dramas, so essential does he think it to the full tragic effect that retribution shall overtake the evildoers. 'The mills of God grind slowly, but they grind exceeding small.' The dramatists are careful to emphasise the moral:

>   Remove the bodies.—See, my honoured Lord,
>   What use you ought make of their punishment;
>   *Let guilty men remember their blacke deedes*
>   *Do leane on crutches made of slender reedes.*
>   *The White Devil*, v. 6. 300-303.
>
>   Let us make noble use
>   Of this great ruin; and join all our force
>   To establish this young hopeful gentleman
>   In his mother's right. These wretched eminent things
>   Leave no more fame behind 'em than should one
>   Fall in a frost and leave his print in snow;
>   As soon as the sun shines, it ever melts
>   Both form and matter. I have ever thought
>   Nature doth nothing so great, for great men,
>   As when she's pleased to make them lords of truth:
>   *'Integrity of life is fame's best friend*
>   *Which nobly beyond Death shall crowne the end.'*
>   *The Duchess of Malfi*, v. v. 111-122.

Even Middleton, who spares his audience no brutal detail in his pictures of lust and murder, closes on the moral note, the lesson:

> *Bianca.* Pride, greatness, honour, beauty, youth, ambition,
>   You must all down together, there's no help for it:
>   Yet this my gladness is that I remove
>   Tasting the same death in a cup of love.

Cardinal. Sir, what thou art these ruins show too piteously;
   Two kings on one throne cannot sit together,
   But one must needs down, for his title's wrong;
   So where lust reigns that prince cannot reign long.
                              Women beware Women.

Of John Ford's tragedies the key-note is certainly not retribution. It is passion, the superiority of passion, which is a law to itself, to all moral saws and scruples. Yet the closing words of his most poignant play are a strange blend of his own and more orthodox morality:

Cardinal. Think on thy life and end, and call for mercy.
Giovanni. Mercy! Why I have found it in this justice.
Cardinal. Strive yet to cry to heaven.
Giovanni.   O, I bleed fast!
   Death, thou'rt a guest long look'd for; I embrace
   Thee and thy wounds: O, my last minute's come!
   Where'er I go let me enjoy this grace
   Freely to view my Annabella's face.
Cardinal. Strange miracle of justice.[1]

Shakespeare's tragedies close on no such note of moral or religious comment—not *Hamlet*, not even *Lear*:
   The weight of this sad time we must obey,
   Speak what we feel, not what we ought to say.
   The oldest hath borne most: we that are young
   Shall never see so much, nor live so long.[2]

'The oldest hath borne most'—it is the human note on which he closes, the tale of suffering. To justify or to arraign the ways of God to men is no task of his; and so in *Othello*:
            O Spartan dog,
   More fell than anguish, hunger, or the sea!

[1] *'Tis Pity*, Act v. sc. vi.
[2] *Lear*, Act v. sc. iii. 324-327.

> Look on the tragic loading of this bed;
> This is thy work: the object poisons sight;
> Let it be hid.[1]

There are indeed comments, religious and moral, in the course of the play, but they are those of the *dramatis personae*, expressions of character or of the mood of the moment:

> There's a divinity that shapes our ends,
> Rough-hew them how we may.

> As flies to wanton boys are we to the gods;
> They kill us for their sport.

> To-morrow and to-morrow and to-morrow
> Creeps in this petty pace from day to day.
> And all our yesterdays have lighted fools
> The way to dusty death.

Speeches such as these cannot be displaced from their context and read as the poet's own comments upon life and the significance of the story. Neither the structure of the play nor any authoritative utterance, like that of the chorus of a Greek tragedy, nor any summing-up such as I have cited from the other dramatists, reveals anything of Shakespeare's own thought about the transcendent background of life. He seems not to be concerned with evil as sin, as the transgression of a divine law, an offence against God. The word 'sin' occurs comparatively seldom in the tragedies.[2] He sees it on the human side, as the wrongs and cruelties that men inflict on one another, 'man's

---

[1] *Othello*, Act v. sc. ii. 360-364.

[2] Judging from Bartlett's Concordance (1894) the word occurs most frequently, as one might expect, in *Measure for Measure*, which turns upon an attempt of the state to punish not only crime but vice, sin. It occurs fairly often in the Histories, which are concerned with the sin of rebellion; in the tragedies seldom, and that not often in a serious sense.

'MACBETH'

inhumanity to man'. Indeed there are plays in which one feels acutely the absence of any reference to religious inhibitions or sanctions. Macbeth, for example, is quite clearly a victim of conscience, of a superstitious shrinking from crime and bloodshed. It is his imagination worked upon by his troubled conscience that evokes the blood-stained dagger and sees the ghost of Banquo; which drives him from crime to crime in the furious quest of the peace of mind which he has forfeited for ever. Yet Macbeth never admits this, if indeed he understands it himself. He scorns the thought of supernatural sanctions:

> But here upon this bank and shoal of time
> We'd jump the life to come.

And some of his commentators have taken him at his word and ascribed to physical fear what is obviously the effect of conscience acting upon a vivid imagination. More than even in *King Lear* one feels the demand for some such religious comment as a chorus in Aeschylus would certainly have given utterance to, some clear indication of the true source of all the mental storm:

> Will all great Neptune's ocean wash this stain
> Clean from my hand; no, this my hand will rather
> The multitudinous seas incarnadine,
> Making the green one red.[1]

We feel ourselves in want of a summing-up that is

---

[1] It would be difficult to find a better or clearer expression of the sense of guilt, of sin, as a feeling uncomplicated by any dogmatic interpretations of the sense, of what it implies. Is the sense of guilt, as Professor Taylor argues, a consciousness of having offended one who is infinitely holy or of having sinned against our common humanity, against the all in each of us from which no one can altogether escape, and which is the ultimate inhibition of our purely egotistic impulses?

not merely political, concerning Scotland, but ethical and religious, that should lift our minds to contemplate with reverence 'the unwritten and unfailing statutes of Heaven whose life is not of to-day or yesterday, but from all time, and no man knows when they were first put forth'. And yet perhaps it is not needed, for the more carefully one reads the play the more evidently is the thought of the supernatural sanctions violated the background of the whole, felt in the part played by the witches, the reported prodigies, and, despite his unwillingness to give it clear expression, his determination to interpret it in terms of earthly fears that may be combated, in the agonised words of Macbeth:

> If 't be so,
> For Banquo's issue have I fil'd my mind;
> For them the gracious Duncan have I murder'd;
> Put rancours in the vessel of my peace,
> Only for them; and mine eternal jewel
> Given to the common enemy of man,
> To make them kings, the seed of Banquo kings!

But this consciousness is never raised above the level of a dark superstition. Shakespeare never raises the thought of divine retribution to a higher level by comment of an onlooker or by confession of the chief actors. The most that Macbeth descries at the last is that witches are liars:

> And be these juggling fiends no more believ'd,
> That palter with us in a double sense;
> That keep the word of promise to the ear,
> And break it to our hope.

And what of *King Lear*, the greatest tragedy of terrible happenings and suffering since *Agamemnon* and *Oedipus Tyrannus*?[1] What is Shakespeare's pronouncement upon the story of folly and ingratitude and inhumanity and the cruel accidents of Chance and Fate? What has he to say of the mysterious power which shipwrecks the lives of the gentle and good as ruthlessly as of the cruel and vicious? Cries do escape the lips of the sufferers; in which of these does one find the mind of the poet?

'These late eclipses in the sun and moon portend no good to us: though the wisdom of nature can reason it thus and thus, yet nature finds itself scourged by the sequent effects. Love cools, friendship falls off, brothers divide; in cities mutinies; in countries discord; in palaces treason; and the bond cracked between son and father.'

'This is the excellent foppery of the world, that, when we are sick in fortune—often the surfeit of our own behaviour—we make guilty of our disasters the sun, the moon, and the stars; as if we were villains by necessity, fools by heavenly compulsion', etc.

> I am a man
> More sinn'd against than sinning.

> World, world, O world!
> But that thy strange mutations make us hate thee,
> Life would not yield to age.

[1] As Aristotle clearly saw, it is not *suffering* terrible things, least of all death, which in great tragedies comes as a relief, that makes a tragic happening. It is *doing* terrible things that makes a tragedy. 'Let us then determine what are the circumstances which strike us as terrible or pitiful. Actions capable of this effect must happen between persons who are either friends or enemies or indifferent to one another. If an enemy kills an enemy there is nothing to excite pity either in the act or the intention—except in so far as suffering itself is pitiful. So again with indifferent persons. But when the tragic incident occurs between those who are near or dear to one another—if, for example, a brother kill a brother, a son his father, a mother her son, a son his mother, or any deed of the kind is done—these are the situations to be looked for by the poet.' Lear suffers at the hands of the children he has loved; and Lear himself brings disaster on the daughter he has loved the best.

THE DRAMA: TRAGEDY

As flies to wanton boys are we to the gods;
They kill us for their sport.

     Heavens, deal so still!
Let the superfluous and lust-dieted man,
That slaves your ordinance, that will not see
Because he doth not feel, feel your power quickly;
So distribution should undo excess,
And each man have enough.

     This shows you are above,
You justicers, that these our nether crimes
So speedily can venge!

      It is the stars,
The stars above us, govern our conditions;
Else one self mate and make could not beget
Such different issues.

      Men must endure
Their going hence, even as their coming hither:
Ripeness is all.

The wheel is come full circle; I am here.

Which of these utterances speaks Shakespeare's mind? They are none of them obviously interjected comments, little adapted to the character of the speaker, like those I have quoted from other dramatists. Each of them is obviously wrung from the speaker by the bent of his character or the intensely felt need of the moment. Whether is Shakespeare on the side of the pious Gloucester, who sees the warnings of Heaven in the eclipses of the sun and moon, or of the sceptical and Machiavellian Edmund? The Greek dramatist would have been on Gloucester's side if the question had concerned the trustworthiness of oracles. And if we look for evidence of divine retribution in the event of the drama, do we feel its presence as we watch Lear bending over the body of the dead Cordelia? 'I was many years ago so shocked by Cordelia's death', says the pious and humane Dr. Johnson, 'that I know not whether I ever endured to read again the last scenes of the play till I undertook to revise them as an editor.' 'We hear much and often from theologians of the light of revelation; and some such thing we find in Aeschylus, but the darkness of revelation is here.' So Swinburne. Shakespeare says nothing. Modern critics, indeed, have undertaken to find in Shakespeare's tragedies a religious significance. Te Winkel[1] even declares that in Shakespeare's tragedies alone do we get again the religious atmosphere of the drama of Aeschylus and Sophocles, the suggestion that the protagonist of the drama is not the human hero, but the divine power behind. 'They are all revelations of the one and the same power over against which they (*i.e.* the human persons) give the impression of poor, wretched creatures if one consider them (as at times the poet makes us do) as independent beings. . . . Fate is put before us by the poet as a living, restless power at work, creating and destroying, and in the end, after the destruction of the old, remaining itself the only indestructible ground for a new future which shall provide the material for a new tragedy.' A strange religion! But such Hegelian determinism would have seemed to the religious mind of the seventeenth century, and not less so, one would think, to Aeschylus, the very negation of religion, for in such a devouring destiny is no shadow of the justice and mercy which we attribute to God.

But on this and other readings of the religious im-

[1] *Bladzijden uit de Geschiedenis der Nederlandsche Letterkunde* door Dr. Jan Te Winkel, Haarlem, 1882; *Vondel als treurspeldichter*, p. 160 ff.

plications of Shakespeare's tragedies, such as Bradley's and Elton's, I do not propose to dwell. My theme is historical, and no one will contend that these interpretations were or would have been accepted by the serious thought of the age as giving to the drama religious significance. The Elizabethan audience saw only the heart-rending story. In his tragedies, as in his comedies and histories, Shakespeare accepted the conditions and limitations of the Elizabethan and Jacobean stage, and refrained from giving to his plays any explicit ethical or religious significance—either that of the Christian feeling of his day, or the crude Senecan religious significance, the doctrine of retribution with which some of his fellow-dramatists essayed, sincerely or otherwise, to justify the horrors of which they invited their audience to sup.

The phenomenon may be considered from another point of view. Great tragedy is both religious and ethical, or, to put it more justly, is religious because it is ethical. It is not concerned with beliefs and rites in themselves, but as these react upon the feelings and conduct of men. Tragedy in Greece, like the prophetic poetry of Israel, was a protest against the religious traditions and myths of their age, against religious beliefs and rites that were or had become divorced from ethics. It is the ethical aspect of religion which is the concern of the poet who is a prophet. 'Bring no more vain oblations; incense is an abomination to me . . . your new moons and your appointed feasts my soul hateth: they are a trouble unto me; I am weary to hear them. . . . Wash you, make you clean; put away the evil of your doings from before mine eyes; cease to do evil; learn to do well; seek justice, relieve the oppressed; judge the fatherless; plead for the widows.'. . .[1] 'Others again cite Homer as a witness that the gods may be influenced by men. . . . "The gods, too, may be moved by prayers; and men pray to them and turn away their wrath by sacrifices and entreaties, and by libations and the odours of fat, when they have sinned and transgressed." Then although we are lovers of Homer we do not love the lying dream which Zeus sent to Agamemnon; neither will we praise the verses of Aeschylus in which Thetis says that Apollo at her nuptials "was celebrating in song her fair progeny whose days were to be long and to know no sickness. And gathering all in one he raised a note of triumph over the blessedness of my lot and cheered my soul. And I thought that the word of Phoebus being prophetic and divine would not fail. And now he himself who uttered the strain . . . he was the very one who slew my son." These are the kinds of sentiments about the gods which will arouse our anger; and he who utters them shall be refused a chorus.'[2] Plato's words mark perhaps a stage in advance of Aeschylus, who will tell the old stories with an effort to suggest that there is a mysterious justice underlying the apparent caprice of the gods; or if there be a latent criticism of Apollo, it is left to be inferred. Plato has reached the next stage in criticism which boldly denies that these stories are true. We have seen the same development in our own treatment of Old Testament stories. But the point I wish to make is this, that the deepest motive of Jewish prophecy and Greek tragedy is ethical, and that this has been the enduring motive, so that as definite mythological and theological conceptions fell into the background, great tragedy has found its favourite theme in the conflict of principle with

[1] Isaiah i. 13-17.   [2] *The Republic*, Book II. (Jowett).

passion, or of contending moral claims and principles ... *Orestes, Antigone, Philoctetes, The Cid, Horace, Cinna, Britannicus, Berenice, Clarissa, Jane Eyre.* 'Iphigenia (in Goethe's play of that name)', says Wolff, 'vacillates between gratitude towards Thoas and longing for home; the heroes of Racine between love and duty; Calderon's Spaniards between the behest of honour and their egotistical impulses. The inner conflict is the soul of these dramas, and Alfieri contends that it is the soul of drama generally.'[1] Yet there is nothing of this in Shakespeare. Even in those tragedies, and there are two of them, where the action does really seem to turn on a conflict of principles, not merely of passion, the issue is never clearly stated. I have already referred to the enigma of Brutus' choice, his decision to join the conspirators. Neither the ethical nor the political principles involved are even adumbrated, for it is impossible to accept as adequate the statement of his motives given in the soliloquy in Act II. Scene i. The speech, like Macbeth's soliloquies, represents rather the turmoil of a mind which does not understand its own impulses and inhibitions, an irresolute mind catching at pretexts for an action to which some almost subconscious process of thought and feeling has determined the speaker. What he says represents but the flotsam and jetsam of his perturbed mind:

> Between the acting of a dreadful thing
> And the first motion, all the interim is
> Like a phantasma or a hideous dream:
> The genius and the mortal instruments
> Are then in council; and the state of man,
> Like to a little kingdom, suffers then
> The nature of an insurrection.

[1] Max J. Wolff: *Shakespeare*, 1907.

INNER CONFLICT

Shakespeare has portrayed vividly the emotions and the actions of a conscientious man, noble but unpractical, tormented by an inward conflict. He has *not* shown us the true character of the principles which have come into conflict with one another. He does not seem to have understood them himself, or was indifferent to them, or did not think his audience would care to have them made explicit; far less has he analysed them. He took the story as he found it in Plutarch's lives of Caesar and Brutus and Antony, and portrayed the characters as feeling and acting rather than as thinking men. Is it very different with Hamlet? A thousand reasons have been given for Hamlet's indecision. One can see or divine, as in Brutus' case, what are the forces at work, the conflict of duty and affection, the paralysing effect of a sudden disillusionment, a sudden revelation of what Sievers calls 'the dark background of life'.[1] But neither Hamlet nor Shakespeare (if one may say so) quite understands what has gone wrong. The main reason of the difficulty lies, it seems to me, just in the fact that Shakespeare did not write a tragedy of conflicting principles and his audience did not wish him to do so.

[1] This statement of the problem of Hamlet's character and mood is not invalidated by accepting Schücking's or Bradley's statement that Hamlet is a 'melancholiker' as described by the Elizabethans (*i.e.* what we should call a neurasthenic), or, in Bradley's words, is suffering from a shock, for this is but to lay stress on the *physical* side of the experience. If there were not a *mental* side, the tragedy would lose value and interest. It would not be a tragedy in the full sense if the catastrophe were simply due to the fact that Hamlet was not well at the time, as one might involve one's life in disaster because at a critical juncture one was confined to bed by an attack of influenza. The spiritual side of Hamlet's melancholy is one that can be appreciated by others, because at times all or many of us can understand what it is to lose faith in life, to feel the worthlessness of any effort we can make. A mystical experience is not entirely invalidated by declaring that the subject is a neurasthenic, if the experience, which his nervous condition has made acute, is yet one which others in full health have in some measure experienced.

The stage in England had not the support even of such a serious and intelligent interest as made it possible for Molière and Racine to elaborate their, if not more imaginative and poetical, yet more intellectual drama. Serious thought and feeling in England was directed towards the pulpit, not the stage, which was a popular entertainment.

The tragic conflict in Shakespeare's tragedies is of a different kind, not a conflict of principles or of principle with passion, but of passion with the limits set to human power. His greatest and most comprehensible and moving tragedies represent a great character swept from his moorings by a storm of passion and finally broken by the circumstances against which passion drives him in headlong career—*Macbeth, Lear, Othello, Coriolanus, Timon*. 'With them', says Wolff, 'passion is so powerful, so prevailing, that every other consideration is smothered in the cradle. . . . If one understands by virtue the conscious pursuit of principles recognised as good, then Shakespeare's characters are never virtuous. They never act on principle.'[1] In *Macbeth*, for example, and *Coriolanus*, the inhibition which wrecks them is a moral *feeling*: Macbeth's sense of guilt driving him from crime to crime in quest of security, Coriolanus' love for his mother, the habit of respect and obedience shattering his resolve. But in each it operates in the same way, as one wave of feeling breaking another. Neither apprehends, or gives value to, the disturbing, inhibiting impulse as a moral principle. A passionate sense of guilt, of innocence forfeited:

> Methought I heard a voice cry 'Sleep no more!
> Macbeth does murder sleep,' the *innocent* sleep,

[1] *Op. cit.*

PRINCIPLE & PASSION

disturbs and deflects the passion of ambition so that the victim rushes headlong to his own destruction. The passion of revenge in *Coriolanus* is met not by reflection on duty to country or to family, but by the passionate upwelling of a deeper, longer established habit of feeling:

> O mother, mother!
> What have you done? Behold, the heavens do ope,
> The gods look down, and this unnatural scene
> They laugh at. O my mother, mother! O!
> You have won a happy victory to Rome;
> But, for your son, believe it, O! believe it,
> Most dangerously you have with him prevail'd,
> If not most mortal to him. But let it come.

It is this very fact that Shakespeare's characters act, not on principle, but on the immediate impulse of feeling, that 'gives to his women a purity that raises them above all their sisters. They shun what is degrading, not because it is forbidden by law or custom, but as something alien to their being, something that runs counter to their inmost nature, and just because they thus surrender themselves to their good instincts, as they surrender themselves to love, they can undergo sacrifices and undertake deeds of heroism which no effort inspired by principles could attain to. They can dare everything like Juliet . . . or suffer everything for their loyalty, like Desdemona and Imogen' (Wolff). Helena in *All's Well that Ends Well* does not stop to ask whether her conduct is right or wrong, how it will appear in the eyes of others. She simply follows the passionate impulse of her love for Bertram. The strange thing to our minds in this instance is that no inhibitory impulses should have been awakened, and that her conduct should have provoked no disapproval. In judging of that we have probably to allow for views of the propertied rights conferred by marriage from which we have drifted far, and to remember that the story comes from a *novella* bringing with it certain recognised conventions which Shakespeare did not trouble himself to modify. What seems clear is that any such conflict as Richardson portrays in *Clarissa* and Charlotte Brontë in *Jane Eyre* was strange to Shakespeare and the Elizabethans.[1] Both of these works are the product of Puritanism. Whatever its errors, it was Puritanism which gave this strength and elevation to a moral principle, a simple perception or conviction of what is right and what is wrong.

In so far, then, as Shakespeare in tragedy never explicitly raised or made any explicit effort, as Aeschylus did, to solve the enigma of life and suffering, to 'justify the ways of God to men'; or took for his theme a definitely stated conflict of moral or religious principles, like that of the *Antigone* or *Clarissa*, it is fair to class Shakespeare with the other dramatists when one speaks, as Schirmer does, of 'das areligiöse Elizabethanische Drama'. Indeed his plays are, as I have argued, on the surface less moral and religious than those of some of his fellows—Heywood's *A Woman*

[1] Emily Brontë's novel is more Elizabethan in spirit than her sister's. Heathcliff and Catherine know nothing of the inhibition of principle. They follow their feelings without disguise or question, but it is a passion which no irregular connection could satisfy, so that when Catherine's pride has driven her to marry Linton the tragic situation is for them absolute. 'It is characteristic of Emily Brontë that she does not waste a moment on the idea of a union outside the law, such as Rochester proposes to Jane Eyre, such a solution is never even named, and the lovers are never united. In life they are parted for good, Heathcliff, by manœuvring with the graves, sees to it that they shall meet in death. The tragic effect would have been spoiled by any other solution; there is nothing puritanical in the treatment, yet there can be no question, in such an atmosphere, of any ordinary scruples' (Elton: *A Survey of English Literature, 1830–1880*, vol. ii. p. 294). Charlotte's comment on her sister's novel and the character of Heathcliff is just a little that of a Victorian on an Elizabethan.

THE ETHICAL & CHRISTIAN SUB-TONE

Killed with Kindness, Massinger's *The Renegade*, Webster's two tragedies and perhaps those of Cyril Tourneur.

Would it then be just to class Shakespeare's tragedies with other characteristic products of the egotistic, non-moral spirit of the Renaissance, as Wolff is inclined to do, tragedies of the unfettered passions dashing themselves against the barriers set to the power of the human individual, 'ein Zwiespalt zwischen dem Wollen und dem Können des Individuums'? Does Shakespeare's drama stand on the same footing as the naturalist novel of to-day? Not I think even to the extent that a drama of Marlowe or of Ford might be classed with a novel by Stendhal. For the naturalist the only passions which count are the animal passions. But in Shakespeare's drama human nature is made up of moral as well as animal passions, even if the immanent principles are not made explicit. Macbeth and Coriolanus are wrecked in the end, not because, like Napoleon, they attain the limit of their power, but because humanity can no longer suffer them. They are the victims of a clash of emotions, a conflict of feelings which on the one hand have their root in moral considerations and on the other in their ambition and desire for a burning vengeance, though they may never state it to themselves in that way. There is a *moral* conflict in Brutus' mind, and we do not doubt when we have read the whole play that it is his conscience which he follows or believes himself to have followed. Even his enemies do not doubt it:

> This was the noblest Roman of them all:
> All the conspirators save only he
> Did that they did in envy of great Caesar;
> He only in *a general honest thought*
> *And common good to all* made one of them.

It is a moral shock which paralyses Hamlet and divides his mind. The difference between Shakespeare and Marlowe becomes clear in those plays where Shakespeare is most obviously the disciple of his young predecessor, and taking over from him as heroes the ambitious, unscrupulous, ruthless Machiavellians. Suffolk, Margaret of Anjou, Clifford, Richard, Duke of York, they rise above one another in a *crescendo* of shrill ferocity and ruthless ambition till the limit is attained in 'the bloody boar', Richard, Duke of Gloucester and later King of England. But Marlowe is in as close imaginative sympathy with these aspiring heroes, whether Tamburlaine or Dr. Faustus, as on one side of his nature Milton is with the dauntless Satan. Marlowe[1] was himself in desire and dream, at any rate, one

> Still climbing after knowledge infinite
> And ever moving with the moving spheres,

sympathetic with the soul which exults in the thought that
> All things that move between the quiet poles
> Shall be at my command.

To Shakespeare this type of character is, when all is said and done, a monster:

---

[1] Of a play one may say as Aristotle does of a speech that it is the work of three factors, the author, the subject, and the audience. Miss Ellis-Fermor in her interesting study of *Christopher Marlowe* (London, 1927) has treated his plays as progressive expressions of his thought about life, which is just what a good deal of Shakespeare criticism to-day finds fault with in the nineteenth-century criticism of Shakespeare. In expressing his own thought and feeling Marlowe has to remember both what his audience will expect or tolerate and the tradition embodied in the story he is dramatising. If Faustus is finally handed over to Lucifer, that need not be taken as evidence of the failure of the poet's own freer thought. Neither the story nor his audience would have permitted of any other close. The poet's sympathies are not entirely at one with the dramatic rendering he gives of the legend. But he could not in the sixteenth century either defy Lucifer with Manfred or save Faustus with Goethe.

'MAN'S INHUMANITY TO MAN'

> Why should a man desire in any way
> To vary from the kindly race of men?

Artistically and ethically he disliked supermen. With whomsoever he may have collaborated, or whoever may have written what he revised, it is he who has given to these plays the final impression they convey, and that is of the horrors of civil war and a greedy wolvish nobility. He might have said of the nobility with Carlyle, substituting English for Scottish, 'A ferocious, selfish, famishing, unprincipled set of hyaenas, from whom at no time and in no way has the country derived any benefit'. His political sympathies were entirely with the strong rule of the Tudors. With *Richard II.* even his politicians become more human—Bolingbroke, Hotspur, Henry V. Compare Falconbridge with the original in the older or earlier play. Even in those plays, again, in which one detects an alloy of bitterness, *Measure for Measure* and *Troilus and Cressida*, there is no criticism of accepted moral standards and no arraignment of Providence. Good is good and evil evil; and the vices for which Shakespeare has least tolerance are cruelty, ingratitude and lightness, licentiousness and heartlessness in women. His two most hateful characters are Iago and Cressida, and Cressida is the viler of the two. It is the same with the tragedies. They are not religious tragedies as those of Aeschylus are religious, or as the tragedies of Seneca and his English disciples, because they do not explicitly envisage evil as sin, 'a transgression of the divine law and an offence against God', nor suffering as divine retribution. That is the religious attitude. For Shakespeare in his drama evil is the wrong that men do to one another, the suffering and ruin brought on men by the aberrations of passion, 'man's inhumanity to man'. The riddle of his tragedies is the riddle of life. That is why they are so modern. They are untouched by the thought, Christian or Stoical, of his day. He stands before the enigma of life in the same attitude as Meredith or Hardy,[1] if less inclined to dogmatise than either; which is not to say that as a private individual he may not have been an orthodox Christian of his day. He did not air his views, whatever they were, in his plays, which, as Carlyle says, contemplated no result beyond drawing audiences to the Globe Theatre.

If one adds to the tragedies the last group of Shakespeare's plays one gets somewhat the impression which the Greek dramatist aimed at by a trilogy of plays, by continuing the story which begins with the *Agamemnon* to its close in the *Eumenides*, by adding to the *Oedipus Tyrannus* the *Oedipus Coloneus*, an effect of reconciliation. If it differs, it is because the effect is ethically (not dogmatically, nor theologically) more Christian; because what Shakespeare lays stress upon is the high virtue of forgiveness. To a Christian mind there is something shocking in the savage hatred for his sons of Oedipus, even if deserved, and the curse which he pronounces upon them. The effect is through and through barbaric. For Shakespeare reconciliation implies forgiveness. Mr. Strachey has justly taken exception to the interpretation of Shakespeare's mood which states or suggests that in them a pessimistic has yielded to a more hopeful, a more optimistic view of humanity and life. That is belied by the characters of the chief persons in the plays. Shakespeare does not deal in

[1] This is not quite just. Implicit in *Macbeth*, *Othello*, even *Lear* is an acceptance of the ideas of God, Sin, Retribution, as there is *not* in Hardy. But it is implicit, even obscure, never made explicit and clear. The main issue is the human protagonist and his doings with his fellowmen. But there is no suggestion of a spirit of religious revolt.

conversions of the type of those of Dickens in the Christmas books. But his eye is not fixed on the evil characters. He does not elaborate them with the fullness with which Iago or Goneril and Regan are drawn. His interest is in another aspect of life and human nature, in the fact that if men and women are egotistic, cruel, and treacherous, there is also in human nature a capacity for love, repentance, and forgiveness,—that these are also facts. There is nothing of the kind in the tragi-comedies which have been said, and to some extent justly, to have turned Shakespeare's attention to another kind of play; for the construction of which he is also not indebted to his younger rivals,[1] but goes back to an earlier type of play which the dramatists had in the main discarded, the long romance which covers a whole lifetime, at which Sidney and Jonson sneered:

> To make a child now swaddled to proceed
> Man, and then shoot up, in one beard, and weed,
> Past threescore years.

The Tempest is probably the most religious, even Christian in spirit, of Shakespeare's plays, though there is not a word in it of dogma or any attempt to interpret the mystery of life. But the root idea is, more clearly than in any other, that of sin and retribution. Prospero himself is Providence controlling the issue and event of everything that happens throughout. He has been deeply wronged and he has meditated revenge, sought the retribution which justice seems to require; and by the power of magic has his enemies in his hand. But love for his daughter has changed the current of his feelings and directed his thoughts

[1] Beaumont and Fletcher. See Thorndike, *The Influence of B. and F. on Shakespeare's Last Plays.*

THE DRAMA: TRAGEDY

towards reparation rather than revenge. Reflection has taught him, in Burke's words, 'what shadows we are and what shadows we pursue':

> We are such stuff
> As dreams are made on, and our little life
> Is rounded with a sleep,

and forgiveness takes the place of vengeance:

> Though with their high wrongs I am struck to the quick,
> Yet with my nobler reason 'gainst my fury
> Do I take part: the rarer action is
> In virtue than in vengeance: they being penitent
> The sole drift of my purpose doth extend
> Not a frown further.

These are almost the words of the Deity in *Paradise Lost*:

> To prayer, repentance, and obedience due,
> Though but endeavoured with sincere intent,
> My ear shall not be slow, mine eye not shut.

But there is no theology in Shakespeare, no definition of predestination and prevenient grace, though Shakespeare recognises as clearly as Milton that there are natures—Caliban, Stephano, Trinculo—who are incapable of moral discipline and understanding, who can only be driven like dumb cattle. If a play may be Christian in sentiment without a note of dogma, only by the value it gives to the Christian virtues of faith, hope, and charity, *The Tempest* is not without a claim to be called a Christian play. Of Christian dogma the poet says nothing, though when he refers to it necessarily in the course of a play it is in a very different tone from Marlowe's. It is for him essentially a religion of atonement and forgiveness. Henry IV. will undertake a crusade:

SHAKESPEARE & CHRISTIANITY

> To chase these pagans in those holy fields
> Over whose acres walk'd those blessed feet
> Which fourteen hundred years ago were nail'd
> For our advantage to the bitter cross.
>
>   Alas! Alas!
> Why all the souls that were were forfeit once;
> And he that might the vantage best have took
> Found out the remedy.

What Shakespeare knew of or thought about dogmatic Christianity we cannot know. One suspects that he did not trouble his head greatly about the Eternal Decrees and the necessity for being able to date exactly the personal experience of conviction of sin and acceptance of mercy; but that he felt and thought as the average man, not a theological expert, of the Middle Ages, viz. that Christianity meant that God had taken on Himself the penalty due by mankind, was the story of the infinite mercy of God:

>   Therefore, Jew,
> Though justice be thy plea, consider this,
> That in the course of justice none of us
> Should see salvation: we do pray for mercy;
> And that same prayer doth teach us all to render
> The deeds of mercy.

A characteristically mediaeval plea to address to a Jew for whom the Lord's Prayer meant nothing. In fact, to call Shakespeare a child of the Renaissance, as Marlowe or Montaigne or Bacon might in various ways be called, is perhaps, after all, misleading. In fact, both he and the world he described are, as Carlyle divined, a product of the Catholic Middle Ages. For him, as for many another man of that age, Christianity and the life he led from day to day only touched one another at certain definite points. The principles of honesty, honour, loyalty, by which he governed his actions, might or might not have Christian sanction (the dictates of personal honour and family loyalty very often had quite definitely *not*), but there was the Faith in the background, the guarantee of forgiveness when he sought it, the only safe conduct to the life beyond the grave. It was not his business—he might leave that to theologians—to square his beliefs either with the mysterious happenings of life or even with a great part of the daily business of life.

But this was not a Christianity that could satisfy a Prynne or a Baxter or a Bunyan, or in a later period a Law or a Foster. For them Christianity was nothing unless it penetrated every phase of life, and that for all men alike. They would hear nothing of 'religious' and 'secular'. And Shakespeare was well aware of the fact. His plays and all plays were a form of 'pastime' in which he would have been as much surprised as another if anyone had required a religious content. That was left for a later age to discover or believe it had discovered. Shakespeare was content with the rôle of purveying amusement for Court and populace, the rôle of master of the revels, not even to mankind but to his own day and generation. Compared with him, one might, in a sense, call Marlowe and Chapman thinkers, Ben Jonson a moralist, Massinger a pietist, Ford an immoralist, whatever one may think of the thought, the morality, the piety or the criticism of morality. For Chapman's and Marlowe's plays are written round an idea, a definite conception of man's will and destiny. Jonson is quite consciously a moralist criticising folly and vice. Massinger is in love with saints and martyrs. Ford is as definitely the antagonist of inhibitory morality as M. André Gide or Mrs.

Bertrand Russell. It is this fact which dates their work, while Shakespeare's is as fresh to-day as it was. We can no longer think as they did. Shakespeare's humorous and passionate and comprehensive picture of life is as vivid and real as ever, the thoughts which the progress of the action evokes, now from this character, now from that, as poignant and significant. We can interpret the whole in the light of our own experience and thought, our philosophy of life and the life of man, remote as these may be from any articulate thought of Shakespeare's own day. Goethe, Coleridge, Schopenhauer, the Freudians have all found in Shakespeare grist for their mills. But not the Puritan of Shakespeare's own day. Even Milton is tempted to apologise for his early enthusiasm, though he can never have been in any real doubt as to the worth of the plays. To the mind not only of a Prynne but also of a Baxter, Shakespeare's plays were an expression of the world and the flesh with which *they* were called on to do battle.

But if that be so, what of his successors, the later Jacobean and Caroline dramatists? It is one of the strangest things in the history of literature, the rapidity with which the Elizabethan drama came to maturity in the work of Marlowe, Shakespeare, Jonson, and their contemporaries, and the equal rapidity with which it, after 1620 or thereabouts at the latest, went downhill to ethical and artistic worthlessness. Beaumont and Fletcher were the direct inheritors of Shakespeare's popularity. They, like him, had no purpose in view but to provide amusement for Court and populace. Beaumont took from Jonson the hint for some of his studies of 'humours'; but they refused to derive from him what with all his pedantry Jonson might have taught them and others, a regard for construction, and some seriousness of purpose in their portrayal of character and manners. Shakespeare was their ancestor, the Shakespeare of *Twelfth Night*, but they had not his imagination, nor yet the fundamental soundness of his judgment of life and character, his deeper interest in human nature, his 'seeing eye'—his creative imagination that not infrequently builds better than the poet had contemplated. Shakespeare is no moralist. He accepts without protest the standards and prejudices of his audience. But when a situation presents itself vividly to his imagination, when a character has come to life in his mind, he cannot help so envisaging it that we are left in no doubt of the real values at stake, even when we may feel that the poet himself is hardly aware of what he has done. Shylock becomes something more than a Jew in caricature. We realise Hamlet's trouble better than himself. But for the drama of Beaumont and Fletcher ethics do not exist, or appear only as fantastic points of honour. Of that element in drama which Aristotle terms *dianoia*, thought, reflection upon life and character, there is practically none. Its place is taken by a florid rhetoric, saved from complete corruption by a vein of poetry, the strange freshness and beauty of the English. There is gaiety and rattle in their comedy—easy, careless dialogue and banter; it is set to a good tune, as Scott declared, but the whole is as shallow, as thin as one's finger-nail. The moral tone has not yet the hard cynicism of the Restoration; it is merely flippant and sentimental. Beaumont's verse has grace and some dignity; Fletcher's, vivacity and volubility; but of dramatic interest and value there is none. Massinger and Ford are less flippant, but the picture they draw is of a life given over to crime and dissoluteness so completely that one understands the Puritan protest. The vices are drawn in unrelieved blackness. The virtues are too sentimental, when they are not perverse. What one feels is that the dramatists live in a world that is more and more their own, unreal, sinister, flippant. When one turns to the real history of some of the characters they portray, as the heroine of Middleton's *Women beware Women*, she is found to be much more human, much less repellent.[1] The dramatists seem to be cut off from any connection with the moral life of the nation. Even their pictures of citizen life are one-sided and monotonous. The same types constantly recur—the gallant, the citizen, the citizen's wife, the bawd, and the punk. Bunyan's picture of Christiana's family affords glimpses of other aspects of humble life than the dramatists could or would afford us, if Dekker and Heywood have shown some appreciation of the nobler side of character. And, after all, the blame does not rest entirely with the dramatists. Those must bear their share who, by their intransigent fanaticism, their preoccupation with high doctrines of eternal decrees and imputed righteousness, would not allow them to give to this great national tradition a larger scope and higher purpose.

[1] See Bax, Clifford: *Bianca Cappella,Representative Women*, 1928.

CHAPTER V

LOVE-POETRY

The Courtly and Petrarchan tradition—Sidney, Spenser, Shakespeare—The reaction of the Renaissance spirit—John Donne—His love-poetry and its influence—The Puritan protest—Wither, Herbert, and Vaughan—Milton, his early poems and his éducation sentimentale—Paradise Lost, The Divorce pamphlets and Samson Agonistes—The Cavaliers and the poetry of the Restoration.

IF one ask oneself what it was in the drama that the Puritan temper condemned, and if one set aside pedantic arguments drawn from texts in Deuteronomy and from the condemnation by the Fathers of the late Roman stage, and make also due allowance for abuses which have always attended and always will attend a professional stage, one finds that it is a particular and striking instance of a condemnation which had a much wider range, including every form of popular amusement that had come down from the later Middle Ages, all that could be brought under the name of 'pastime'. 'Nor have I', says Baxter, 'been tempted to any of the sins which go under the name of pastime.' Playing tip-cat and ringing the church bells were the sins that tormented the sensitive conscience of the young Bunyan. 'The town,' says Baxter again, speaking of Kidderminster, 'having been formerly eminent for Vanity, had yearly a Show in which they brought forth the painted forms of Giants and such-like fooleries to walk about the streets with';[1] and, speaking of the attitude of the town towards himself and others at the outbreak of the Civil War, he says: 'And just as at their Shows and Wakes and Stage-plays, when the Drink and the Spirit of Ryot did work together in their Heads, and the Crowd encouraged one another, so was it with them now.'[2] The life of the later Middle Ages had been full of popular festivals and gaiety. The Catholic Church had conquered paganism as a religion, but it had in doing so found it necessary to absorb or find a place for much of older belief and cult, to find saints to take the place of tutelary gods; and it tolerated among the common people much of revelry and many seasonal rites which undoubtedly had their roots in the licence of Nature-worship. The Church had tolerated, if it had not always approved; and at intervals not only individuals but Councils protested. Nor were the English Puritans the only reformers who found such things a source of moral evil. Savonarola, in Florence, a city (says the *Cambridge History*) morally superior to every other Italian capital, had striven to put down the fêtes of the city, which were 'a gross survival of mediaeval or pagan license'. 'Savonarola knew, as all earnest reformers knew, that such holidays not only contained possibilities of irreparable evil in themselves, but taint the preceding and succeeding months, and permanently lower the standard of national purity and sobriety. He insisted on the suppression by the State of the horse-races, the bonfires and allegorical processions, the gross carnival songs, which would have been tolerated at no other season; in the country towns the podestà was to forbid the public dances.'[3] I quote this to re-

---

[1] *Reliquiae Baxterianae*, 1696, p. 20.   [2] *Ibid.*
[3] *Cambridge Modern History*, vol. i. chap. v. Florence (1), Savonarola.

mind you that Puritan ill-will to the May-days and Wakes and Festivals and Church-ales, which gave so much colour to popular life, was not a new thing; that these festivities had in them an element of grossness and debauchery which popular festivities have not lost altogether in our own day, but which had then a still recognised root in older beliefs and rites no one would dream of to-day. And the drama, even Shakespeare's comedy, the wit of a Mercutio, the jests of Falstaff have a strain of the same spirit of licence and phallic gaiety. The mistake of the Puritans was that they did not, even to the same extent as Savonarola, or perhaps Calvin, recognise that 'men and children cannot live without amusements', and Butler's *Hudibras* depicts the natural man's revolt against a régime of prohibition and overstrained morality. Some gaiety went out of the world forever with the suppression of mediaeval seasonal celebrations whose roots lay so deep in an older Nature-worship. No songs written or sung since the fifteenth century have quite the perfect gaiety and lightness of touch of the popular songs, or songs half popular, half courtly, whether of Latin or German countries; but a breath of their gaiety still lingers in the earlier Elizabethan song:

> Spring, the year's spring, is the year's pleasant king;
> Then blooms each thing, then maids dance in a ring;
> Cold doth not sting, the pretty birds do sing,
>   Cuckoo, jug-jug, pu-wee, to-witta-woo.

But what is true of popular festivities and rites and songs is true also of much in the courtly literature of the Middle Ages—romance and allegory and courtly lyric. If a Christian background is taken for granted, if there is no conscious paganism of worship or belief, yet the spirit is more pagan than Christian. However it may be sublimated or disguised, the mediaeval 'dream of love and chivalry' is a glorification of free love and personal prowess, and derives as much from the cult of Venus and Cupid as from the worship of Christ and the Virgin—if religious and erotic feeling have ever acted and reacted upon one another. Spenser could not reconcile the pagan spirit of the *Romance of the Rose* with the Christian Puritan spirit in which he began to compose his poem and to sing of the Red Cross knight and Una. Justify it as he might by the high allegoric teaching of which his poem is the vehicle, it is love, romantic, human love, that becomes more and more his subject as he goes on to tell of Florimell and Amoret, of Britomart and Calidore, and Pastorella and Serena. If he deepens and purifies the passion of which he sings with so much ardour and sweetness, it is in virtue of his own ardent yet virginal spirit, the Platonic strain in his allegory, and the finer humanism which strove to unite passion and affection as ancient literature had not succeeded in doing. He was faithful to the Protestant insistence on marriage as the end and aim of love, but his poem still breathed too much of the freer spirit of the Rose tradition to be always acceptable to the Puritan mind. And Spenser's poetry was not the only channel through which the tradition of mediaeval love-poetry flowed into the Elizabethan. That tradition continued to be the inspiration of all the love-poetry composed in sonnet or song or pastoral or romance or romantic comedy; and what I have to consider is how that tradition was affected by the influence of Latin poetry on the one hand, and on the other by the intensified moral temper of the religious reaction. However sublimated or disguised as a worship of the ideal—a disguise which the franker spirit of a poet like Donne and some of his followers impatiently rejects—courtly love-poetry from the Troubadours to the *Romance of the Rose* and onwards to the last songs of the courtiers of Charles II. was a poetry of free love. When the love-poetry of the Troubadours was transferred to Italy, the sensuous and the ideal strains were both intensified and in consequence tended to part company: so that we have on the one hand the transcendentally spiritualised love of Dante and Guinicelli and Cavalcanti, and on the other the quite frankly sensuous love which Boccaccio portrays in the *Filostrato* and which Chaucer transferred to his *Troilus and Criseyde*. In Petrarch there was a little of both tendencies, and they came at times into conflict with one another. This is the tradition which the Elizabethan sonneteers inherited, if for most of them it was a purely literary fashion. Sidney's Stella was, like Petrarch's Laura, a married woman. He does not address her in the language of religious reverence which Dante and his school had taught others to do—who did not share their mystical conception of the love of a woman as the first rung on a ladder that led to the love of God; but Sidney does, like Petrarch, speak of her as the sum of all perfections and the inspiration of every virtue he possesses:

> Alas! have I not pain enough, my friend,
>   Upon whose breast a fiercer gripe doth tire
>   Than did on him who first stole down the fire,
> While Love on me doth all his quiver spend,
>   But with your rhubarb words you must contend
>   To grieve me worse in saying that desire
>   Doth plunge my well form'd soul even in the mire
> Of sinful thoughts which do in ruin end?

PETRARCHISM

> If that be sin which doth the manners frame,
> Well stayed with truth in word and faith of deed,
>   Ready of wit and fearing nought but shame;
> If it be sin which in fix'd hearts doth breed
>   A loathing of all loose unchastity:
>   Then love is sin, and let me sinful be.[1]

But Stella who thus inspires even chastity is yet the object of desire, and is reproached for her coldness, and praised when she yields so far at least as to admit her lover's service, which in Criseyde's case was the end of the siege:

> My spring appears, O see what here doth grow,
>   For Stella hath with words where faith doth shine
> Of her high heart given me the monarchy:
> I, I, O I may say that she is mine.
> And though she give but this conditionally,
>   This realm of bliss, while virtue's course I take,
>   No kings be crowned but they some covenant make.[2]

And we all know that kings seldom observe their covenants. When Sidney turns serious, he, like Petrarch, bids farewell to earthly love:

> Leave me, O Love, that reachest but to dust.

Spenser's beautiful sonnets to the lady he hopes to marry and Shakespeare's wonderful sequence to his friend and patron are, by these very facts, debarred from the sense of any conflict between love and any religious or ethical inhibition such as one is aware of in Petrarch and Sidney. Spenser's virginal and pious mind blends in a simpler fashion the theme of her perfection, her influence, her cruelty in refusing, with quite Christian digressions on Holy Week;

---
[1] *Astrophel and Stella*, Sonnet xiv.
[2] *Ibid.* Sonnet lxix.

but he, too, uses the language of devotion and adoration:

> The glorious image of the makers beautie,
>   my souerayne saynt, the Idoll of my thought,
>   dare not henceforth, aboue the bounds of dewtie,
>   t' accuse of pride, or rashly blame for ought.
> For being as she is, diuinely wrought,
>   and of the brood of Angels heu'nly borne:
>   and with the crew of blessed Saynts vpbrought,
>   each of which did her with theyr guifts adorne;
> The bud of ioy, the blossome of the morne,
>   the beame of light, whom mortal eyes admyre:
>   what reason is it then but she should scorne
>   base things, that to her loue too bold aspire?
> Such heau'nly formes ought rather worshipt be,
>   then dare be lou'd by men of meane degree.[1]

Shakespeare's sonnets to his friend have only one theme, the depth and entireness of his devotion, his self-abnegating love:

> Being your slave, what should I do but tend
>   Upon the hours and times of your desire?
> I have no precious time at all to spend,
>   Nor services to do, till you require.[2]

Absence, injury, long separation, nothing can qualify his devotion; and in his heart love knows no rival. Nor does he use the language of religion to express a passion entirely human and sincere. It is in the shorter sequence of sonnets to the dark lady that one finds the only poems which strike a moral or religious note:

> The expense of spirit in a waste of shame
> Is lust in action.

> Poor soul, the centre of my sinful earth,
>   Fool'd by those rebel powers that thee array,

[1] *Amoretti*, Sonnet lxi.   [2] Sonnet lvii.

RELIGIOUS IMAGERY IN LOVE-POETRY

>   Why dost thou pine within, and suffer dearth,
>   Painting thy outward walls so costly gay?

Of the use of religious imagery one cannot accuse the greater Elizabethans. One does find it, however, and, as perhaps might have been expected, in a Catholic poet, Henry Constable. His *Diana* is no more than a literary exercise after the manner of Petrarch and Desportes. But he repeats the more extravagant hyperboles of the fashion—the divinity of his lady, the resemblance of the lover to the martyr and the saint:

>   Dear! seek revenge and him a liar prove!
>   Gods only do impossibilities.
>   'Impossible', saith he, 'thy grace to gain.'
>   Show then the power of thy divinities
>   By granting me thy favour to obtain!
>   So shall thy foe give to himself the lie:
>   A goddess thou shalt prove, and happy I.[1]

In the ninth sonnet of the second decade he compares himself, wounded by his lady's hand, to St. Francis bearing the stigmata:

>   Saint Francis had the like yet felt no smart,
>   Where I in living torments never die;
>   His wounds were in his hands and feete, where I
>   All these same helplesse wounds feele in my heart.

It is not strange that a serious Catholic like Southwell the martyr will have nothing to do with love-poetry:

>   Vayne loves avaunt! infamous is your pleasure,
>   Your joye deceite;
>   Your jewells, jestes, and worthless trash your treasure,
>   Fooles common baite.
>   Your pallace is a prison that allureth
>   To sweete mishap, and rest that payne procureth.[2]

---
[1] *Diana*, Sonnet iv.   [2] Southwell: *Loves Gardyne Greife*.

And so in 'Love's Servile Lot':

> Loves house is sloth, her dore deceite,
>   And slippery hope her staires;
> Unbashful boldnes bidds her guests,
>   And every vice repayres.
>
> . . . . .
>
> Plowe not the seas, sowe not the sands,
>   Leave off your idel payne;
> Seeke other mistresse for your myndes,
>   Loves service is in vayne.

If therefore we find later an Anglican like Vaughan denouncing the love-poetry of his contemporaries, it does not necessarily mean that such poetry had grown more licentious, but that to the religious mind of the century, whatever its particular stamp, the hyperboles of courtly poetry, its idealisation, or rather idolisation, of the lady, its concentrated intensity, its application to the service of love of the language of worship and theology were reprehensible. Nor would it blunt the edge of a serious Catholic's or Puritan's anger that the poet should plead that such poetry was in the nature of a pastime. Such pastimes were no fit occupation for a man intent on his salvation, hearing ever in his ears, like Christian, the cry, 'What shall I do to be saved?' All such verse was a vanity, all this love-poetry merited the title 'lascivious', which is used in a wider sense than we should give to it. For Vaughan includes his own early verses, which are innocuous to the verge of insipidity, though with some apology. 'I must remember, that I myself have for many years together, languished of this very sickness; and it is no long time since I have recovered. But (blessed be God for it!) I have by his saving assistance suppresst my greatest follies, and those which escaped from me are (I think) as innoxious, as most of that vein use to be; besides, they are interlined with many virtuous, and some pious mixtures. What I speak of them is truth: but let no man mistake it for an extenuation of faults, as if I intended an Apology for them, or myself, who am conscious of so much guilt in both, as can never be expiated without special sorrows.'[1] Among the faults of such poetry Vaughan reckons that 'certain Authors have been so irreverendly bold, as to dash Scriptures and the sacred Relatives of God with their impious conceits; and . . . some of these desperate adventurers may (I think) be reckoned amongst the principal or most learned Writers of English verse'.[2] What Vaughan has in view I take to be such religious conceits and phraseology in love-poetry as Constable's sonnets on the divinity of his lady, and the likening the wounds of the lover to the stigmata of St. Francis are superficial and purely literary examples of, but which continue into the more flippant and even licentious poetry of the seventeenth-century 'metaphysicals'. Donne, in a daringly sensual poem, finds proof of his lady's divinity in that she is not only true but truth itself, and that she can read the thoughts of his heart:

> But when I saw thou sawest my heart,
> And knew'st my thoughts, beyond an Angel's art.[3]

Vaughan's own love verses show the influence of Donne, but it is the Platonic Donne of the later poems addressed to his wife:

---

[1] *The Author's Preface to the following Hymns* ('Silex Scintillans: Sacred Poems and Private Ejaculations').
[2] *Loc. cit.* [3] *The Dreame,* vv. 15-16.

LOVE-POETRY

> Whil'st I by pow'rfull Love so much refin'd
> That my absent soule the same is,
>   Carelesse to misse
>   A glaunce or kisse,
> Can with those Elements of lust and sense
>   Freely dispense,
> And court the mind.[1]

There were two things which might and did happen to this Courtly love-poetry at the Renaissance, as in Italy earlier. It might grow more spiritual or more sensual. The more ideal element might under Platonic influence be detached and treated more abstractly and intellectually. One can hardly say that in this process the poetry was elevated or ennobled, for no love-poetry of the Renaissance breathes so pure and passionate a strain as that of Dante in the *Vita Nuova*. The Platonism of the new poetry is too drily intellectual, or else it conveys a suspicion of insincerity. The lover protests too much his indifference to the physical. But it is some such purified and intellectual passion that Spenser quite sincerely exalts in his *Hymn in honour of Love*:

> For loue is Lord of truth and loialtie,
> Lifting himselfe out of the lowly dust,
> On golden plumes vp to the purest skie,
> Aboue the reach of loathly sinfull lust,
> Whose base affect through cowardly distrust
>   Of his weake wings, dare not to heauen fly,
>   But like a moldwarpe in the earth doth ly.
>
> His dunghill thoughts, which do themselues enure
> To dirtie drosse, no higher dare aspyre,
> Ne can his feeble earthly eyes endure
> The flaming light of that celestiall fyre,

---

[1] *To* Amoret, *of the Difference 'twixt him, and other Lovers, and what True Love is*, vv. 22-28.

GEORGE CHAPMAN

>Which kindleth loue in generous desyre,
> And makes him mount aboue his natiue might
>Of heauie earth, vp to the heauens hight.

But Spenser's vein is more Petrarchan than Platonic; has a touch even of Dante's spirit, if more airy, less intense. With all his love of love, Spenser had something of a virginal mind. His ideal of love is not abstract and intellectual, but it is pure. The intellectual Platonic vein is better illustrated from Chapman's pedantic and tormented, yet in their own way forcible, sonnets:

>Muses that sing loues sensual empery,
> And lovers kindling your enraged fires
>At Cupids bonfires burning in the eye,
> Blown with the empty breath of vain desires,
>You that prefer the painted cabinet
> Before the wealthy jewels it doth store yee,
>That all your joys in dying figures set,
> And stain the living substance of your glory,
>Abjure those joys, abhor their memory,
> And let my love the honour'd subject be
>Of love, and honour's complete history;
> Your eyes were never yet let in to see
>The majesty and riches of the mind,
>But dwell in darkness; for your God is blind.[1]

Spenser never writes in that vein; but Spenser too, it must be remembered, repents, like Vaughan, of having composed love verses. 'Having in the greener Times of my youth composed these former two Hymnes in the praise of Love and Beautie, and finding that the same too much pleased those of like age and disposition, which being too vehemently caried with that kind of affection, do rather sucke out poyson to their strong passion, then hony to their honest delight, I

---

[1] *A Coronet for his Mistress Philosophy*, Sonnet i.

was mooued by the one of you two most excellent Ladies to call in the same';[1] and by way of retractation he composed his Hymns of Heavenly Love and of Heavenly Beautie, in which all earthly love is laid upon the altar of the love of Christ:

> With all thy hart, with all thy soule and mind
> Thou must him loue, and his beheasts embrace;
> All other loues, with which the world doth blind
> Weake fancies, and stirre vp affections base,
> Thou must renounce, and vtterly displace,
> And giue thy selfe vnto him full and free,
> That full and freely gaue himselfe to thee.[2]

But if it was possible to detach abstractly one, the more ideal, aspect of Courtly love, it was still easier for poets of the Renaissance, familiar with Ovid and the whole range of Latin erotic elegy and lyric, to detach or accentuate the other, the sensual. Even Milton in his Latin poems, to say nothing of Beza or Buchanan, gives freer play to a sensuous, voluptuous fancy than he was willing to do either in Italian or English. The Courtly extravagances were a challenge to the more realistic bent of mind to detach the silken covering and show what was the real nature of the passion so elegantly veiled as a worship of an unapproachable Laura. Jean de Meung had already done so in his Swiftian continuation of Guillaume de Lorris' refined allegory, and Shakespeare does so in *Troilus and Cressida* and the sonnets to the dark lady. That strange play has puzzled the critics, and it certainly contains discordant elements and perhaps some work that is not Shakespeare's. But the main drift is clear

---

[1] Dedicatory epistle *To the Right Honorable and most Vertuous Ladies, the Lady Margaret Countesse of Cumberland, and the Ladie Marie Countesse of Warwicke.*

[2] *An Hymne of Heavenly Love*, vv. 260-266.

enough. Shakespeare reads Chaucer's charming but ambiguous story of the lovers and Pandarus, and says to himself, this refined and pathetic treatment of Criseyde is all very charming, but what are the real facts underlying Chaucer's sympathetic irony? Just this: Your chivalrous knights are lustful brutes and stupid bullies, and the lady whom the one true knight and lover of the poem adores is a heartless light-skirts:

> Fie, fie upon her!
> There's language in her eye, her cheek, her lip,
> Nay, her foot speaks; her wanton spirits look out
> At every joint and motive of her body.
> O these encounterers, so glib of tongue,
> That give accosting welcome ere it comes,
> And wide unclasp the tables of their thoughts
> To every ticklish reader, set them down
> For sluttish spoils of opportunity
> And daughters of the game.[1]

The strangest of Shakespeare's plays, it is to my mind one of the most powerful, the satire redeemed from cynicism by the wisdom and humanity of Ulysses and the intensity of Troilus' love for Cressida:

> I am giddy, expectation whirls me round.
> The imaginary relish is so sweet
> That it enchants my sense. What will it be
> When that the watery palate tastes indeed
> Love's thrice-repured nectar? death, I fear me;
> Swounding destruction, or some joy too fine,
> Too subtle-potent, tun'd too sharp in sweetness
> For the capacity of my ruder powers.[2]

But in lyrical and elegiac poetry the great rebel against the tradition of Petrarchan idealism, the

---
[1] *Troilus and Cressida*, Act IV. sc. v. 54-63.
[2] *Ibid.* Act III. sc. ii. 17-24.

'mincing poetry' which Hotspur hated, was John Donne; and a reader of some of Donne's elegies and songs will feel that he has indeed passed from one extreme to another, has quitted the peaks of self-abnegation and adoration to immerse himself in the mud-baths of sensual passion and cynical scorn of woman:

> Hope not for minde in women; at their best
> Sweetnesse and wit, they are but Mummy, possest.[1]

But if he can bring himself to read on he will begin to discover that this is not the whole truth, that these strange and startling, sometimes revolting, poems have in them at their worst a quality which distinguishes them from the more voluptuous, more cynical because more cold-blooded, sensuousness of Elizabethan idylls and of such imitations of Donne's extravagances as Carew's *Rapture* or Cartwright's *Song of Dalliance*, to say nothing of the flippant indecencies of many of his followers before and after the Restoration, which if not always printed are scattered through manuscript collections and may be sampled in the late Mr. Bullen's *Musa Proterva*. The difference is that between the coarsest and most savage of Catullus' verses and Ovid's *Amores* and *Art of Love*. Catullus and Donne are passionate. Passionate sincerity of feeling redeems to some extent the sensuality and cynical savagery of their poems. For if one is, with the late Sir Walter Raleigh, to call Donne a sensualist, it must be with a distinction. He is not a voluptuary, a Sir Epicure Mammon or Volpone, for whose kind love is a pleasure of the same class as eating and drinking, women things to be classed with wine and sauces and soft raiment:

---

[1] *Love's Alchymie*, 23-24.

JOHN DONNE

> O sir, the wonder,
> The blazing star of Italy! a wench
> Of the first year, a beauty ripe as harvest!
> Whose skin is whiter than a swan all over,
> Than silver, snow, or lilies; a soft lip,
> Would tempt you to eternity of kissing!
> And flesh that melteth in the touch to blood!
> Bright as your gold, and lovely as your gold![1]

Donne is almost an ascetic in his disregard of physical beauty, a quality in the woman of his adoration or scorn which he never mentions. He was a sensualist as Tolstoi was, one for whom woman was a curious and perpetual interest at once attracting and repelling, but never to be regarded with indifference. And in virtue of this hot-blooded sincerity of feeling his poetry reveals on a closer study a greater complexity of moods, a wider dramatic range, than the first impression suggests, so much so that one comes at moments to the conviction that this poetry is a more complete mirror than any other one can recall of love as a complex passion in which sense and soul are inextricably blended. It is pedantically witty, and one may easily take some of it too seriously. It is sensual, coarse, and cynical, and yet can speak the language of passion which is neither sensual nor cynical:

> All kings, and all their favourites,
> All glory of honours, beauties, wits,
> The sun itself, which makes times, as they pass,
> Is elder by a year now, than it was
> When thou and I first one another saw:
> All other things to their destruction draw,
>   Only our love hath no decay;
> This, no tomorrow hath, nor yesterday,
> Running it never runs from us away,
> But truly keepes his first, last, everlasting day.[2]

[1] *Volpone*, i. 1.   [2] *The Anniversarie*, vv. 1-10.

And lastly there are poems in which passion is silent and the language is that of affection only:

> Sweetest love I do not go
> For weariness of thee,
> Nor in hope the world can show
> A fitter love for me;
> But since that I
> Must die at last, 'tis best
> To use myself in jest
> Thus by fain'd deaths to die.

These poems were addressed to his wife, and in them Donne speaks a language which is not that of Courtly love-poetry, but of simpler people, and it is well to remember that now, as in the Middle Ages, there is love-poetry which is not Courtly or 'metaphysical', and in which it is idle to talk of the influence of either Renaissance or Reformation. Courtly love-poetry was the product of the leisure of the upper class of Feudal society. Idleness is the portress to the garden of the Rose. 'In the days of Racine', Napoleon said, 'love was the whole content of life. That happens in a society where no great deeds are being done.' It happens nowhere in reality, but it is only in a society to which wealth gives leisure that it can be accepted even as a convention. The long-drawn-out woes of a Petrarch, the conventional anxieties about 'onestà' and secrecy which complicate the loves of Troilus and Criseyde, have no place in the experience of the characters in a popular love story. The love of the more popular romances and lyrics is of a simpler, franker character, the love of a young man and maid, and the ideal end is their happy marriage. *King Horn*, *Havelok the Dane*, *The Squire of Low Degree*, *Floris and Blanchfleur*, and many others, all turn on the same theme. The loves of Lancelot and Tristram and Isolt and Troilus and Criseyde are of a different type, and were told, in the first place, for a different audience, more curious of the contradictions and fluctuations of feeling, manners, and the subtilities of 'chevalerie et courtoisie'. Now it was just the simpler, more normal feeling and attitude towards the purpose and significance of love that was the theme of the early Elizabethan drama, and notably of Shakespeare's romantic comedy and tragedy. 'His lovers look forward to marriage as a matter of course, and they neither anticipate its rights nor turn their affections elsewhere. They commonly love at first sight, and once for all. Love-relations which do not contemplate marriage occur rarely, and in subordination to other dramatic purposes. Tragedy like that of Gretchen does not attract him.'[1] So Professor Herford, and I need not follow him in his analysis of Shakespeare's individual treatment. My point is that this was the treatment of love as a motive in a story which his audience desired and expected. They were not prudish, and got from Shakespeare, as well as other dramatists, plenty of coarse and bawdy jests. Nor were they averse to tragedies of lust and murder. But both were crimes; and if in the later drama of Beaumont and Fletcher and Massinger and Ford the influence of the Court encouraged a taste for more piquant situations and emotions, yet no play dealt with courtly love and its peculiar conventions and conflict with 'onestà' as Chaucer had dealt in *Troilus and Criseyde*. Even Ford's sombre plays justify illicit love only on the ground of the transcendent claims of a consuming passion. Their motto is not that of Boccaccio's Criseida:

---

[1] Herford: *Shakespeare's Treatment of Love and Marriage*, 1921.

> L' acqua furtiva, assai più dolce cosa
> È che il vin con abbondanza avuto:
> Così d'amor la gioia che nascosa
> Trapassa assai del sempre mai tenuto
> Marito in braccio;

which might or should have been the motto inscribed over the portals of the Garden of the Rose.

This simpler, more natural, popular, or bourgeois love-poetry has nothing in it of the metaphysical strain of Courtly love-poetry, no doctrine of the gentle heart and its relation to love, of the high duties of patience and sleeplessness and secrecy and the avoidance of 'villainy', or still less of the transcendental doctrines of the mystical identity of lover and the relation of spiritual to sensuous love, or of the cynical reactions from these extravagances. But it was a conception of love which might be reflected on and developed by those who, while condemning the extravagances of Petrarchan worship and the sensuality of Latin poetry, classical and of the Revival of Learning, were not at all inclined to an ascetic exaltation of virginity. Puritans could be lovers like other people. Mrs. Hutchinson tells the story of her wooing with a naïve and somewhat priggish vanity. And there were Puritan love-poets.

George Wither, in his later years the author of endless diffuse didactic and pious poems, if they can be called poems, wrote in his early days, besides some natural and charming pastorals, two poems on love in which, if they have little of the passion of Donne's, one can see what the Puritan thought of the significance of love. The first is *Fidelia*, a long Heroical Epistle, after Ovid and Michael Drayton, the second a still longer poem, in short trochaic lines, on the theme of the perfect woman, *Fair Virtue, The Mistresse of Philarete.* For Wither the only true love is virtuous love. *The Mistresse of Philarete* must have every virtue of body, but still more of spirit:

> Malice never lets she in,
> Neither hates she aught but sin.
> Envy if she could admit,
> There's no means to nourish it,
> For her gentle heart is pleased
> When she knows another's eased:
> And there's none who ever got
> That perfection she hath not,
> So that no cause is there why
> She should anyone envy.

Like all these very chaste poets, Wither protests a little too much for our taste. One suspects that a poet actually in love would be less exacting in what he requires of his mistress, and be more reserved on the subject of chaste and unchaste love. There is more of the actuality of love in Donne's turbid elegies than in Wither's airy flights. But his poetry is not coldly intellectual, nor narrowly virtuous. He has no patience with the Petrarchan worship of a remote mistress:

> Shall I wasting in despair
> Die because a woman's fair?
> Or make pale my cheeks with care
> 'Cause another's rosy are?
> Be she fairer than the day,
> Or the flow'ry meads in May,
> If she be not fair to me
> What care I how fair she be?

That his mistress should love and be constant is her highest virtue:

> Constancy, I mean, the purest
> Of all beauties and the surest;
> For who'er doth that profess
> Hath an endless loveliness.

But *Fidelia* is even more significant of the Puritan lover, for its theme is that of the great Puritan novel of a century later. It is a letter from an earlier Clarissa or Pamela to an earlier Lovelace who has forsaken her, forsaken her because she would not transgress the bounds of chastity:

> Oh, what of me by this time had become
> If my desires with thine had happ'd to roam,
> Or I unwisely had consented to
> What, shameless, once thou did'st attempt to do?
> I might have fallen by those immodest tricks,
> Had not some power been stronger than my sex.

She loves him still, and meditates what may be the causes which keep him away. Is it another love, or is it his parents' unwillingness that he should marry beneath him? And, like Richardson, she protests against the claim of parents to sunder lovers:

> Can there be any friend that hath the power
> To disunite hearts so conjoined as ours?
> Ere I would so have done by thee, I'ld rather
> Have parted with one dearer than my father.
> For though the will of our Creator binds
> Each child to learn and know his parents' minds,
> Yet sure am I so just a deity
> Commandeth nothing against piety;
> Nor doth that band of duty give them leave
> To violate their faith or to deceive.
> And though that parents have authority
> To rule their children in minority,
> Yet they are never granted such power on them
> That will allow to tyrannize upon them,
> Or use them under their command so ill
> To force them without reason to their will.
>   .   .   .   .   .   .
> For I do think it is not only meant
> Children should ask but parents should consent;

> And that they err, their duty as much breaking
> For not consenting, as we not for speaking.[1]

There you have, however poorly expressed, the theme or themes on which so many later novels were to turn, from *Clarissa* to most Victorian novels, English and American—young love, fidelity or infidelity, harsh parents or other untoward circumstances. It is an old motive in popular story:

> The course of true love never did run smooth,
> For either it was different in blood,
> Or else misgraffed in respect to years,
> Or else it stood upon the choice of friends.

But in the mediaeval Courtly circles for whom romance and allegory were composed this type of story was not so piquant as that of Lancelot's love for the wife of Arthur, or Tristram's for the wife of Mark. Marriage was a prudential arrangement

---

[1] But Wither is speaking the language of rebellion, anticipating Richardson. It was the accepted view that no child should marry without the leave of his or her parents. See Schücking in *Englische Studien*, vol. 62. *Die Familie bei Shakespeare*. Nobody could state the view of a right-thinking child more explicitly than Dorothy Osborne. She will not marry one whom she does not esteem unless by her father's injunction, but she is quite prepared to submit to his will, and she thinks that Temple owes the same duty to his father. 'Sure the whole world could not perswade mee (unlesse a Parent comanded it) to marry one that I had no esteeme for, and where I have any, I am not less scrupulous then your father, for I should never bee brought to doe them the injury as to give them a wife whose affections they could never hope for, besydes that I must sacrifice myself int and live a walking missery till the only hope that would then be left mee, were perfected. O mee this is soe sad, it hath put mee out of all I had to say besydes.' The reference to his father is to the fact that Temple's father had not insisted on his son marrying the woman he had offered him. She will not marry one whom she cannot esteem, and will not marry one she does esteem, unless she can also love him. But she will do even the first if her father commands. Clarissa has advanced a little farther. She will not marry without her parents' consent, but she will not, even at their command, marry a Solmes whom she cannot esteem. See also the poor play by George Wilkins, *The Miseries of Enforced Marriage*, 1637.

entered into mainly with a view to property. 'No married pair can really love each other.' Love must be free:

> Love wol nat be constreyned by maistrye;
> When maistrye comth, the god of love anon
> Beteth his winges and farwel he is gon.

'Shal noon housbonde seyn to me chekmat', says Criseyde to herself when meditating whether she shall give her heart to Troilus:

> For either they ben ful of Ialousye,
> Or maisterful or loven novelrye,

and marriage is never mentioned by the lovers as even a possibility.

Marriage was not otherwise regarded at the Court of Elizabeth or James than in the fourteenth century. In his letters to Dudley Carleton, Chamberlayne seldom mentions the death of a nobleman or wealthy citizen without speculating as to who will be the likeliest inheritor of his wealthy widow. The subject of Spenser's glowing *Epithalamion*, she that was

> Clad all in white that seems a virgin best,

had already been (if we may credit recent research) twice married and was to have a fourth 'husband at chirche dore' after Spenser's death. Marriages recur in the records between widows and widowers, each bringing children into the joint family, and then there are further marriages among these children, so that properties may be secured and enlarged. Donne married his daughter at the age of twenty-three to Edward Alleyn, then fifty-eight, and the bargaining was, on a smaller scale, just such as Coulton[1] describes between greater people in the four-

[1] Coulton: *Chaucer and his England*.

teenth century. The majority of wives were doubtless as chaste and respectable as to-day; still, if one wishes to realise the general level of thought and feeling about marriage, one need only recall, I will not say Elizabethan comedy, for comedy is never a very trustworthy guide to social conditions, but a tragedy like *Othello*, not laying too much stress upon the Venetian setting. Shakespeare's Venice in many respects was London. What shocks us in the play, the readiness with which Othello entertains Iago's suggestions, is partly explicable if one recall the common estimate of the risks a man was running who married and so put his personal honour in the keeping of another:

> Cuckoo, Cuckoo! O word of fear
> Unpleasing to the married ear.

Othello knows it, and has only married because love swept him off his feet:

> For know, Iago,
> But that I love the gentle Desdemona,
> I would not my unhoused free condition
> Put into circumscription and confine
> For the sea's worth.

Iago thinks all wives are the same; and his wife, who is no cynic, is quite sure that all husbands are unfaithful, and is not to be persuaded by Desdemona that wives should be more strict. Spenser's idealisation of romantic love found little to support it as he came to know the Court more closely:

> And is loue, then (said Corylas), once knowne
> In Court, and his sweet lore professed there?
> I weened sure he was our God alone:
> And only woond in fields and forests here.

> Not so (quoth he), loue most aboundeth there.
> For all the walls and windows there are writ,
> All full of loue, and loue, and loue, my deare,
> And all their talke and studie is of it.
> Ne any there doth braue or valiant seeme,
> Vnlesse that some gay Mistresse badge he beares;
> Ne any one himselfe doth ought esteeme,
> Vnlesse he swim in loue vp to the eares.
> But they of loue and of his sacred lere,
> (As it should be) all otherwise deuise
> Then we poore shepheards are accustomd here,
> And him do sue and serue all otherwise.
> For with lewd speeches and licentious deeds,
> His mightie mysteries they do prophane,
> And vse his ydle name to other needs,
> But as a complement for courting vaine.
> So him they do not serue as they professe,
> But make him serue to them for sordid vses.
> Ah my dread Lord, that doest liege hearts possesse,
> Avenge thy selfe on them for their abuses.[1]

If then serious feeling in Puritan and other circles was in revolt against the licentiousness of which Petrarchan idealism and refinement were often only the thin veil, it was inevitable that they should also demur to a too utilitarian conception of marriage. It was not in an ascetic spirit that Herbert and Vaughan condemned the love-poetry of the day. Their feeling was not that of Guinicelli and Dante who sublimated Court love-poetry by making the love of a woman a love that sought no earthly fulfilment, a prelibation of the love of God. Their protest was ethical, not mystical. The sanction of love, they said, and so Spenser and Wither, is marriage. But, and this was practically, at any rate, a new idea, the sanction of marriage is love, or should be. Some of the best minds were disposed to feel, like Clarissa,

[1] *Colin Clout's Come Home Againe*, 771-794.

that parents, if they may forbid an unsuitable marriage, have no right to compel a daughter to marry a Solmes or a Barnes Newcome, when her own heart does not consent. Puritanism was the hot-bed from which was to spring and blossom the sentimentalism, the moving conflict between the conscience and the heart, of *Pamela* and *Clarissa* and *Jane Eyre* and of *The Mill on the Floss*, and other novels of the kind, against which we are witnessing in our own day in the novels of men, and still more of women, so remarkable a reaction. In support of my thesis let me appeal, not to Wither, but to a greater poet and more rebellious thinker than he—to John Milton.

Milton, like many other poets, made such a sad mess of his adventures in love and matrimony, and his failure made him such a sore, angry, intolerant, and arrogant critic of women, that it is easy to do injustice to him as a lover. There is no subject on which he thought and felt more passionately, not even politics. 'Milton', a critic and woman has said, 'is an example of a great lover spoiled by wrong opinions. He was disobedient to the heavenly vision: he turned his back upon the radiant form: he shut his ears to the appealing voice. Yet he could not forget the vision; the glamour of love's presence made pale his daylight, the appeal of love's melodious voice made vocal his silences.'[1] What the vision had been before a too hasty choice brought disillusionment he has adumbrated in an interesting digression in one of the polemical pamphlets. His character had been attacked; he had been accused of a disorderly and licentious life while at the University and after he went down. His answer to the charge or insinua-

[1] *Wordsworth and Tolstoi and Other Papers*, by Anna M. B. Guthrie, Edinburgh, 1922.

tion is to show how the twin ideas of love and chastity had developed side by side in his heart and mind. In early youth he had read and loved—he might have added 'and imitated'—the 'smooth elegiac poets whereof the schools are not scarce', but 'if I found these authors anywhere speaking unworthy things of themselves or unchaste of those names which before they had extolled; this effect it wrought with me, from that time forward their art I still applauded, but the men I deplored; and above them all I preferred' (he is probably leaping forward some years; Milton is a little disposed, when he resumes his past life, to give to things an appearance of more logical development than was quite exact) 'the two famous renowners of Beatrice and Laura, who never write but honour of them to whom they devote their verse, displaying sublime and pure thoughts without transgression'. 'Next (for hear me out now, readers) I betook me among those lofty fables and romances which recount in solemn cantos the deeds of knighthood founded by our victorious kings, and from hence had in renown over all Christendom. There I read in the oath of every knight, that he should defend to the expense of his best blood, or of his life, if it so befell him, the honour and chastity of virgin or matron; from whence even then I learned what a noble virtue chastity sure must be, to the defence of which so many worthies, by such a dear adventure of themselves, had sworn; and if I found in the story afterwards any of them by word or deed breaking that oath, I judged it the same fault of the poet as that which is attributed to Homer, to have written indecent things of the Gods: only this my mind gave me, that every free and gentle spirit, without that oath, ought to be born a knight, nor needed to expect the gilt spur, or the laying of a sword upon a shoulder, to stir him up both by his counsel and his arms to secure and protect the weakness of any attempted chastity. So that even these books, which to many others have been the fuel of wantonness and loose living, I cannot think how, unless by divine indulgence, proved to me so many incitements, as you have heard, to the love and steadfast observation of that virtue which abhors the society of bordelloes.'[1] That is a passage of singular interest and beauty; to Milton as to Spenser the ideal element in the love of the romances had made appeal, if his disillusionment came in a different way, not from experience of the contrast between the ideal and the real in the amours of courtiers, but from the personal experience of the power of love to blind and to mislead, of the fate that lies in store for the idealist who believes that the vision has taken concrete form in a woman of quite ordinary mould; and the consequences are bitter for her too, be she Mary Powell or Harriet Westbrook. In a later pamphlet Milton complains that the man of the world is not seldom a better judge of a fit wife than the idealist who has garnered up his heart: 'And lastly it is not strange though many, who have spent their youth chastely, are in some things not so quick-sighted, while they haste too eagerly to light the nuptial torch ... while they who have lived most loosely, by reason of their bold accustoming, prove most successful in their matches, because their wild affections, unsettling at will, have been so many divorces to teach them experience.'[2]

But to return to the history of the young Milton's

[1] *An Apology for Smectymnuus*, Introduction.
[2] *The Doctrine and Discipline of Divorce*, Book I. chap. iii.

éducation sentimentale. From poetry and romance he passed to 'the shady spaces of philosophy, but chiefly to the divine volumes of Plato, and his equal' (*i.e.* 'his contemporary') 'Xenophon, where if I should tell ye what I learned of chastity and love, I mean that which is truly so, whose charming cup is only virtue, which she bears in her hand to those that are worthy; (the rest are cheated with a thick intoxicating potion, which a certain sorceress, the abuser of Love's name, carries about) and how the first and chiefest office of love begins and ends in the soul, producing those happy twins of her divine generation, knowledge and virtue: with such abstract sublimities as these it might be worth your listening, readers, as I may one day hope to have ye in a still time, when there shall be no more chiding'. So he writes, mindful of the great poem he is meditating, the theme of which at this time was to be the wars and loves of Arthur and his knights. 'Last of all' in his education as a lover, 'not in time but as perfection is last', he reckons his 'careful training in the precepts of Christian religion ... the doctrine of Holy Scripture, unfolding those chaste and high mysteries with timeliest care infused that "the body is for the Lord and the Lord for the body", thus also I argued to myself that if unchastity in a woman, whom St. Paul terms the glory of man, be such a scandal and dishonour, then certainly in a man, who is both the image and glory of God, it must, though not commonly so thought, be much more deflowering and dishonourable. Nor did I slumber over that place[1] expressing such high rewards of ever accompanying the Lamb, with those Celestial songs

---

[1] *Revelation,* xxii. 17. Cf.
    And hears the unexpressive Nuptiall song.
                                     Lycidas, l. 176.

to others inapprehensible but not to those who were not defiled with women, which doubtless means fornication; for marriage must not be called a defilement.' Thus speaks the young idealist, at once Humanist and Puritan, one who has sucked from the flowers of poetry romantic and classical only the purest honey, a more ardent devotee of purity than even the courtier Spenser, and equally convinced that 'marriage is no defilement'. To that opinion he was, through all his disappointment, to be faithful:

> Hail wedded Love, mysterious law, true source
> Of human offspring, sole propriety
> In Paradise of all things common else.
> By thee adulterous lust was driven from men
> Among the bestial herds to range, by thee
> Founded in reason Loyal, Just, and Pure,
> Relations dear, and all the Charities
> Of Father, Son, and Brother first were known.
> Far be it that I should write thee sin or blame,
> Or think thee unbefitting holiest place,
> Perpetual fountain of domestic sweets,
> Whose bed is undefil'd and chaste pronounc'd
> Present or past, as Saints and Patriarchs us'd.
> Here Love his golden shafts employs, here lights
> His constant lamp and waves his purple wings,
> Reigns here and revels; not in the bought smile
> Of Harlots loveless, joyless, unindear'd,
> Casual fruition; nor in Court Amours,
> Mixt Dance, or wanton Mask, or Midnight Ball,
> Or Serenate, which the starv'd Lover sings
> To his proud fair, best quitted with disdain.[1]

There are in these lines touches of the angry controversialist and a significance to which I shall recur. But taken together these passages of prose and verse are the noblest expression one can point to of the Protestant ideal of love and marriage, of marriage

[1] *Paradise Lost*, IV. 750 ff.

which, despite the high sacramental doctrine of the Catholic Church, the Middle Ages with their diverse cults of asceticism and free-love had been too apt to belittle, but in which Milton honours not only the union of hearts but the enrichment that it brings in all the charities of the family. But between the writing of the earlier prose confession of faith and of *Paradise Lost* had come the great disillusionment; and the passionate eulogist of love, protected by chastity and sanctioned by marriage, had discovered that love thus canalised, instead of at once deepening and enriching the affections, might wreck a man's whole life, if he had chosen amiss. And so in the Divorce pamphlets, the last phase of Milton's enlightenment on this great theme, he became an early champion of what we now mean by free-love, not that of the Courtly tradition of the Rose in which the assumption was that marriage is a social arrangement to secure property and transmit it, but that the love of another man's wife is a liberal education. Free-love for Milton and for modern reformers means a relaxation of the marriage laws. Donne half-humorously, half-cynically defends change as the very life of love:

> Waters stink soon if in one place they bide,
> And in the vast sea are more putrifi'd:
> But when they kiss one bank and, leaving this,
> Never look back but the next bank do kiss,
> Then are they purest; Change is the nursery
> Of music, joy, life, and eternity.[1]

That was not Milton's mood when he wrote the pamphlets. If later he came to defend polygamy, so that in the lines quoted he defends the Patriarchs, that was when his ideal of womanhood had become a

[1] *Elegie*, III. 31-36.

much more Judaic one than that of the early reader of romances and 'the two famous renowners of Beatrice and Laura'. In the pamphlets it is still as the champion of love that he advocates freedom of divorce, love not lust, 'this pure and more inbred joy of joining to itself a fit conversing soul (which desire is properly called love) and is stronger than death, as the Spouse of Christ thought; many waters cannot quench it, neither can the floods drown it'.[1] Plato's myth of Eros and Anteros 'is a deep and serious verity shewing us that love in marriage cannot live nor subsist unless it be mutual; and where love cannot be there can be left of wedlock nothing but the empty husks of an outside matrimony, as undelightful and unpleasing to God as any other kind of hypocrisy'.[2]

The way of idealists is hard, especially if they be also poets and egotists, and the Milton who composed *Paradise Lost* was an angry and embittered man who had travelled far from the position still maintained in the Divorce pamphlets, had become, theoretically at least, a polygamist and at times a misogynist:

> O why did God
> Creator wise, that peopled highest Heaven
> With Spirits Masculine, create at last
> This novelty on Earth, this fair defect
> Of Nature, and not fill the World at once
> With Men as Angels, without Feminine.[3]

And so Milton sets out to show that man's chief enemies had from the first been two—the devil and woman, Satan and Eve. But the lover in Milton was not dead though suppressed. His second marriage

---

[1] *Doctrine and Discipline*, etc., Book I. chap. iv.
[2] *Ibid.* Book I. chap. vi.
[3] *Paradise Lose*, x. 888 ff.

seems to have brought some promise of assuagement to the immedicable wound the first had left behind, but 'the blind fury' intervened:

> Methought I saw my late espoused Saint
> Brought to me like Alcestis from the grave.
>   .   .   .   .   .   .
> But O, as to embrace me she inclin'd,
> I wak'd, she fled, and day brought back my night.

And so, by something of the same strange inversion as made Satan more impressive and even sympathetic to us than those against whom he fought, Eve, the origin of all our woe, became infinitely more attractive than Adam. 'The more she is slighted and undervalued the more attractive does Milton's Eve appear in her beauty, her gentleness, her helpless dependence on Adam; in her touching fondness for her impossible husband. Her love is as unselfish as his is selfish. She resents nothing, demands nothing, but is content to give all.... She glories in her humiliation. ... Her love is to her all in all:

> With thee conversing I forget all time,
> All seasons and their change please all alike.'[1]

The most pathetic speech in the poem is Eve's:

> Forsake me not thus, Adam, witness Heav'n
> What love sincere, and reverence in my heart
> I bear thee, and unweeting have offended,
> Unhappily deceiv'd; thy suppliant
> I beg, and clasp thy knees; bereave me not,
> Whereon I live, thy gentle looks, thy aid,
> Thy counsel in this uttermost distress,
> My only strength and stay: forlorn of thee,
> Whither shall I betake me, where subsist?[2]

[1] Guthrie, *op. cit.*   [2] *Paradise Lost*, x. 914 ff.

It cannot, I think, be said that either the complex, passionate, realistic vein of Donne's poetry or the idealistic, virtuous love whose sanction and completion is marriage (of which Milton and Wither in different strains sing the glories, if Milton discovers also the perils), represents the general tenor of love-poetry throughout the century, before and after the Restoration. It is easy to exaggerate the influence of Donne, within whose circle none durst move but he, though he doubtless is responsible for the character of the conceits in the so-called 'metaphysical' poetry. The poets played with conceits as the Elizabethans had played with words. But none of them had Donne's passionate feeling and curiously analytic mind, neither his nor Milton's profound interest in love as a power to make or to mar a man's life. For both these a hasty marriage was the critical step in life, and it is symptomatic of the temperament of which one feels the vibration in their poetry. The Courtly poets of the century were light-o'-love young gallants, if the word may be transferred to the male sex, charming singers at their best of the old joys and sorrows and paradoxes, taken less seriously. Once or twice they strike a more resonant note as in Rochester's:

> When wearied with a world of woes
>   To thy safe bosom I retire,
> Where Love and peace and honour flow,
>   May I contented there expire.
>
> Lest once more wandering from that heaven,
>   I fall on some base heart unblessed,
> Faithless to thee, false, unforgiven,
>   And lose my everlasting rest.

Not infrequently their tone is frankly licentious. It is from the post-Restoration lyrists that Bullen gathered the greater number of the songs in his *Musa Proterva*, though there are contributions from the earlier period too, even from Marvell. In the drama too the romantic tradition dominates the later plays. Shakespeare's *Antony and Cleopatra* is a magnificent apotheosis of the romantic love which admits no inhibitions, all for love or the world well lost; though the amazing comprehensiveness and justice of his imagination and thought enables him to glorify the passion without obscuring its ethical significance, with none of Dryden's sentiment. The most serious dramatist of the school of Beaumont and Fletcher, John Ford, has treated the same theme in a more intense and confined vein, if in less splendid poetry. Passion is itself a justification of whatever action it may prompt; the victim of a *crime passionnel* is Love's Martyr.

'The wild affections', says the late Professor Raleigh, 'unsettling at will, wrote better love-songs than the steadfast principles of the sober and well governed. Roystering libertines like Sir Charles Sedley were more edifying lovers than the austere husbands of Mary Powell and of Eve.' They were better songsters certainly. Few poets have given to English song a more splendid *élan* than the metaphysicals in songs written in simple measures:

> Love in fantastic triumph sat
>   While bleeding hearts around him flowed,
> For whom fresh pains he did create,
>   And strange tyrannic power he showed.

or

> My love is of a birth as rare
>   As 'tis for object strange and high,
> It was begotten by despair,
>   Upon impossibility.

But they sang all the better that they did not take

the passion too seriously. They had not felt, like Donne, its subterranean currents. They had not, like Milton, staked their whole life and happiness on the hope of realising a love 'stronger than death... many waters cannot quench it, neither can the floods drown it'. The courtly, romantic tradition of love made its last appearance in the tirades of Dryden's Heroic Dramas, as perfectly empty as the verse is at times stirring and sonorous. It was not in poetry that the deeper feeling, the more serious interest in love, and its conflicts with ethical ideals and inhibitions or social prejudices and institutions, was to be heard, but in the work of the English novelists from Richardson to George Eliot and George Meredith and Charlotte and Emily Brontë and Thomas Hardy and D. H. Lawrence. In their novels we find again the complexities and conflicts of which Donne's strange songs and elegies and Milton's divorce pamphlets were in their different ways the evidences and interpreters.

CHAPTER VI

HUMANISM AND THE CHURCHES

The Court as the focus of Polite Letters, whether secular or devout—The Populace—The Godly—The infallible Churches, Roman and Presbyterian—The Eternal Decrees and Pastoral Discipline—Baxter—The Sects—Bunyan and Milton—The Via Media of the Church of England and its appeal to the Humanist spirit—Hooker—The Poets and others—Hales, Chillingworth, and the Cambridge Platonists—Cudworth's sermon to the House of Commons.

THE drama of Shakespeare, Marlowe, Jonson, Webster, Beaumont and Fletcher, Massinger; the poetry of love, romantic, pastoral, in sonnet and song, of Spenser, Sidney, Shakespeare, Daniel, Drayton, Donne,—these were the chief forms of imaginative, secular literature (for the prose novel was not yet a fully developed vehicle for the imaginative portrayal of life), and on both the religious spirit of the age looked with either doubtful approbation or quite definite condemnation, so that the drama, the most sensitive in its reaction to the taste of the audience, was driven steadily downhill after its splendid opening, owing to the lack of support from an audience at once cultured and serious. It was as a religious allegory, a sermon in poetic form, that *The Faerie Queene* could gain admission to a pious household like that of John Milton or Henry More, whatever extraneous delight it might bring with it, even as the title of Borrow's *Bible in Spain* gained for Mr. Birrell the benefit of a pleasant Sunday afternoon. Spenser's disciples, the Fletchers, discarded the romantic, chivalrous story, retaining only the edifying, if wearisome, allegory. Browne wove moral allegory into his pastoral strain. Wither is pious and didactic. Milton's secular poems, Latin and English, are the pastime of his youth. If a poet turns serious, he condemns and repents of his love-poems. If he does not burn them, then, like Donne, he leaves them unprinted, or makes amends by writing pious sonnets and hymns, Divine Poems, or Noble Numbers. It is the Court which keeps alive secular imaginative literature—drama and sonnet and song and courtly eulogy and elegy and witty audacities in prose and verse—the Court, or what one might call the 'galleries' to the Court, the Universities and the Inns where young lawyers forgathered. All polite literature is Courtly, and continued to be so even throughout the Commonwealth. It was only after the Revolution that the Town took the place of the Court, and gave us *The Tatler* and *The Spectator*, to give way itself in time to that more indefinable audience and arbiter, the general reading public.

In the century with which we are dealing, the Court, whether as an object of flattery or of satire, is the focus of interest to poet and dramatist; and not only for these, but for preachers too like Andrewes and Donne and Taylor and others. Even the pious young George Herbert regarded Cambridge and the Public Oratorship there as but a portico to the Court. He inaugurated his term of office by commenting, not on an oration by Demosthenes or Cicero, but one by the Scottish Solomon himself; and when he obtained a small sinecure at Court, Walton tells us how, 'with the advantage of his college and of his Oratorship, he enjoyed his genteel humour for clothes and court-like company and seldom looked towards Cambridge unless the King was there, but then he never failed'.[1] It was only when, like Donne, he found the path of preferment barred that he forsook 'the painted pleasures of a Court life' and made an ever-severer piety the practice of his short life, and in religious verse and music consecrated his Muse. Richard Baxter, later the leader of the presbyterians, tells us that when he was eighteen a friend of his parents persuaded them and him 'to lay by preparations for the ministry, and to go to London and get acquaintance at Court and get some office as being the only rising way.... I would not be disobedient but went up and stayed at Whitehall with Sir Henry Herbert (then Master of the Revels) about a month. But I had quickly enough of the Court, when I saw a Stage-Play instead of a sermon on the Lord's Day in the afternoon, and saw what course was there in fashion, and heard little preaching but what was against the Puritans.'[2]

That is the Court as the Puritans saw it: 'The Court of this King', says Mrs. Hutchinson, speaking of James, 'was a nursery of lust and intemperance ... the generality of the gentry and of the land soon learned the Court fashion and every great house in the country became a sty of uncleanness. To keep the people in their deplorable security, till vengeance overtook them, they were entertained with masks and stage-plays and sorts of ruder sports.'[3] But even she admits that there was another side at least to the Court of his successor. 'The face of the Court

[1] *Life of Mr. George Herbert.*   [2] *Reliquiae Baxterianae*, 1696, p. 11.
[3] *Memoirs of the Life of Colonel Hutchinson*, ed. C. H. Firth, 1906, p. 64.

THE COURT

was much changed in the change of the King, for King Charles was temperate, chaste, and serious. . . . Men of learning and ingenuity in all the arts were in esteem, and received encouragement of the king, who was a most excellent judge and a great lover of paintings, carvings, gravings, and many other ingenuities, less offensive than the bawdry and profane abusive wit of the other Court.'[1] And whatever the Puritan thought, it was on the Court that the eyes of a young Bacon or Donne or Herbert were directed. It is from the Court that favour and promotion come. It is the Court that a Carew or a Herrick seeks to delight with songs or complimentary epistles or elegies or even, it may be, epigrams and satires. The Court, the City, the Country,—that is the poet's threefold division of life, and however he may pose as a lover of philosophic leisure and self-sufficiency, it is to the Court he looks in hope and expectancy, for there

> All is warmth and light and good desire.

'Wotton', cries Thomas Bastard when he and others have mooted the question which life is best,

> The country and the country swain,
> How can they yield a poet any sense?
> How can they stir him up or heat his vein?
> How can they feed him with intelligence?
> You have that fire which can a wit inflame
> In happy London, England's fairest eye:
> Well may you Poets have of worthy name,
> Which have the food and life of Poetry.
> And yet the country or the town may sway,
> Or bear a part, as clowns do in a play.[2]

---

[1] *Memoirs of the Life of Colonel Hutchinson*, ed. C. H. Firth, 1906, p. 64.
[2] *Chrestoleros*, Lib. II. Epigram iv.

In Donne's poem on the wedding of Somerset one catches a glimpse of the warmth and splendour of a festive season at Court:

> At Court the spring already advanced is,
> The sun stays longer up; and yet not his
> The glory is; far other, other fires.
> First zeal to Prince and State; then love's desires
> Burn in one breast, and like Heaven's two great lights
> The one doth govern days, the other nights.
> And then that early light which did appear
> Before the sun and moon created were,
> The Prince's favour is diffus'd o'er all,
> From which all Fortunes, Names, and Natures fall;
> Then from those wombs of stars, the Bride's bright eyes,
> At every glance a constellation flies,
> And sows the Court with stars, and doth prevent
> In light and power the all-eyed firmament;
> First her eyes kindle other ladies' eyes,
> Then from their beams their jewels' lustres rise,
> And from their jewels torches do take fire,
> And all is warmth and light and good desire.[1]

Even Milton in his youth felt the glamour of Court pageantry:

> Tow'red cities please us then,
> And the busy hum of men,
> Where throngs of Knights and Barons bold
> In weeds of peace high triumph hold,
> With store of Ladies whose bright eyes
> Rain influence and adjudge the prize
> Of wit and arms while both contend
> To win her grace whom all commend.
> There let Hymen oft appear
> In saffron robe, with taper clear,
> And pomp and feast and revelry,
> With mask and antique pageantry.

[1] *Eclogue*, 1613, December 26, ll. 15-32.

THE COURT

But in the later *Comus* Milton has become, like Spenser in *Colin Clout's Come Home Againe,* the censor of the Court which is the ominous wood where Amoret and the Lady of the Mask are exposed to the wiles and persecutions of Busyrane or the Enchanter:

> Shepherd, I take thy word
> And trust thy honest offer'd courtesy,
> Which oft is sooner found in lowly sheds
> With smoky rafters, than in tapst'ry halls
> And courts of princes, where it first was nam'd
> And yet is most pretended.

But it was not Puritans alone who became aware of the seamy side of Court life. The Court was the epitome of the world which has ever had two faces. The poet who laid *The Faerie Queene* at the feet of the Court, a sustained and elaborate piece of flattery, had no illusions as to the true character of Court life:

> For sooth to say it is no sort of life
> For shepheards fit to lead in that same place,
> Where each one seeks with malice and with strife,
> To thrust down other into foule disgrace,
> Himselfe to raise; and he doth soonest rise
> That best can handle his deceitfull wit,
> In subtle shifts, and finest sleights devise,
> Either by slaundering his well-deemed name
> Through leasings lewd, and fained forgerie, etc.[1]

And Donne writes in the same key:

> At home in wholesome solitariness
> My precious soul began the wretchedness
> Of suitors at Court to mourn, and a trance
> Like his who dreamt he saw Hell did advance
> Itself on me; such men as he saw there
> I saw at Court and worse, and more, etc.[2]

[1] *Colin Clout's Come Home Againe*, 686-696.
[2] Satyre IV. 155-160.

If one did not write for the Court and those whose tastes were courtly, what other audience might one cater for? To understand any literature one must know something of the audience as well as, at times even more than, of the author. Ben Jonson addressing the Court declares that 'In thee the whole kingdom dresseth itself, and is ambitious to use thee as her glass'. But Jonson knew that there was another glass in which he and Shakespeare and their fellows must contemplate their work and study its effect, and that was the populace of London and the towns they visited, but especially of London. These with young courtiers and lawyers made up the chief part of their audience, and at times the dramatists resent the fact: 'Oh, it offends me to the soul to hear a robustious fellow tear a passion to tatters, to very rags, to split the ears of the groundlings, who for the most part are capable of nothing but inexplicable dumb-shows and noise.'[1] 'And now that you may see I will be out of humour for company, I stand wholly to your kind approbation, and indeed am nothing so peremptory as in the beginning: marry I will not do as Plautus in his *Amphitruo* for all this, *Summi Jovis causa plaudite*, beg a plaudit for God's sake; but if you, out of the bounty of your good liking, will bestow it, why, you may, in time, make lean Macilente as fat as Sir John Falstaff. *Non ego ventosae plebis suffragia venor*;'[2] and again:

> Come leave the loathed stage,
> And the more loathsome age,
> Where pride and impudence in faction knit,
> Usurp the chair of wit!

[1] *Hamlet* III. ii.
[2] Jonson: *Every Man out of his Humour*, Grex.

THE POPULACE

> Indicting and arraigning every day
>   Something they call a play;
> Let their fastidious, vain
>   Commission of the brain
> Run on and rage, sweat, censure and condemn;
> They were not made for thee, less thou for them.[1]

But Jonson was as contemptuous of courtiers as of the populace. We must not think that the latter alone constituted what Mr. Bridges calls 'those wretched beings who can never be forgiven for their share in preventing the greatest poet and dramatist of the world from being the best artist'.[2] Well, the idle rich and the idle poor have always had a great many tastes in common. An Elizabethan theatre audience was probably not much unlike the attendance at a race-course to-day. The same classes of people were present and the same absent. If these lectures have a thesis, beyond a purely historical one, it is that blame must also attach to those who in an excess of righteousness withdrew their support from one of the great means of satisfying the craving of the human heart for a fuller and more intelligibly motived and ordered life than the flux of experience will generally allow us. 'The use of this feigned history hath been to give some shadow of satisfaction to the mind of man in those points where the nature of things doth deny it, the world being in proportion inferior to the soul, by reason whereof there is agreeable to the spirit of man a more ample greatness, a more exact goodness, and a more absolute variety than can be found in the nature of things. . . . And therefore it (*i.e.* poetry) was ever thought to have some participation of divineness, because it doth

[1] Jonson: *Ode to Himself*.
[2] Bridges: *Collected Essays*, 1927, p. 29. Compare the whole essay with Chapters III. and IV. *ante*.

173

HUMANISM & THE CHURCHES

raise and erect the mind by submitting the shows of things to the desires of the mind.'[1] It was these 'wretched beings' after all who gave Shakespeare the opportunity that the Godly would have denied him.

But plays and bear-fights and shows were not the sole entertainments provided for the populace. They read or they listened to readers, for the *Stationers' Register* and such a catalogue as Professor Hyder Rollins has compiled from it will show what an enormous output there was of ballads, calendars, and other sorts of purely popular literature.

There remain the serious, the godly. For them, whether within or without the Court of the pious if drunken James or the grave and dignified Charles, the predominant interest was theology. To turn over the pages of Arber's reprint of the *Stationers' Register* or to browse in Anthony à Wood's *Athenae Oxonienses* is a revelation of the enormous output of sermons and theological treatises. It is difficult to understand where all the purchasers and readers were to be found of these learned treatises in Latin or English, the folio volumes of sermons, the innumerable polemical tracts. Beside this great river one has to think of the plays and poems, which interest us so much more to-day, as a sparkling side-stream; and of the poetry, much was also religious. What I wish to consider now is how the humanist spirit, as I have described it, fared in the Churches, as one may call them at once—remembering always that those who were called Nonconformists and from whom later denominations derive were still within the Anglican Church, hopeful of imposing upon her and the nation a reform of theology, ritual, and government. How far did the spirit of Erasmus or Montaigne or Bacon or

[1] Bacon, Lord: *Advancement of Learning*, II.

174

RELIGIOUS DIVISIONS

Shakespeare succeed or fail to mellow or modify the Christian temper of these great treatises and these innumerable sermons? It is a difficult question, and one to which my answer, I fear, will be somewhat incomplete.

For to open the portals and look in again even for a moment or two upon the controversies and passionate disquisitions of the seventeenth century is to contemplate almost such a scene as greeted Satan when he looked out from the gate of Hell:

> For hot, cold, moist and dry, four Champions fierce
> Strive here for Maistry, and to Battle bring
> Their embryon Atoms; they around the flag
> Of each his faction, in their several Clans,
> Light arm'd or heavy, sharp, smooth, swift or slow,
> Swarm populous. . . .
>   Nor was his ear less peel'd
> With noises loud and ruinous (to compare
> Great things with small) than when Bellona storms
> With all her battering Engines bent to rase
> Some Capital City; or less than if this frame
> Of Heav'n were falling, and these Elements
> In mutiny had from her Axle torn
> The steadfast Earth.[1]

For hot, cold, moist and dry we have to substitute Roman, Anglican, Presbyterian, and what were generally called the Separatists or Sectarians, including all varieties of opinion from Brownists or Independents to Ranters and Quakers. Dryden has described these in *The Hind and the Panther*:

> The bloody Boar, an independent beast,
> Unlicked to form, in groans his hate express'd.
> Among the timorous kind, the quaking Hare
> Profess'd neutrality but would not swear.

[1] *Paradise Lost*, II. ll. 898-900 and 920-927.

> The bristled baptist Boar, impure as he
> But whiten'd with the foam of sanctity,
> With fat pollutions fill'd the sacred place,
> And mountains levell'd in his furious race.

But Baptist or Anabaptist was a word thrown around as indiscriminately as Bolshevist to-day.

Of the Romanists in England I do not propose to speak at length. Theirs was in England an oppressed and persecuted Church, whatever it may have been in the reign of Mary, or was in Spain and Italy. For the orthodox Protestant, the Roman Church was not merely in error and corrupt, she was Anti-Christ. But for my special purpose, the interest for the humanist mind of the spirit or temper of a Church as that finds expression in literature, the thing of importance to trace is the effects of the Counter-Reformation on art and poetry, even so far as these could show themselves in a Protestant, Catholic-hating, persecuting country. Of art, I need say little: because, apart from its being outside my scope, there was no permitted use of Catholic architecture, decoration, or ritual. The practising Catholic had to hide his head in dens and caves of the earth, watched for by pursuivants. The influence of the Counter-Reformation in this field must be sought in its effects upon Anglican architecture and ritual after Andrews and Laud began to reassert the claims of the Church of England to catholicity, *i.e.* in the re-edifying, re-decorating, and re-elaboration of ritual in Cambridge and Oxford Churches.

But Protestant England, like Protestant Holland, did have poets who were Catholics, and the poetry of Crashaw, like the poetry of Vondel, is influenced by the genius and spirit of the Church of Rome as reformed and reanimated by the Council of Trent.

COUNTER-REFORMATION

'It was', says Neumann in his study of Rembrandt,[1] 'one of the great impulses in the new propaganda in the restored Catholic Church to adapt itself to popular instincts, and to fascinate them by methods and appeals to sensation of a kind adapted to popular tastes. From this new democratisation of the Church sprang the cult of the ugly and the exciting, drawing its materials from the effect on the imagination of ascetic practice and the cruelties of the scaffold. Gladiatorial games belonged to the past; but here were the new Circenses which through coarseness and horror, blood and murder, if confined to imagery, attracted and thrilled the populace. Representations of the most hideous martyrdoms, the most exquisite tortures, the horrible and the hideous, were the themes of the aristocratic art of Italy, which brought itself down to the level of the taste of the masses and so gained a hold upon them.' That is one aspect of baroque art, if another is the pretty, the voluptuous, the sentimental, equally fitted to appeal to the people. Both aspects are traceable in English Catholic poetry in the seventeenth century.

Two characteristics of that poetry set it in sharp opposition to the Protestant sentiment of the day. The first is—and here the Anglicans followed in a more restrained, more humanist spirit—the emphasis laid upon the recorded or imagined incidents of Christ's life and death upon earth. For the orthodox Protestant preachers, I have already pointed out, this was superseded by the great fundamental doctrines of Predestination, Effectual Calling, Imputed Righteousness, and the rigid enforcement of a purely Scriptural worship and a strict congregational discipline. From the Anglicans the Romans differed

[1] Carl Neumann: *Rembrandt*, 1902.

by the greater stress they laid upon the physical. One sees it in the well-known verses of the young poet, priest, and martyr, Robert Southwell:

As I in hoary Winter's night stood shivering in the snowe,
Surpris'd I was with sodayne heat, which made my heart to glow;
And lifting up a fearfull eye to vewe what fire was nere,
A pretty Babe all burning bright, did in the ayre appear,
Who scorchèd with excessive heat, such floodes of teares did shed
As though his floodes should quench his flames, which with his tears were fedd;
Alas, quoth He, but newly borne, in fiery heates I frye,
Yet none approach to warme their harts or feel my fire but I!
My faultless brest the fornace is, the fuell wounding thornes,
Love is the fire, and sighes the smoke, the ashes shame and scornes;
The fuell Justice layeth on, and Mercy blowes the coales,
The metall in this fornace wrought are men's defilèd soules,
For which as nowe on fire I am, to worke them to their good,
So will I melt into a bath to washe them in my bloode!
With this He vanisht out of sight, and swiftly shroncke awaye,
And straight I callèd unto mind that it was Christmas-daye.

Southwell had been educated at Douay and Paris, and entered the Jesuit order at Rome in 1578. His longer poem, *Saint Peter's Complaynt*, was inspired by (begun, indeed, as translation[1] from) the *Lacrime di San Pietro* of Luigi Tansillo, which it far surpasses; but the influence of the spirit of Italian poetry is as clear in the poem I have quoted as in the longer one—the, to our English temperament, somewhat hectic emotion, the sensuous elaboration of the imagery of sighs and tears and fire and blood, the delight in conceited antitheses, and the choice of subject. Other poems deal

---

[1] Mario Praz: *Robert Southwell's 'Saint Peter's Complaynt' and its Italian Source. Modern Language Review,* xix., 1924, 273.

with 'Our Ladies' Salutation' (that favourite theme of mediaeval art), 'The Epiphany', 'The Virgin Mary to Christ on the Cross':

> What mist hath dimm'd that glorious face,
>   What seas of grief my Son doth toss!

The child Christ is, as always, a favourite theme:

> His chilling cold doth heat require,
> Come, seraphims, in lieu of fire;
> This little ark no cover hath,
> Let cherubs wings his body swath;
> Come Raphael, this babe must eat,
> Provide our little Toby meat.
> . . . . .
> With tears he fights and wins the field,
> His naked breast stands for a shield;
> His battering shots are babish cries,
> His arrows, looks of weeping eyes;
> His martial ensigns, cold and need,
> And feeble flesh his warrior's steed.[1]

There are, however, among Southwell's poems those of a more ethical, a less sentimental strain, as the dissuasive against earthly love which I quoted earlier, and others in which the spirit of the martyr contemplates the vanity and fleetingness of life—'Life is but Loss', 'Seek Flowers in Heaven,' 'At Home in Heaven':

> Give not assent to muddy-minded skill
>   That deems the features of a pleasing face
> To be the sweetest bait to lure the will,
>   Not valuing right the worth of ghostly grace;
> Let God's and Angels' censure win belief
> That, of all beauties, judge our souls the chief.

'Upon the Image of Death', on the other hand, illustrates that love of the ugly, the horrible, to which

---

[1] *New Heaven, New Warre.*

Neumann refers and which had already appeared in mediaeval religious poetry:

> I often look upon a face
> Most ugly, grisly, bare and thin;
> I often view the hollow place
> Where eyes and nose had sometime bin:
> I see the bones across that lie,
> Yet little think that I must die.

But the chief representative of the Catholic reaction, of the temper of the new Catholicism, is Richard Crashaw, the son of a Puritan preacher to whom the Church of Rome was Anti-Christ and stage-plays an abomination. In Crashaw's long, irregular, ecstatic, pirouetting odes, one hears, as in the very similar poems of the Dutch poet Vondel (the dedication, for example, of his strange series of pious Heroical Epistles, *Heilighe Maegden*, or the poem on Christ exposed to the soldiers)—one hears the voice of the poet who has found his way back to Rome and cannot give too passionate utterance to his sense of regained security, his emotional, sensuous delight in sacraments and ritual and cults, his complete surrender to an unquestioning faith and obedience:

> Faith can believe
> As fast as Love new laws can give.
> Faith is my force: Faith strength affords
> To keep pace with those powerful words.
> And words more sure, more sweet than they,
> Love could not think, Truth could not say.[1]

Crashaw's raptures are at least as sensuous as they are spiritual. His themes are the favourite ones of Christ's

[1] The Hymne of Sainte Thomas in Adoration of the Blessed Sacrament, 11-16.

life and death, and the life and death of saint and martyr; and in his poetry one sees very clearly the tendency of Catholicism, since the Council of Trent, to revel in the cults of the Sacred Heart, the Name of Christ, His Wounds, and all the antitheses of God and man, strength and weakness, life and death, in which the whole subject of Christian faith abounds. Crashaw sings of the Nativity in the same strain as Southwell:

> I saw the curl'd drops soft and slow
>   Come hovering o'er the place's head;
> Offering their whitest sheets of snow
>   To furnish the fair infant's bed:
> Forbear, said I, be not too bold,
> Your fleece is white but 'tis too cold.[1]

One need not dwell on the ecstasies and extravagances of his poems on the tears of Mary Magdalen—the favourite saint of the Counter-Reformation, suggesting images at once voluptuous and pious [2]—nor his

---

[1] A Hymne of the Nativity, sung by the Shepheards, st. vii.

[2] 'One of the most typical expressions of the phenomenon' (*i.e.* of the secentistic art of the Jesuits) 'is the pervasive cult of the Magdalen. In plastic art, as in literature, the motive is unwearyingly repeated. In the fair sinner, represented in the flower of youth, who despoils herself of mundane pomp, and, ungirt and clad in rough garments, pours the silver river of her tears on the feet of the Redeemer and dries them with the golden river of her hair, the period must recognise itself as in a mirror. Contrition and indulgence were the hinges of Jesuit morality: remorse for the life of the flesh, repentance at the eleventh hour, the gesture of the last refusal, the *coup de théâtre* of conversion, the gracious acceptance accorded to the erring soul in the affectionate bosom of the Divinity—all these were the most popular elements of that faith tormented and sophisticated by the confessional. At that erotic epoch the great amorous penitent—Venus in sackcloth—indicated the way of redemption, the possibility of eternal glory; and to many minds it must have appeared that she was nearest to Christ not only who had suffered much but also who had sinned much.' (Mario Praz: *Secentismo e Marinismo in Inghilterra. John Donne—Richard Crashaw.* Firenze: La Voce, 1925. A valuable and interesting study.)

passionate celebration of Saint Teresa and her spiritual martyrdom:

> How kindly will thy gentle heart
> Kiss the sweetly killing dart!
> And close in his embraces keep
> Those delicious wounds that weep
> Balsam to heal themselves with.

'Delicious wounds', 'intolerable joys', these are the ever recurring themes. Whatever one may think of these ecstasies as poetry or of their power of appeal to the popular mind, at least of Latin countries, one can hardly call them an expression of the humanist spirit of Montaigne or Erasmus, the spirit which loves reason, moderation, balance, culture, and dreads extravagance and other-worldly aspirations and ardours. One cannot even speak of Crashaw as a mystic, for mysticism implies thought—and Crashaw does not think, he accepts.

From the 'sects', Dryden passes in his description to the Presbyterians:

> More haughty than the rest, the wolfish race
> Appears with belly gaunt and famish'd face;
> Never was so deform'd a beast of grace,
> His ragged tail betwixt his legs he bears
> Close clapp'd for shame; but his rough crest he rears,
> And pricks up his predestinating ears.[1]

It would be manifestly unjust to accept a satirist and a convert to Catholicism as a trustworthy authority on the character of the various Churches and sects which had divided and torn England for more than a century. But Dryden, whose earliest ties had been with the Independents, expresses the feeling of a great part

---

[1] *The Hind and the Panther*, 1. 160-165.

of the nation when it looked back on the horrors of civil war and the rule of the Saints—in nothing more so than in the special bitterness with which he speaks of the Presbyterians. Butler in his *Hudibras* writes in the same tone. His Presbyterian knight is not ignorant, like the sectarian squire Ralph, who trusts to the guidance of the inner light and scorns learning:

> A light that falls down from on high
> For spiritual trades to cozen by:
> An *ignis fatuus* that bewitches,
> And leads men into pools and ditches.[1]

Hudibras, the Presbyterian, is a learned but intolerant, infallible, bitter, hypocritical enemy of every amusement and adornment of life:

> For his religion, it was fit
> To match his learning and his wit:
> 'Twas Presbyterian true blew,
> For he was of that stubborn crew
> Of Errant Saints whom all men grant
> To be the true Church Militant:
> Such as do build their Faith upon
> The holy text of Pike and Gun;
> Decide all Controversies by
> Infallible Artillery;
> And prove their Doctrine Orthodox
> By Apostolic Blows and Knocks;
> Call Fire and Sword and Desolation,
> A godly—thorough—Reformation,
> Which always must be carried on
> And still be doing, never done:
> As if Religion were intended
> For nothing else but to be mended.
> A Sect whose chief Devotion lies
> In odd perverse Antipathies.

[1] *Hudibras*, I. vii. 507-510.

> In falling out with that or this,
> And finding somewhat still amiss:
> More peevish, cross, and splenetick
> Than dog distrest or monkey sick.[1]

If this is the language of bitter enemies, Milton, who had been trained in the Presbyterian school, the school of Cartwright and those who hoped to reform the Church of England on Calvinist and Presbyterian lines, came to speak of them with no less bitterness; and, though he speaks for himself, he is uttering the sentiments of many others who, under the Commonwealth, discovered that Presbyter was but Priest writ large.

For of all the Protestant Churches that arose in antagonism to the Anti-Christian Church of Rome, none claimed so absolutely to be the inheritor of the spiritual infallibility and secular authority of that Church as the Calvinist and Presbyterian Church of Geneva, Scotland, and New England. They claimed not only, with other Churches and sects, to have substituted an infallible Bible for an infallible historical Church, but to have furnished, in Calvin's *Institutes*, an infallible interpretation, doctrinal and ecclesiastical. It was not toleration for which the Puritans, from Cartwright's manifestoes to the Savoy Conference, were contending, but for the substitution of their theology and their scheme of Church government and worship for that established, on the ground that these had for their sanction the infallible authority of Scripture. But there were two things in Presbyterian doctrine and discipline which brought them into sharp conflict with the humanist spirit, more even than their requirement of such a naked, unlovely form of service as at a later period sent Sir Walter Scott over to the Scottish Episcopalians. They were

[1] *Ibid.* 1. i. 189-212.

things on which even a man conciliatory in details, like Baxter, never fails to lay the fullest stress, in support of which he is quite prepared to resist toleration as a national sin. These were (1) the doctrine of predestination, and (2) the exercise of congregational discipline, a theme to which he is never tired of returning. 'Discipline I wanted in the Church, and saw the sad effect of its neglect.'[1] We are apt to think

[1] It is not what Laud did that Baxter seems to complain of, so much as of what he would not allow them, the parish pastors, to do, viz., to exercise a moral discipline co-extensive with the parish. Discipline is the very root of his grievance against the Episcopal Anglican Church. His view is clearly elaborated in the *Reliquiae Baxterianae*, Lib. I. Part I. The Anglican Diocesan government of the Church, which he describes at length (pp. 396-7), 'destroyeth the Pastoral Office, which is of divine institution and was known in the Primitive Church: for it doth deprive the Presbyters of the third essential part of their office: for it is clear in Scripture, that Christ appointed no Presbyters that were not subservient to Him in all the three parts of his office as Prophet, Priest, and King, to stand between the people and Him in Teaching, Worshipping, and Governing.' Diocesan Prelacy 'introduceth a New Humane Species of Presbyters or Spiritual Officers instead of Christ's which it destroyeth: that is a sort of meer Subject Presbyters that have no power of Government but merely to Teach and Worship' (pp. 397 ff.). The system expounded here by Baxter implies that each minister was in his congregation and parish, if he had a parish, a Bishop, one might almost say a Pope. For what other sects during the Commonwealth thought of this Presbyterian claim to infallibility and authority, see Barclay's *Inner Life of the Religious Societies of the Commonwealth*, pp. 194 ff. But for Cromwell, many would have found the little finger of the Presbyterians thicker than the loins of the Bishops:

'Rejoice, rejoice, good people, for the blessed Reformation, which is ready, like an evening wolf, to seize upon you and your loving friend and neighbours; stand still gaping with your mouths, and quietly bow down your backs, whilst you are bridled and saddled, and let the holy, humble, and gentle Presbyters get up and ride; they will doubtless deal very meekly with you, and not put you out of your pace, though the Proverb be, set a beggar on a horse back and he'll ride to the Devil, though they have spurs yet they will not use them. You remember how the bishops posted you furiously to and fro like Jehu the son of Nimshi, until with soundring and surbates they had even wearied you of your lives; the gentle Presbyters will in no wise ride you so hard, though some Malignants would make you believe that Sir John will never be off your backs, because it is intended he shall have his holy spiritual courts in every parish in the kingdom; but this benefit you are like to have, that if by his continual riding he so gaul your backs and shoulders that you can no longer

of the Puritans as suffering under and complaining of the tyrannous discipline of Laud's Diocesan courts and the Court of High Commission. They did; but Baxter complains much more of the restraint put on the exercise of congregational discipline. What he condemned in the Anglican Episcopal discipline was its exercise by 'a lay Chancellor's Court . . . and that in a Secular manner by abundance of secular officers unknown to the Primitive Church'. What he wanted

endure but cry out by reason of your sore oppression, you shall have liberty granted you to leap out of the frying-pan into the fire, by making your appeal to the Common Council of Presbyters forsooth, where, when you shall come with the complaint, 'Your fathers the bishops made our work grievous, and our parochial Presbyters (those lyons' whelps) do add thereto, now do you ease somewhat the grievous servitude and heavy yoke put upon us", you may expect from this honourable court an answer like unto that of Rehoboam's to those distressed people that cried unto him: "Our fathers made your yokes heavy but we will add thereto . . . mend yourselves as you can, for we are the divine power and, consequently, the Lawgivers both of Church and State, and therefore you are to be content, and submit yourselves to your superiors; your Presbyters . . . that have the rule over you must in no wise be resisted . . . for the same power which lately was resident and confin'd to the breast of one man, to wit an archbishop, is inherent and of divine right in the body of the Presbytery, and convey'd equally to every particular Presbyter; therefore if their Episcopal power be offensive to you, never expect to have it otherwise, for your Parliament themselves cannot lawfully help you." Now, have you not cause to rejoice for this jubilee, this year of deliverance from your antichristian servitude to Egyptian bondage? . . . But in plain terms (loving friends, neighbours, and countrymen), let us a little reason together seriously. Have not you borne the brunt and heat of this unnatural war,' and he goes on to urge that it was not for this fresh bondage they had fought, and to utter the prayer that the clergy themselves should be left to fight it out: 'Should but the King set his Episcopal clergy and the Parliament their Presbyterian clergy in the forefront of their battle's forlorn hope, and put them instead of other lambs, honest, innocent souls, upon all their desperate attempts, without doubt they would as zealously preach for peace as they now do for war, they would quickly agree and turn as they were rather than lose all. I am confident this would prove the most effectual means of our reconciliation.'

Martin's Echo, or a Remonstrance from his Holiness reverend young Martin Mar-priest, responsory to the late Sacred Synodical Decretal, in all humility presented to the reverend, pious and grave consideration of the Right Reverend Father in God the Universal Bishop of our Souls, his superlative Holiness Sir Simon Synod. 1645.

was the congregational discipline which he exercised himself at Kidderminster, whose operation in Presbyterian countries as Scotland and New England is known to most of us, if only from the life of poor Robert Burns and from the novels of Nathaniel Hawthorne. What such discipline meant has been described by a recent sympathetic but candid biographer of Baxter:[1] 'In fact, the town cannot have been an easy place for the natural man. After his long day at the loom in stifling air, he had no outlet except the alehouse. This was his club. But as the opinions of his neighbours grew increasingly antagonistic to any pleasure not derived from religion, he must have felt as if he were in an iron chamber which slowly narrowed to crush him. There was no escape unless he got converted. He had no means of escape to other towns or parishes. . . . And his case was worse if he happened to be a church-member, for then he was liable to suspension or excommunication, with the horror of social ostracism which this entailed.' What the pleasures derived from religion by the regenerate were, Baxter himself describes: 'Every Thursday evening my neighbours that were most desirous and had opportunity met at my house, and there one of them repeated the sermon, and afterwards they proposed what doubts any of them had about the sermon, or any case of conscience, and I resolved their doubts; and last of all I prayed with them myself, which beside singing a psalm was all they did. And once a week also some of the younger sort who were not fit to pray in so great an assembly met among a few, more privately, where they spent three hours in prayer together. Every Saturday night they met at some of their houses to repeat the sermon

[1] Powicke: *Life of the Reverend Richard Baxter*, 1924.

of the last Lord's Day and to prepare themselves for the following day. Once in a few weeks we had a day of humiliation on one occasion or other. Every religious woman that was safely delivered—instead of the feastings and gossipings—did keep a day of thanksgiving with some of their neighbours with them, praising God and singing Psalms, and soberly feasting together. Two days every week my assistant and I myself took 14 families between us for private Catechism.' The meeting for Parish Discipline was held 'every first Wednesday of the month'.[1] This was the life expected, not of those who had retired from the world to live a life of devotion, but of everyone who made profession of a Christian life. Whatever differences in doctrine and theology distinguished the other sects for which Cromwell secured toleration, despite the anger of the Presbyterians, congregational discipline was severe in them all. The first dissension in the English separatist church at Amsterdam arose, not over any point of doctrine or ritual, but over the lace on Mrs. Francis Johnson's sleeve. Mrs. Johnson was 'a godly woman' who continued to wear such dresses as she had worn before she was 'a godly woman', the dress of her rank. 'Her husband's father and brother, because Mrs. Johnson would not cut her garments to the precise degree of plainness which they deemed Christian simplicity, kept up a pertinacious opposition. The controversy raged for eleven years and ... the Church excommunicated George Johnson and his father, whom no reasonable "reformation in apparel" would satisfy.'[2] Baxter's own admission was that discipline, while

---

[1] *Reliquiae Baxterianae*, 1696, p. 83.
[2] R. Barclay: *The Inner Life of the Religious Societies of the Commonwealth*, 1876, pp. 65-66.

necessary for the congregation, 'an ordinance of Christ, and greatly conducing to the honour of the Church, which is not a common prophane society, nor a sty of swine, but must be cleaner than the societies of infidels and heathens', had no beneficial effect on the individual. On Burns we know that the effect was entirely bad.

It is little wonder that Baxter's neighbour, Sir Ralph Clare, preferred the Book of Common Prayer, and expressed his disrelish of 'precisians and extempore praying and making such ado for heaven'. Nor was the doctrine of Predestination,[1] which for Presbyterians and all sects other than the Quakers was cardinal, that 'great point of predestination', 'of God's absolute decrees', 'generally embraced by all religious persons in the land', of a kind to make a strong appeal to a humanist mind. The two most eminent of religious poets of protestant countries whom the century produced, the Dutch poet Vondel and the English poet Milton, repudiated the doctrine violently. Von-

---

[1] 'By God's decree a certain number of angels and men are predestinated, out of God's mere good grace and love, without any foresight of faith or good works in them, to everlasting life; and others foreordained according to the unsearchable counsel of his will, whereby he extends or withholds mercy as he pleases, to everlasting death.

'Deus ab aeterno praedestinavit quosdam ad vitam: quosdam reprobravit ad mortem.'—*Lambeth Articles.*

'The general and received doctrine of England in that age,' *i.e.* the latter years of the sixteenth century.—FULLER: *op. cit.*

'In the interest of assurance of salvation the doctrine of Predestination becomes the central doctrine of Protestantism—whether with Luther, Zwingli, or Calvin, equally original and equally necessary. Calvinism, however, more and more made this doctrine the focus of its system, and in its great historical conflicts drew thence the strong support of their consciousness of election; sacrificing, however, for this, Rationality and Universal Love as elements of its conception of God; whereas Lutheranism, in defending the two latter interests, progressively weakened the doctrine of predestination, thereby, however, taking from its thought the heroic, the iron element.'—TROELTSCH: *Renaissance u. Reformation,* Gesammelte Werker, vol. iv.

del's *Decretum Horribile*[1] is the fierce denunciation of a doctrine which consigned newly-born infants to eternal perdition, a doctrine that made Calvin, he thought, a greater slanderer of God than Servetus whom he burned. The central thesis of *Paradise Lost*, as a didactic poem, is the freedom of the will. That is the beginning and the end of Milton's justification of God's ways to men:

I form'd them free and free they must remain.

Nor would Milton accept the orthodox Protestant doctrine that since the Fall man is naturally incapable of even the aspiration after good, his will free only to do evil and incur the penalty. God's image was not totally extinguished: 'This is evident, not only from the wisdom and holiness of many of the heathen, manifested both in words and deeds, but also from what is said in Gen. ix. 2—The dread of you shall be

---

[1] 'God snatches the innocent child even from its mother's breast, and hurls it into everlasting fire! O gulf! O yawning grave! Where shall I escape your stench? And dares this monster strike his claws into Servetus and dash him to the ground as a slanderer of God, after this scandalous book had spewed its loathsome curse in the face of heaven? Where am I? under the light of lamps that God has kindled or under Lucifer, in the black realm of smoke? Is this the providence of which the chosen vessel of God (*i.e.* St. Paul) spoke? Is this the consolation of the sick? Is this the treasure Christ has brought to light?' So Vondel's poem opens. He goes on to put appropriate words of horror into the mouth of a mother expecting the birth of her child. 'Is God the crocodile who devours as a luxury the new-born child on the bank of the Nile? ... Is God a hypocrite who welcomes the Star in the East with chant and organ and paints the streets of Bethlehem with the colours of murder? ... Is God a Moloch, a stranger to mercy, who takes the offered child in his red-hot arms and gives at the breast to drink of fire and flaming oil? But that would be an act of mercy, a sleeping draught. The child would rest released from terror.' He goes on to attack Gommarus and others, and closes in a strain of lofty consolation. 'Faith has never had aught in common with despair.' 'Be of good comfort, mother, you have for you Jehovah who loves your child more than yourself. ... He gathers the children in the bosom of the New Jerusalem with more love than a hen gathers her young ones. There they taste of all joys and laugh at the heresy of Beza.'

upon every beast of the earth; v. 6—Whoso sheddeth man's blood, by man shall his blood be shed; for in the image of God made He man. These vestiges of original excellence are visible first in the understanding, Psalm xix. 1—The heavens declare the glory of God, which could not be if man were incapable of hearing their voice . . . nor is the liberty of the will entirely destroyed.'[1] So the Humanist Milton asserts the excellence of individual men of antiquity, and the Puritan looks round for texts to confirm his conviction. The more orthodox Henry Smith thought otherwise: 'For all the philosophical virtues and good deeds which men do before they have faith, which is a gift of God, are Sin and not acceptable to God. John vi. 29.'

The Eternal Decrees, the complete corruption of Human Nature, Justification through the Imputed Righteousness of Christ, congregational discipline confining the Church to the faithful, and the conviction that the Church of Rome is Anti-Christ—these are (with the requirement of a strictly scriptural worship) the cardinal principles of the Presbyterian church of Baxter and Scotland and New England. They are doctrines and practices which produced some very remarkable and good men and women, not least the last. They are compatible with a high degree of culture. The Presbyterian has never despised learning or, like some of the sects, found a virtue in ignorance. But they are (allowing for the splendid inconsistencies of which the human mind is fortunately capable) incompatible with a genial and tolerant humanism which recognises the virtues as well as the vices of human nature, accepts pleasure as in itself a good, and recognises in the arts, whatever their aberrations, the fullest expression of man's sense

[1] *De Doctrina Christiana*, chap. xii., translated by Charles R. Sumner.

of values. The humanist spirit could breathe with difficulty in the atmosphere of Puritan Christianity.[1]

[1] The failure of Protestantism, especially the Calvinist Reformed faith, to find any place for the arts, the free play of the human spirit, has been fully recognised by all recent historians even in Protestant countries. Protestantism did give a new sanction to *work*, to the serious callings and professions of secular life, which Mediaeval Catholicism had reckoned of no intrinsic value, useful as they were or rather necessary. The Christian life proper was the life of those who abandoned the world for the cloister. To the Protestant mind serious work was itself a Christian ascesis, and so was begotten the finer element in the temper of later Anglo-Saxon capitalism. Many of the great capitalists were serious religious men whose ideal was not gain but work. 'Service' is the phrase to-day. But for art and science Protestantism found no logical place. The art of the Renaissance found a safer and more productive shelter under the wing of the Catholic Church of the Counter-Reformation. 'Under the Church', says Troeltsch, 'the Renaissance discarded certain pagan attractions. She consecrated her art and laid upon science the bridle of prudence or scepticism, but otherwise she displayed all the rich culture of the Counter-Renaissance in the work of poets like Tasso, Cervantes, Corneille, and Racine, of philosophers like Gassendi, Charron, Sanchez, Campanella, and Descartes, scientists as Galileo and Pascal, artists like Rubens and Bernini. It is just this Catholic culture of the Counter-Reformation which forms the foundation of the modern scientific and philosophic, juristic and aesthetic development, and not Protestantism. That has always to be insisted on, and is not difficult to understand if one keeps in mind that Protestantism is the newer, more radical, blunter, more one-sided Christianity, while Catholicism carried on the *coincidentia oppositorum* which she has achieved from the first, and was in the Middle Ages.' The breach with the Church came, as he goes on to point out, with the French Revolution. Carlyle inherited from his Puritan ancestry just two things, the sanctification of work and a deep distrust of the arts, except when in the artist he can hail the prophet. 'Two men I honour and no third. First the toilworn craftsman that with earth-made implement laboriously conquers the Earth and makes her man's. Venerable to me is the hard hand.... A second man I honour and still more highly—him who is seen toiling for the spiritually indispensable, not daily bread but the bread of Life.... Highest of all when his outward and his inward endeavours are one: when we can name him artist: not earthly craftsman only, but inspired thinker, who with Heaven-made implement conquers Heaven for us! ... These two in all their degree I honour; all else is chaff and dust, which let the wind blow whither it listeth.'

Now a similar shelter for the arts was found, as Troeltsch and Huizinga (*op. cit.* p. 282 note) admit, in England under Elizabeth and the Anglican Church. Continental historians are coming to recognise that there was more in the conflict that led to the Civil War than merely haughty prelates and liberty-loving Puritans. Hooker, Andrews, Laud, and Charles were also on the side of the spirit of man.

TERRORISM

Freedom of mind and, what is even more essential, freedom of imagination, is denied it. Milton's imagination becomes cramped as his great poem comes under the control of orthodox doctrine and biblical literalism. His poem is greatest in the opening books, where his imagination operates most freely. Even in the sphere of religion there was little to give wings to the imagination except it be the contemplation of sin and death and Hell. Effects of terror are those in which the Puritan preacher excels. Read Henry Smith on a gnawing conscience, or even Baxter, after he has described the nature of the *Saint's Everlasting Rest* and passes on to describe 'the greatness of the torments of the damned'. 'As it was no less than God whom the sinner has offended, it is no less than God that will punish their offences. He hath prepared those torments for his enemies. His continued anger will still be devouring them. His breath of indignation will kindle the flames. His wrath will be an intolerable burden to their souls. . . . Oh they that could not bear a prison or a gibbet or fire for Christ, no not scarce a few scores, how will they now bear the devouring fire,' etc. 'Oh, woe to the soul that is thus set up for a butt for the wrath of the Almighty to shoot at! And for a bush that must burn in the flames of His jealousy, and never to be consumed.' On those aspects of the Christian story which make most appeal to the imagination, the gracious acts, the beautiful words of Christ, the Puritan preachers seldom touch, just as they abolished the seasonal feasts in which they were recalled, equally condemnatory of their religious significance and of the fanciful and festive embroidery which older traditions of nature worship had woven around them. Nor do they dwell greatly, as one might have hoped and expected, on the social implications of Christianity. *Piers Plowman* as an appeal to bring Christian charity into every relation of life, to make Do Wel the test of true faith:

> And Pieres at his preyere the perdoun unfoldeth,
> And i behynde hem both bihelde al the bulle
> Al in two lynes it lay and nouht a leef more
> And was writen riht thus in witnesse of treuthe:
> *Et qui bona egerunt ibunt in vitam eternam;*
> *Qui vero mala in ignem eternam;*

has more of the Humanist spirit of Christianity than whole folios of Puritan sermons, though Adams' sermons, if Adams was a Puritan, and such a book as Baxter's *Christian Directory* and the attacks of Puritan divines, as Capel and Moore, on enclosing, and Ames' *De Conscientia* and Bunyan's *Life and Death of Mr. Badman*, show that this aspect of Christianity was not entirely neglected. But the main themes of sermons are doctrinal—sin, chiefly sins of sense and the taste for frivolity and pastimes, repentance and effectual calling, perseverance, the evils of Papacy and Prelacy, the imputed righteousness of Christ. Puritan poetry is almost confined to Scriptural paraphrases or pious emblems and allegory like those of Francis Quarles. Even Milton has to lay his singing robes aside when he translates the Psalms, lest he give offence to the brethren by merely human interpolations, though here also Baxter is less narrow than his associates. He wished to have a better translation of the psalms than Sternhold and Hopkins (not neglecting the poetical sweetness under the pretence of exact translating), and he would have welcomed hymns in addition to the Psalms. But this is startling boldness. Some extremists even doubted the legitimacy of singing Psalms, since they expressed the feelings of David and not the worshippers, and indeed it is hard to see why, if congregational prayers must be extempore, congregational singing should not have to be the same. The Puritan distrust of music and human inventions cut them off from the winning and passionate expression of their feelings which the later Puritans of the Methodist and Evangelical revival found in the hymns of Charles Wesley, Isaac Watts, John Newton, Cowper, Toplady, and others.

That the sermons and treatises of men like Owen, Baxter, Henry Smith, and others had real merits no one who examines them with any sympathy will deny, and their repeated re-issue till almost our own day proves that they continued to find students and admirers. But these were confined to those who accepted the essentials of their teaching. Has any work of theirs, even Baxter's *Saint's Everlasting Rest*, made any such appeal to readers outside their communion as Thomas à Kempis' *De Imitatione Christi*? The spirit of man, disengaged from the trammels of a rigid theology, finds little on which it can dwell with any satisfaction in these great tomes. He feels, as he surveys them, like the dove sent forth from the ark voyaging over a hoarse sea of dogmas and denunciations and ecstasies and terrors that have in great measure lost their power to attract or awe; or if the sea be an inappropriate metaphor for many of the treatises, one finds oneself in a sandy desert of didactic exhortations and Scriptural paraphrases.

But Puritanism produced one great poet, whom I shall consider more fully later, John Milton, for though Milton moved more and more away from the presbyterian, orthodox wing of the anti-prelatists, he was educated in its school of infallibility, doctrinal and ecclesiastical. He retained the spirit of that infallibility to the end though the church of which he was finally priest and pope was the Church of John Milton. 'John Milton to all the Churches' is his dedication to the *De Doctrina*. His humanism made it impossible for him to accept the cardinal doctrine of the school, the doctrine of predestination and the complete corruption of human nature. That doctrine, as Troeltsch says, emptied God of the attributes of reason and love, but, for Milton the humanist, reason was the supreme gift of God to man, and 'Reason also is choice', is freedom. Nor, stern and harsh as Milton was in polemical pamphlets from the very first, can any candid reader doubt his aversion from anything that savoured of irrational cruelty? But the Humanist and the Puritan in Milton fought a hard battle, with the result that his great poem, despite all its beauty of language and verse, has never made the appeal to the heart of Virgil and Dante.

Bunyan is at the opposite pole from Milton, Puritans as they may both be called. Like Fox, he represents the religious movement as it worked in and on the common people, the unlearned. 'Blessed are the ignorant, for they alone know.' What Bunyan knew he knew and embraced without a doubt. Such doubts as he knew were not those of the intellect but of a tormented and tormenting imagination. From the nervous terrors so vividly described in the *Grace Abounding to the Chief of Sinners* he found shelter in just those doctrines which the Puritan poet in England and the Catholic poet in Holland rejected —Election, Effectual Calling, Imputed Righteousness, the Perseverance of the Saints. These were the coat, the mark on his forehead, and the sealed roll given to Christian by the Shining Ones, the guarantee of his election, and his salvation by the imputed righteousness of Christ: 'One day as I was passing in the field, and that too with some dashes on my conscience, fearing lest all was not yet right, suddenly this sentence fell upon my soul, *Thy Righteousness is in Heaven*; and methought I saw with the eyes of my Soul, Jesus Christ at God's right hand. There, I saw, was my righteousness; so that wherever I was, or what ever I was doing, God could not say of me, *He wants my Righteousness*, for that was just before him. I also saw moreover, that it was not my good frame of Heart that made my Righteousness better, nor yet my bad frame that made my Righteousness worse; for my Righteousness was Jesus Christ himself, *the same yesterday, to-day and for ever*; Heb. xiii. 9.'[1] Like Johannes Agricola, Bunyan believed that:

> Ere stars were thundergirt, or pil'd
> The heavens, God thought on me his child;
> Ordained a life for me, arrayed
> Its circumstances every one
> To the minutest.

But he did not believe with Browning's hero that he was thereby made incapable of sin, far from it. He was a sinner and could do no good thing, but he was accepted of God and pardoned, his sins annulled, in virtue of the righteousness of Christ and that alone. It was in virtue of no merits of his, foreseen before the world was made, that he had been elected. Such graces as he may have are themselves the consequences of that election. 'I believe that the decree of election is so far off from making works in us foreseen the ground or cause of the choice that it containeth in the bowels of it, not only the persons, but the

---

[1] *Grace Abounding to the Chief of Sinners*, Par. 230.

graces that accompany their salvation.'[1] The necessary converse of this would seem to be that God in reprobating the wicked decreed also the vices which accompany their damnation, that these are contained in the bowels of the reprobation; but this in *Reprobation Asserted* he strenuously denies. Freewill, which is the cardinal principle of Milton's justification of God's ways to men, is for Bunyan the greatest of heresies.

To such a mind and temper Humanism, with its acceptance of the good things of life, its belief in at least a strain of goodness in man, its recognition of pastime, the Muses and the Graces that

> round about Jove's altar sing,

could seem to be only one of those distracting voices which, like Atalanta's apples, delay the Christian runner in his race so that he does *not* attain: 'I give thee notice of this betimes knowing that thou shalt have enough call after thee, even the devil, sin, this world, vain company, pleasures, profits, esteem among men, ease, pomp, pride, together with an innumerable company of such companions; one crying, stay for me; the other saying do not leave me behind; a third saying, And take me along with you' (*The Heavenly Footman*). The appeal of Hooker to reason and experience was for Bunyan nothing; the literal interpretation of the Bible everything. There is more of the spirit of a free and reasonable humanity in the work of a cultured Quaker like Barclay, who will not accept a doctrine that seems to deprive God alike of reason and love. But to Bunyan Quakers were anathema: 'Keep company with the soundest Christians, that have most experience of Christ; and

[1] *A Confession of my Faith*, Of Election, 3.

be sure thou have a care of Quakers, Ranters, Freewillers; also do not too much company with some Anabaptists, though I go under that name myself.' Nor was Bunyan in any manner or measure a mystic. He was an intensely practical English peasant, for whom his religion is first and foremost an escape from the real and practical terrors of death and Hell.

Is there anything, then, in his work that touches Humanism at all? What has given it a measure of appeal to many who share neither the doctrines nor the temper of the author? In a way I think that, despite all that has been said in its praise, the genuine popularity of even *The Pilgrim's Progress* has been exaggerated. One must recall two things, the strength and duration of the Evangelical tradition which was revived in the eighteenth century and remained a force till almost our own day. It is to Evangelical readers that it makes the most direct appeal, for in it are written clearly the cardinal doctrines of effectual calling and imputed righteousness. One must recall also the limited range of reading which was allowed on Sundays in Evangelical Scotland and England. One read *The Pilgrim's Progress* because *Robinson Crusoe* and all other secular books were absolutely prohibited. Still, Bunyan's great allegory, and in some measure the lesser ones too, have appealed to readers who did not share, nor always detect in the works, the fundamental doctrines of the writer. For such readers Bunyan is saved, despite these terrible doctrines, by the grace of his humanity, his ethical honesty and sanity, his sweet-blooded interest in human nature, and the power of his imagination and his beautiful prose. Notwithstanding his condemnation of Freewillers and rejection of human righteousness, his practical ethics assume human freedom, and he is quite sure that imputed righteousness will show itself in right conduct. Nor are his ethics those of a retreat from life, a monastic pursuit of holiness. Christian's abandonment of his wife and children has nothing in common with Gautama's or Count Tolstoi's flight from home. It means no more than that he has to take his own way in the Christian life he has resolved to live. The ethics of *The Life and Death of Mr. Badman* are the ethics of the world, humanist ethics—honesty, justice, and charity in all the relationships of life. Bunyan's allegory is, one suspects, the inspiration of Defoe's picaresque tales which differ from their Spanish predecessors just by their at least professed purpose of edification. The book is a strange blend of denunciations, divine judgements (always emphasised by a pointing hand in the margin), and everyday ethics, nor are the vices condemned, as so often in puritan and evangelical sermons and tracts, only the sins of sense and pastimes. The weightiest paragraphs deal with the dishonesty of traders and the absolute incompatibility with Christian morals of the economic principle that one should buy in the cheapest and sell in the dearest market: 'He that will sell . . . his commodity as dear as he can, must sometimes make a prey of the ignorance of the Chapman: but that he cannot do with a good conscience . . . he that will sell his commodity as dear, or for as much, as he can must, if need be, make a prey of his neighbours fondness [*i.e.* folly] but that a man cannot doe with a good conscience. . . . The same may also be said for buying: no man must always buy as cheap as he can, but must also use good conscience in buying: That which by no means he can use and keep if he buys always as cheap as he can. . . . Secondly, if it be lawful for me always to sell my commodity as dear, or for as much as I can, then it is lawful for me to deal with my neighbour without the use of charity; but it is not lawful for me to *lay aside* or to deal with my neighbour *without* the use of charity. . . . Let all your things be done in charity. But that a man cannot live in the exercise of charity that selleth . . . as dear or that buyeth as cheap as he can is evident by these reasons. . . . God hath given thee more skill, more knowledge, and understanding in thy commodity than he hath given to him that would buy of thee. But what? canst thou think that God hath given thee this that thou mightest make a prey of thy neighbour? No verily; but he hath given thee it for *his* help; that thou mightest in *this*, be *eyes to the blind*, and save thy neighbour from that damage that his ignorance, or necessity, or fondness would betray him into the hands of.' So Bunyan arraigns, in the name of justice and charity, the great doctrine of *caveat emptor*, and the basal principle of the industrial civilisation which was coming; and if these are Christian they are also sound Humanist principles, which cannot be said of all the other injunctions regarding Sunday observance and communicating only with saints which are part of that 'ado for heaven' of which Sir Ralph Clare complained. The humanist principle was laid down in the famous words of Bunyan's Master: 'the Sabbath was made for man, not man for the Sabbath.' It is a source of much distress to Bunyan that many 'professors', whose observance of Sunday was probably rigid, were not guiltless of such profitable but unjust practices in trading as he arraigns.

In allegory one is tempted to think Bunyan found,

not only an effective means of preaching the fundamental doctrines of his evangelical Christianity, but an escape in some degree for the innate love of pastime, of play, which in his youth had led him into the baneful practice of playing tip-cat or ringing church-bells. He enjoyed writing and creating scenes and characters, drawing on his knowledge of the human heart and human character, and also a little on those 'beastly romances' which he had read in his youth. It is a partial emancipation. The main issue is never lost sight of as in Defoe's stories. Fear is the dominant emotion. The first picture that Christian sees in the Interpreter's House is that of St. Paul, 'the only man whom the Lord of the place whither thou art going hath authorised to be thy guide in all difficult places thou mayest meet with in the way', and St. Paul is without doubt his guide rather than the Christ of the Gospels; and two other symbols in the same house are typical of Bunyan's mind, the man who has awakened from the dream of the day of judgement and the valiant man 'of a very stout countenance' who forced his way into the Palace. Bunyan's fear of the wrath to come made him afraid of nothing else, despite his vivid imagination and sensitive nerves; and it is this that arrests a young reader who may not appreciate all the theological doctrines stated or expressed symbolically, this picture of a fearful yet dauntless man making his way through perils and seductions, along English morasses and fields and hills, and meeting on his way real types of humanity, to a glorious end—the romance of the Christian venture. The second part is less rich in terrors and ecstasies, draws nearer to a novel, even a comedy of everyday life, and, like the *Life and Death of Mr. Badman*, it was a contributor to the development of the modern novel. Schirmer[1] has emphasised the interesting fact that the Puritans, despite their condemnation of the drama and general disapproval of all secular literature that had only pastime for its end, were vital contributors to the rise of the novel, the novel as a realistic picture of everyday life and character and also as a vivid portrayal of the inner conflict of conscience and passion. It is a direct line of descent that runs from *Grace Abounding to the Chief of Sinners* to Rousseau's *Confessions* and *The Artist as Young Man* of James Joyce.

But Bunyan and Fox and the Sectaries had even less sympathy than the Presbyterians with other interests than the religious. For them the world of business and pleasure was a Vanity Fair; man's sole concern to escape from the world to come when 'the day shall burn as an oven, and the evil shall be as stubble. Ah, my friends, put a red-hot oven and stubble together and what work there will be.' Bunyan and Baxter might preach mutual tolerance among like-minded Christians, but there was no tolerance in their hearts for papist and prelatist and man of the world. The Bishop of Gloucester's *Design of Christianity*, with its talk of reformation rather than of regeneration, is, Bunyan contends, a pale, shadowy gospel proved not from Scripture but from the Cambridge thinker John Smith, while 'John Smith goes in turn to Plato, and so they wrap the business up'. Cambridge and Platonism has no appeal for Bunyan or Fox or their followers, who had small use for Universities. 'At another time', says Fox, 'on a First Day morning the Lord opened unto me, that being bred at Oxford and Cambridge was not enough to fit and qualify men to be minister

[1] Walter F. Schirmer: *Antike, Renaissance und Puritanismus*, München, 1924.

of Christ'[1]—which is true enough, but it is equally true that *not* being bred at Oxford or Cambridge is no guarantee either, that some learning is at least a check upon the aberrations of inspiration and self-conceit. 'That other attribute of God', says Sir Thomas Browne, 'wherewith I recreate my devotion is His wisdom, in which I am happy; and for the contemplation of this only do I not repent me that I was bred in the way of study; the advantage I have of the vulgar, with the happiness and content I conceive therein, is an ample recompense for all my endeavours in what part of knowledge soever. Wisdom is His most beauteous attribute, no man can attain unto it, yet Solomon pleased God when he desired it.'[2]

But Browne was an Anglican: 'there is no Church whose every part so squares unto my conscience; whose Articles, Constitutions, and Customs seem so consonant unto reason, and as it were framed to my particular Devotion, as this whereof I hold my belief, the Church of England.'[3] As Matthew Arnold has pointed out, the fact that the Puritan side in the Civil War was that which gained for England ultimately constitutional liberty, whatever that may have meant of *real* liberty for the unprotected labourer, has obscured the fact that the Anglican Church was nevertheless the champion of spiritual freedom in a larger sense than merely a mutual toleration of difference of opinion. By accident, perhaps, rather than by design she defended the English people from the tyranny of the 'Eternal Decrees', and of that presbyterian and congregational discipline which so many others than merely Anglicans found during the Commonwealth

---

[1] 'Next, it is a fond error . . . to think that the University makes a minister of the gospel.'—MILTON: *Means to remove Hirelings out of the Church*, 1659.
[2] *Religio Medici*, Sect. 13.   [3] *Ibid.* Sect. 5.

as bad as or worse than Laud and the Court of High Commission; and would have found much worse but for the restraining hand of Cromwell; that moral and doctrinal discipline which lay so heavy upon Scotland and New England long after the Commonwealth had passed away. If this be so, I do not ascribe it specifically to Anglican doctrine or to Anglican bishops generally—who were often as narrow and at heart as puritan as their opponents—but to the political situation, and not least to Queen Elizabeth. That strong-minded, worldly-minded, unscrupulous little lady it was who saved Shakespeare for us and gave him the chance, if under somewhat humiliating conditions:

> O for my sake do you with Fortune chide,
> The guilty goddess of my harmful deeds
> That did not better for my life provide
> Than public means which public manners breeds:

the chance to present his picture of life which, whatever be its imperfections, is instinct with the finest spirit of a humanism penetrating, just, and sympathetic. And it was she who saved England from passing from an infallible Pope to an infallible John Calvin; who in her endeavour to keep the door open for Catholic as well as Protestant made it possible for the English Church to retain and recover some of the most attractive and humane features of the old faith, and, which is for our purpose more important, to cultivate reasonableness, to dispense with infallibility, and to appeal to history and reason, and so to produce men like Hooker, George Herbert, Henry Vaughan, Andrewes, Cosin, Hammond, Hales, Chillingworth, Walton, and the Cambridge Platonists—men who in different ways come near to the realisation of what Erasmus desired when he spoke of the 'philosophy of Christ', by which he meant, Professor Preserved Smith says, 'a simple, rational, and classical Christianity'.

And just here it seems to me that Anglicanism had in some measure the advantage of Catholicism, gave, if not so great a direct inspiration to art—and that was coming in Church and university and under the patronage of the Court, had not Parliament and Cromwell's troopers trodden it so brutally underfoot— yet a freer play to the human mind. The rigid orthodoxy of Rome, of which the Jesuits made themselves the champions, *did* fetter men's minds in Italy, and to some extent in France. Men had to speak very guardedly. A premium was put upon hypocrisy. Marino could plead that the *Adone* was a pious and moral allegory. The art and poetry of the Counter-Reformation are a strange blend of sentimental piety and sensuous suggestion. It was serious thinking that was regarded with the greater jealousy. 'I could recount what I have seen and heard in other countries, where this kind of inquisition tyrannises; when I have sat among their learned men (for this honour I had) and been counted happy to be born in such a place of philosophic freedom as they supposed England was, while themselves did nothing but bemoan the servile condition into which learning amongst them was brought; that this was it which had damped the glory of Italian wits; that nothing had been there written now these many years but flattery and fustian. There it was that I found and visited the famous Galileo grown old, a prisoner to the Inquisition, for thinking in astronomy otherwise than the Franciscan and Dominican licensers thought.'[1] So Milton, who was already finding that he thought quite otherwise

[1] *Areopagitica.*

about the aims and justifications of the revolution that was in process ('such a deliverance as shall never be forgotten by any revolution of time that this world hath to finish') than did his presbyterian friends, for it was not liberty or toleration *they* were concerned about, but the enforcement of 'the Lord's Discipline'. Galileo was in prison; Descartes thought it safer to retreat from France into more tolerant Holland. But it lies out of my way to consider further the effect of ecclesiastical or royal tyranny on thought and literature in Italy and France. What I wish to suggest is simply that the very fact that the Anglican Church made no claim to infallibility ('Two things there are which trouble greatly these later times: one that the Church of Rome cannot, another that Geneva will not, erre ' (Hooker)), but pursued a *via media*, that this fact gave a freer play to reason, not the too rigid reasoning of *a priori* logic, 'the dead reckoning of logic', but that reasonable consideration of history and probability guided by the lantern of learning, 'those finer feelings of moral evidence which must determine the actions and opinions of our lives'.

The *via media* to which Queen Elizabeth committed the Church, despite the protests of reformers returned from the continent and eager to establish 'the Lord's Discipline', was more of a political compromise than a religious reformation, than a deliberate return to a more primitive Christianity. It was Hooker who, in defending it against the fierce and, for popular purposes, well-directed attack of the Martin Marprelate tracts and the arguments of Cartwright, gave the English Church a philosophical basis. With the Catholic elements in Hooker's view of Church government and the sacraments, which Keble stresses, admitting that Hooker has sometimes rather suggested than stressed them, we are not concerned, but with the essentially humanist strain in his defence. Three things Hooker sees to be threatened by the Puritan claim to be the guardians of an infallible discipline—reason, history, and learning. It is in the very spirit of humanism that Hooker defends reason against the bibliolatry of Cartwright: 'But so it is, the name of the light of Nature is made hateful with men; the star of Reason and learning, and all other such like helps, beginneth no otherwise to be thought of than if it were an unlucky comet; or as if God had so accursed it, that it should never shine or give light in things concerning our duty any way towards Him, but be esteemed as that star in Revelation called Wormwood: which being fallen from Heaven maketh rivers and waters in which it falleth so bitter, that men tasting them die thereof. A number there are who think they cannot admire as they ought the power and authority of the Word of God if in things divine they should attribute any force to man's Reason: for which cause they never use Reason so willingly as to disgrace Reason. . . . No man cometh unto God to offer Him sacrifice, to pour out supplications and prayers before Him, or to do Him any service which doth not first believe Him both to be, and to be a Rewarder of them who seek Him. Let men be taught this either by revelation from Heaven, or by instruction on earth; by labour, study, and meditation, or by the secret inspiration of the Holy Ghost; whatsoever the mean be they know it by, if the knowledge thereof were possible without discourse of natural reason, why should none be found capable thereof but only men; nor men till such time as they come unto ripe and full ability to work by reasonable understanding? The whole drift of the

Scripture of God, what is it but only to teach theology? Theology, what is it but the science of things divine? What science can be attained unto without the help of natural discourse and reason? "Judge you of that which I speak", saith the Apostle. In vain it were to speak anything of God but that by Reason men are able somewhat to judge of that they hear, and by discourse to discern how consonant it is to truth. Scripture indeed teacheth things above Nature, things which our Reason by itself could not reach unto. Yet those things also we believe knowing by Reason that Scripture is the Word of God.'[1]

That is the spirit in which the greater of the Anglican divines were to defend their position—divines such as Andrewes, Hales, Chillingworth, Benjamin Whichcote, Jeremy Taylor, and others—and if they invoked or enjoyed the support of the secular arm, and Laud tried to enforce on Englishmen a discipline such as they will never submit to, it must be remembered that they were fighting adversaries who had as little belief in toleration as themselves, who were convinced that their discipline was among 'the peremptory commands of God; that no mortal man can dispense with them, and that the magistrate grievously sinneth in not constraining thereunto. Will ye blame any man for doing that of his own accord which all men should be compelled to do that are not willing of themselves?'[2] The Anglican Church has no such splendours of the devotional spirit to point to as the Roman Church of the Council of Trent, no great mystics like John of the Cross or Saint Teresa, no such great leaders and missionaries as Ignatius and Francis Xavier. A reasonable

[1] Hooker: *Ecclesiastical Polity*, Book III.
[2] *Ibid. To the Reader*, p. 177 in vol. i. of Keble's edition, 1841.

Christianity may, as the next century was to prove, easily enough become a prudential, utilitarian, somewhat worldly, 'profit and loss' Christianity, the Christianity of Addison's essays and the 'moderates', the Whig bishops, against which the Oxford movement in England and the Disruption in Scotland were both reactions. But that was not the 'reasonableness' for which Hooker and the Cambridge Platonists contended, but an ardent, devotional 'philosophy of Christ', and whatever be the rights and wrongs of the doctrinal questions involved, with which the present writer is not concerned, there is no doubt that to the humanist mind some of the sweetest spots in the tormented life of that stormy century are due to the influence of the Church of Hooker and Andrewes and Laud and Taylor—the recovery of the idea of beauty as an element in religious architecture and ritual, the revival of discipline in the Universities, the rebuilding and redecoration of colleges and chapels; great scholars like Selden; gentle, quaint students and antiquarians like Burton and Sir Thomas Browne and John Earle and Izaak Walton. Most of the sermons of the seventeenth century have lost interest for us because of an old-fashioned exegesis, an excess of emphasis on subtle points of doctrine and polemics, a rigour that is sometimes terrifying, a style of wit against which later comers like Eachard were to protest. But the Anglican Preaching is more humane than the Puritan. They lay less monotonous stress on the great points of doctrine to which we have so often referred, the eternal decrees, the corruption of human nature, imputed righteousness. Even when they dwell on the terrors of retribution it is in a less material fashion than Baxter and Bunyan. For Donne, the most sombre of them all, the final penalty is, as for Marlowe's Mephistophelis, the loss of the presence of God: 'that God should let my soul fall out of his hand into a bottomless pit, and roll an unremovable stone upon it, and leave it to that which it finds there ... and never think more of that soul, never have more to do with it'. And Donne had been bred a Catholic. In general the Anglican preachers love to dwell upon the story of the Gospel in their seasonal sermons, the Nativity on which Andrewes preached some of his most beautiful sermons, the Resurrection, the Crucifixion. They do so, of course, doctrinally rather than historically. It is the Christian doctrine of the Incarnation, the two natures and one person, of the Passion as the revelation of man's sin and the love of God, the Resurrection and the Christian hope that are the themes of Andrewes' sermons, devotionally the greatest of Anglican preachers. To me this Anglican preaching at its best is at once less and more practical than that of the Evangelical Puritans. It calls the listener more out of himself, the consideration of his own salvation. That is never lost sight of, but they do not so confine themselves to the doctrines of effectual calling, human corruption, imputed righteousness. They call their audience to contemplate the great Catholic doctrines of the Incarnation, the Passion and the Resurrection, and the appeal that these make to love as well as to fear. 'And to conclude, if we ask how we shall know when Christ doth thus respect us? Then truly, when fixing both the eyes of our meditation "upon Him that was pierced" we, as it were with one eye upon the grief, the other upon the love wherewith he was pierced, we find by both, or one of these, some motion of grace arise in our hearts; the consideration of grief piercing our hearts with sorrow, the consideration of

His love piercing our hearts with love again. The one is the compunction which they felt, who when they heard such things, were pricked in their hearts. The other the motion of comfort which they felt who when Christ spake to them of the necessity of his piercing said: "Did we not feel our hearts warm within us?" That from the sin and pain He suffered for us; this from the comforts and benefits He thereby procured for us' (Andrewes, *Of the Passion*, March 26, 1617: 'and they shall look upon me whom they have pierced'). And they are more practical. It is on the practical significance of the doctrine that Andrewes closes. And further, the Anglican preachers do not lay such easily dangerous stress on the worthlessness of human nature and conduct. Repentance, Chillingworth insists, is not remorse, sorrow for wrong done and confidence in Christ's merits, it is a new life, a turning from all sin, and keeping all God's statutes, and doing that which is lawful and right; and with the antinomian tendency of Puritan ethics in his mind he goes on: 'But is not this to preach works, as the Papists do? No, certainly it is not; but to preach works, as Christ and his apostles do: it is to preach the necessity of them which no good Protestant, no good Christian ever denied; but it is not to preach the merit of them, which is the error of the Papists.'[1] To Chillingworth Christianity is a fuller Humanism because it is a fulfilling of the law, not so much in Bunyan's sense that Christ has fulfilled the law and God accepts His righteousness for ours, but because in the Christian life the Greek moralists' idea of moral prudence is raised to a higher power: Plato's Justice is taken up into Christian Charity: 'In 1 Corinthians xiii. we may behold almost all the virtues that can be

[1] Chillingworth: *Sermon* I.

named enwrapped in one virtue of charity and love
... it suffereth long, and so it is longanimity: it is
kind, and so it is courtesy; it vaunteth not itself, and
so it is modesty; it is not puffed up, and so it is
humility; it is not easily provoked, and so it is lenity;
it thinketh no evil, and so it is simplicity; it rejoiceth
in the truth, and so it is verity; it beareth all things,
and so it is fortitude; it believeth all things, and so
it is faith; it hopeth all things, and so it is confidence;
it endureth all things, and so it is patience; it never
faileth and so it is perseverance. You see two glorious
and Divine virtues, namely, faith and charity, though
not naturally expressed, yet pretty well counterfeited
by the moralist. And to make up the analogy complete, we have the third royal virtue, which is hope,
reasonably well shadowed out in that which they call
intentio finis: which is nothing else but a foretasting
of the happiness which they propose to themselves
as a sufficient reward for all their severe and melancholic endeavours.

'What shall we say, my beloved, shall the heathenish moralist merely out of the strength of natural
reason conclude the knowledge of what is good and
fit to be done, without a practice of it upon our
affections and outward actions, to be nothing worth,
nay, ridiculous and contemptible; and shall we, who
have the oracles of God ... shall we, I say, content
ourselves any longer with bare hearing and knowing
of the word, and no more? God forbid! ... Will it
avail anyone then to say, Lord, we confess we have
not done these works, but we have spent many an
hour in hearing and talking of thy word; nay, we
have maintained to the utmost of our power, and to
our own great prejudice, many opinions and tenets.
Alas! we little thought that any spotted, imperfect

work of ours was requisite; we were resolved that, for working, thou hadst done enough for us to get us to heaven. Will any such excuses as these serve our turn? Far be it from us to think so.'[1] In like manner Jeremy Taylor, a more diffuse preacher, diffuse and florid, *humanises* his sermons on Christian morals by appeals to Cicero and Plutarch and ancient authors, Greek and Roman, even the poets, adorning his style with their golden words and cadences.

And I seem to myself to find this note as of a Christian Humanism in the religious poetry of the century which is most distinctively Anglican, the poetry, say, of Herbert and Vaughan. This poetry has not the ardours and ecstasies of the Catholic poetry of Southwell and Crashaw, nor even of such a Protestant poet as the Spenserian Giles Fletcher, who combines Spenser's imagery and phrasing and rhythms with the overstrained hyperboles and endless antitheses of Southwell and Italian poetry. It does not dwell so passionately and sensuously on the physical —the tears of Mary Magdalen, the wounds of Christ, the bleeding Crucifix, the torments and ecstasies of saints. It is less didactic and Scriptural than most Protestant poetry. Despite their often quaint imagery the dominant note of the Anglican poems is sincerity and simplicity of feeling. It is their own personal experience they are trying to record. The poet's tone is more moderate, more reserved, and less didactic, because he is speaking to himself and to God rather than to a larger audience. It was Donne who first struck quite clearly this personal note, but Donne is not entirely characteristic because, whether as love-poet or religious poet, Donne never is typical. 'Within that circle none durst walk but he.' Donne

[1] Chillingworth: *Sermon* II. pars. 36, 37, 39.

and Milton are the two most striking individualities among the poets of the century. The most characteristic Anglican is Herbert, and this not in virtue of his doctrine, with which I am not concerned and of which there is little obtruded in *The Temple*, but of his feeling. His theme is the humanist aspect of Christianity, Christ's sacrifice, not as a doctrine of substitution and imputed righteousness, but as a history of human goodness and suffering, of how a man who was also God gave his life for erring, ungrateful humanity:

> Having been tenant long to a rich Lord
>   Not thriving I resolved to be bold,
>   And made a suit unto him to afford
> A new small rented lease and cancell the old.
> In heaven at his manor I him sought:
> They told me there that he was lately gone
> About some land, which he had dearly bought
> Long since on earth, to take possession.
> I straight return'd, and knowing his great birth,
> Sought him accordingly in great resorts;
> In cities, theatres, gardens, parks, and courts:
> At length I heard a ragged noise and mirth
> Of theeves and murderers: there I him espied
> Who straight, *your suit is granted,* said, and died.[1]

Love is in Herbert's poetry the centre and circumference of his Christianity, not the sensuous ecstasies of Crashaw, nor the hard-won, tormented hope of Donne, nor the love which is more a doctrine than an experience of Milton, not even the passionate gratitude of Bunyan for being 'saved', but the tempered, disciplined, pure and deep yet gentle passion which the spirit in and behind nature awoke in Wordsworth:

---

[1] *Redemption.*

Love bade me welcome: yet my soul drew back
    Guilty of dust and sinne.
But quick-ey'd Love, observing me grow slack
    From my first entrance in,
Drew nearer to me, sweetly questioning
    If I lack'd anything.

A guest, I answer'd, worthy to be here:
    Love said, you shall be he.
I th' unkind, ungrateful? Ah my deare,
    I cannot look on thee.
Love took my hand, and smiling did reply,
    Who made the eyes but I?

Truth, Lord, but I have marr'd them: let my shame
    Go where it doth deserve.
And know you not, sayes Love, who bore the blame?
    My deare, then I will serve.
You must sit down, sayes Love, and taste my meat:
    So I did sit and eat.[1]

The just parallel to Herbert's *The Temple* is not Keble's *Christian Year* or any collection of hymns but a sonnet sequence such as Petrarch's *Laura* or Shakespeare's sonnets to his friend and patron. It is the record of God's wooing of the soul of Herbert recorded in the Christian story and the seasons and symbols of the Church, and Herbert's wooing of God, a record of conflict and fluctuating moods, and expostulations with God and himself, with occasional digressions to preach a short sermon or elaborate a parable—a series of metaphysical love poems. Indeed the two sonnets, *Love* (No. 24), show that Herbert is quite aware of the resemblance, that he is writing love poems to a different subject, and so in *Dulnesse*:

---

[1] *Love.*

GEORGE HERBERT

> The wanton lover in a curious strain
>   Can praise his fairest fair
> And with quaint metaphors her curled hair
>   Curl o'er again.
>
> Thou art my loveliness, my life, my light,
>   Beautie alone to me:
> Thy bloodie death and undeserv'd, makes thee
>   Pure red and white.

For the subtleties of dogma Herbert has no taste:

> Could not that wisdom which first broach'd the wine
>   Have thicken'd it with definitions?
> And jagg'd his seamless coat, had that been fine
>   With curious questions and divisions?
>
> But all the doctrine which he taught and gave
>   Was cleare as heav'n from whence it came.
> At least those beams of truth, which only save,
>   Surpass in brightness any flame.
>
> *Love God, and love your neighbour. Watch and pray.*
>   *Do as ye would be done unto.*
> O dark instructions; even as dark as day!
>   Who can these Gordian knots undo?
>
> But he doth bid us take his blood for wine?
>   Bid what he please; I am sure,
> To take and taste what he doth there designe,
>   Is all that saves, and not obscure.[1]

It was Herbert, as an earlier chapter has indicated, who turned Vaughan from profane to divine love, if his passion had never been of an overwhelming character; and his *Silex Scintillans* is just such a sequent record as *The Temple* of Vaughan's experience as a lover. But he is less ecclesiastical than

[1] *Divinitie.*

Herbert, less confined for the sense of the presence he desires to the Church and its symbolism. In nature and in human nature, his own childhood and the childhood of the world, the veil that divides the soul from God trembles at moments with the consciousness of His presence:

> Were now that chronicle alive,
> Those white designs which children drive,
> And the thoughts of each harmless hour,
> With their content too in my pow'r,
> Quickly would I make my path even,
> And by meer playing go to Heaven.
>
> . . . . .
>
> How do I study now, and scan
> Thee more than ere I studied man,
> And only see through a long night
> Thy edges, and thy bordering light!
> O for thy center and mid-day!
> For sure that is the *narrow way*.[1]

To men of the temper of Herbert and Vaughan and Traherne and Walton and many another for whom Christianity was not an insurance against Hell-fire but a new experience of love for God and Man, the outbreak of the Civil War came as a profound shock, whether their sympathies had been with Parliament or King in the political and ecclesiastical struggle which led up to that calamity. In the Latin verses which were prefixed to his *Olor Iscanus* (1651), *Ad Posteros*, Vaughan describes his own attitude:

> Sed ut mea Certus
> Tempora Cognoscas, dura fuere, scias.
> Vixi, divisos cum fregerat haeresis Anglos
> Inter Tysiphonas presbyteri et populi.
> His primum miseris per amoena furentibus arva
> Prostravit sanctam vilis avena rosam,

[1] *Childe-hood.*

HENRY VAUGHAN

Turbârunt fontes, et fusis pax perit undis,
    Moestaque Coelestes obruit umbra dies.
Duret ut Integritas tamen, et pia gloria, partem
    Me nullam in tanta strage fuisse, scias;
Credidimus nempe insonti vocem esse Cruori,
    Et vires quae post funera flere docent.
Hinc Castae, fidaeque; pati me more parentis
    Commonui, et Lachrymis fata levare meis;
Hinc nusquam horrendis violavi Sacra procellis,
    Nec mihi mens unquam, nec manus atra fuit.
Si pius es, ne plura petas; Satur Ile recedat
    Qui sapit, et nos non Scripsimus Insipidis.[1]

But it was not Anglicans alone who felt that Civil War was an outrage which brought with it more evils than it could cure. The presbyterian Richard Baxter

---

[1] *Ad Posteros.* Mr. Blunden has kindly allowed me to give here his rendering of the poem amended by himself in some lines.

    Time soon forgets; and yet I would not have
    This present wholly mouldering in the grave.
    Hear, then, posterity; from Wales I drew
    My life, and first its airy mountains knew,
    And Usk below them winding; then I went
    To learned Herbert's kind encouragement,
    Herbert, the pride of our Latinity;
    Six years with double gifts he guided me,
    Method and love, and mind and heart conspired,
    Nor ever flagged his mind, nor his hand tired.
    This was my shaping season; but the times
    In which it fell were torn with public crimes;
    When schism had scattered England in the storms
    Of Presbyterian hate and Rebel swarms.
    Through happy fields went these demented foes,
    And the coarse rush beat down the holy rose;
    They fouled the fountains, peace died gasping there,
    Glooms wept above and veiled heaven's glittering air.
    But Honour led me, and a pious heart:
    In the great ravenous heat I had no part;
    It was my faith, that guiltless blood will cry
    Aloud, and has a power which does not die.
    My mother's pure and patient pattern showed
    How best with weeping I should bear my load;
    So never with wild insult did I smite
    The holy down; my heart and hand were white.
    Forbear, O friend, to ask me more than this;
    Let the wise weigh my words; the fool may miss.
            On the Poems of Henry Vaughan, 1927.

expresses the same sentiment, or much the same, though his sympathies were with Parliament. He had no doubt that the fundamental cause of the war was religion. 'But though it must be confessed that the public safety and liberty wrought very much with most, especially the Nobility and Gentry who adhered to the Parliament, yet was it principally the difference about religious matters that filled up the Parliament's armies and put the resolution and valour into their soldiers which carried them on in another manner than mercenary soldiers are carried on.' 'I make no doubt that both parties were to blame (as commonly falleth out in most wars and contentions) and I will not be he that shall justify either of them. I doubt not but the readiness and rashness of the younger unexperienced sort of religious people made many Parliament men and ministers overgo themselves to keep pace with those hot spurs, no doubt but much indiscretion appeared and worse than indiscretion in the tumultuous petitioners and much sin was committed in dishonouring of the King and provocation of him and in the uncivil language against the Bishops and Liturgy of the Church.' 'I confess for my part I have not such censorious thoughts of those that were neuters as formerly I had; for he that either thinketh both sides raised an unlawful war, or that could not tell which (if either) was in the right might well be excused if he defended neither.'[1] Andrew Marvell, the friend of Milton and Fairfax, and after the Restoration a savage critic of the Court, was of the same opinion. 'Whether it be a war of religion or of liberty is not worth the labour to inquire. Whatsoever was at the top the other was at the bottom, but upon considering

[1] *Reliquiae Baxterianae*, 1696, pp. 31, 39.

all I think the cause was too good to have been fought for. Men ought to have trusted God: they ought and might have trusted the King with the whole matter. The arms of the Church are prayers and tears: the arms of the subject are patience and petitions.'[1]

But if the war destroyed some things, if it checked the development of the drama and music, so that these great factors in the life of the English people never quite recovered the place they might have occupied in our life and culture, made us a nation of shopkeepers, a people without music, as a recent German writer describes us, it on the other hand promoted by its excesses and the suffering it occasioned, the spirit of reasonableness and toleration, so that a little more adroit and generous handling of the situation on the part of the restored Church might conceivably have gained for her a larger section of the nation than was the case. But the lesson of toleration was slowly learned, and was learned too late to allow a healing spirit to work.

For even before the war broke out a process of reaction was at work in the very heart of Puritanism, a movement that led many Puritans to a clearer recognition and fuller appreciation of the value of the Anglican *via media*, the spirit of reasonableness and moderation, the appeal to reason and history and learning for which Hooker had pleaded. Emmanuel College was a definitely Puritan foundation. 'The first Master, Lawrence Chaderton (one of the translators of the Bible), gave on more than one occasion ample proof of his sympathies with the Puritan party. Thomas Hooker, John Cotton, Thomas Shepherd, and not a few other names which occupy a conspicuous place in the pages of Cotton Mather's New

[1] Marvell: *The Rehearsal Transpros'd.*

England (among them the founder of Harvard College) were some of those who received their earliest education within its walls' (Powicke). Yet it was in this college that there originated the movement which we associate with the name of the Cambridge Platonists, a determined effort to associate Christianity with philosophy, to vindicate the place of reason in religion, to disintegrate Puritan Bibliolatry and the Calvinist doctrine of Reprobation, and revindicate the Platonic identification of God with the Idea of Goodness. 'He is that unstained beauty and supreme good to which our wills are perpetually aspiring, and wheresoever we find true beauty, love and goodness, we may say there is God.'[1]

These men, even under the rule of the Commonwealth, were sympathetically loyal to the Church of England, even if they disapproved of the narrow and harsh discipline of Laud. The last master of Emmanuel College, before Cromwell's troopers rabbled Cambridge, in his oration *In Vesperiis Comitiorum*, declared: 'Our Church is happier than others, who traces back her origin to no popular insurrection, has inherited no maimed and mutilated priesthood, no novel discipline soon to disappear, but whatsoever stands forth to view as confirmed by Councils and defined by ancient Fathers, and originating in Apostolic times—this she has restored, maintained, and handed down for our observance.'[2] And of the more definitely Platonist group a contemporary wrote: 'Nor is it credible that they should hold any other doctrine than the Church, since they derive it from the same fountains, viz., from the sacred writings of the Apostles and Evangelists in interpreting whereof they carefully attend to the sense of

---
[1] F. J. Powicke: *The Cambridge Platonists*, 1926, p. 36.   [2] *Ibid.* p. 5.

the Ancient Church by which they conceive the modern ought to be guided.' The quest of the philosophy of Christ landed some of them, as Henry More, in a somewhat fantastic theosophy. Cudworth's great reply to Hobbes, *The True Intellectual System of the Universe*, was never finished and never could have been finished. But what they were in quest of was not the toleration which is enforced by the state and accepted by those who have grown weary of endless dissensions and warfare, but a reconciling conception of Christianity as, not a religion of dogmas and rites, but of the spirit, a finer humanism satisfying alike to the reason and the imagination. And such a Christianity, though this never came consciously within their scope, would have left a freer and fairer field to the activity of thought and imagination in other spheres than the definitely religious, to a degree that it is hard to imagine that a religion which included among its chief tenets the doctrine of Reprobation, and had for ever in its ears the roar of Hell fire, possibly could. A Bunyan could hardly have permitted himself to write, or approved of a serious Christian writing, a *Microcosmographie* or a *Compleat Angler* or an *Anatomy of Melancholy* or *Religio Medici* and *Hydriotaphia*.

Any such union of Puritan and Anglican as Baxter sought at the Savoy Conference was impossible. One has only to read the full statement of the different points of view in the *Reliquiae Baxterianae* to see that what the Puritans wished was not a wider but a narrower Church, not a freedom from ecclesiastical discipline but a closer, more searching test of membership and enforcement of discipline. As Matthew Arnold says, 'the persistence of the

Church in pressing for conformity arose, not as the political historians have it, from the lust of haughty ecclesiastics, but from a real sense that their formularies were made so large and open, and the sense put upon subscription to them was so indulgent, that any reasonable man could honestly conform; and that it was perverseness and determination to impose their special ideas on the Church and to narrow the Church's latitude which made the Puritans stand out'. Yet one cannot but regret that it was not thought best to let the Nonconformists go their own way in peace before feeling was finally embittered by persecution. So slow were men to learn the lesson of toleration and confidence in the appeal of reason and experience, and Baxter himself, be it remembered, rejected all thought of toleration for Catholics and Rationalists. But the Anglican persecution was political; that of the Puritans was religious. Even Milton could, after pleading that 'it is not lawful for any power on earth to compel in matters of religion', yet declare that the Catholics were to be excepted because their religion was idolatry, 'popery, as being idolatrous, is not to be tolerated either in public or in private'. The Church had to pay a heavy penalty, and not altogether unjustly, for her courtly subservience and political intolerance.

But if the Cambridge thinkers failed in the impossible task of effecting a reconciliation of parties by a deeper philosophy of Christianity, they did something of great service. They transferred the emphasis from doctrine, 'the eternal decrees', 'justification by faith', 'effectual calling', 'imputed righteousness', to the Christian life. The finest literary expression of the new spirit is probably the great sermon preached by Ralph Cudworth before the House of Commons on March 31, 1646, on the text, 'And hereby we know that we do know him if we keep his commandments. He that saith I know him and keepeth not his commandments is a liar and the truth is not in him.' After the aridities and terrors of the Puritan preachers, after the wit of Andrewes and the ornate, fanciful eloquence of Taylor, even after the sombre splendours of Donne, one comes with an extraordinary sense of relief on this great and humane sermon. Cudworth has shed altogether the fantastic wit and the fantastic exegesis that have made unreadable the great bulk of seventeenth-century sermons. He is not witty, but eloquent, with the eloquence of a passionate sincerity, an eloquence less akin to that of Donne and Taylor than to that of Burke.

One cannot but wonder that the House of Commons, their minds full of predestination and imputed righteousness, convinced that Rome is Anti-Christ and Prelacy no better, but many of them equally convinced of the iniquity of Independency, the tyranny of Presbyterianism, the blasphemy of the sects that were springing up like mushrooms,—that the House should have given a vote of thanks to the preacher whose burden was that these things were nothing, that the Christian life was everything. 'Ink and paper can never make us Christians, can never beget a new nature, a living principle in us; can never form Christ or any true notion of spiritual things in our hearts. The gospel, that new law which Christ delivered to the world, it is not merely a dead letter without us, but a quickening spirit within us. Cold theorems and maxims, dry and jejune disputes . . . all this is but the groping of the poor dark spirit of man after truth, to find it out with his own endeavours, and feel it with his own cold benumbed hands. Words and syllables, which are but dead things,[1] cannot possibly convey the living notions of heavenly truths to us.' 'Would we know whether we know Christ aright let us consider whether the life of Christ be in us. *Qui non habet vitam Christi, Christum non habet.* . . . He that builds his house upon this foundation, and not an airy notion of Christ swimming in his brain, but Christ really dwelling and living in his heart, as our Saviour himself witnesseth, he "buildeth his house upon a rock; and when the winds blow and the rains descend and beat upon it, it shall stand impregnably". But he that builds all his comfort upon an ungrounded persuasion that God from all eternity hath loved him, and absolutely decreed him to life and happiness, and seeketh not for God really dwelling in his soul; he builds his house upon a quicksand and it shall suddenly sink and be swallowed up: "his hope shall be cut off and his trust shall be a spider's web; he shall lean upon his house but it shall not stand; he shall hold it fast but it shall not endure".'

'He that endeavours really to mortify his lusts and to comply with that truth in his life, which his conscience is convinced of, is nearer a Christian, though he never heard of Christ, than he that believes all the vulgar articles of the Christian faith, and plainly denieth Christ in his life.'

'But I wish it were not the distemper of our times to scare and fright men only with opinions and make men only solicitous about the entertainment of this

---

[1] One recalls Burke: 'These things do not make your government. Dead instruments, passive tools as they are, it is the spirit of the English communion that gives all their life and efficacy to them. It is the spirit of the English constitution which, infused through the mighty mass, pervades, feeds, unites, invigorates, vivifies every part of the empire, even down to the minutest member.'

and that speculation, which will not render them any thing the better in their lives or the liker unto God. ... We say "Lo, here is Christ" and "Lo, there is Christ" in these and these opinions; whereas, in truth, Christ is neither here nor there nor anywhere but where the Spirit of Christ, the life of Christ is.'

'Knowledge indeed is a thing far more excellent than riches, outward pleasures, worldly dignities, or anything else in the world besides holiness, and the conformity of our wills to the will of God; but yet our happiness consisteth not in it but in a certain Divine temper and constitution of soul, which is far above it.'

'But it is a piece of corruption, that runneth through human nature, that we naturally prize truth more than goodness, knowledge more than holiness. We think it a gallant thing to be fluttering up to heaven with our wings of knowledge and speculation; whereas, the highest mystery of a divine life here, and of perfect happiness hereafter, consisteth in nothing but mere obedience to the Divine will. Happiness is that inward sweet delight that will arise from the harmonious agreement between our wills and God's will. There is nothing contrary to God in the whole world, nothing that fights against him but self-will. ... It was by reason of this self-will that Adam fell in Paradise; that those glorious angels, those morning stars, kept not their first station, but dropped down from Heaven like falling stars, and sunk into this condition of bitterness, anxiety and wretchedness, in which now they are. They all entangled themselves with the length of their own wings, they would needs will more and otherwise than God would will in them; and going about to make their wills wider, and to enlarge them into greater amplitude, the more they struggled they found themselves the faster pinioned, and crowded up into narrowness and servility; insomuch that now they are not able to use any wings at all, but inheriting the serpent's curse, can only creep with their bellies upon the earth.'[1]

The high doctrine of the Eternal Decrees, that is one of the wings which Cudworth's hearers were fain to stretch too wide; another was the imputed righteousness of Christ. This was the doctrine under whose wing a sincere and tormented soul like that of Bunyan found shelter: 'At this I was greatly lightened in my mind and made to understand that God could justify a sinner at any time, it was but his looking upon Christ and imputing of his benefits to us and the work was forthwith done.... Now was I set on high, I saw myself within the arms of Grace and mercy, and though before I was afraid to think of a dying hour, yet now I cried, *Let me die*: now Death was a lovely and beautiful sight, for I saw we *shall never live indeed till we be gone to the other World*.'[2] Cromwell also, one gathers from his letters, found in the doctrine of imputed righteousness a support while he walked in the crooked ways of revolutionary politics. To Cudworth, nourished on Plato, it seemed not only a dangerous doctrine, with whose effects he was doubtless familiar, but to betray a misunderstanding, a materialistic conception of the doctrine of redemption which was a redemption not from Hell and the consequences of sin, but from sin itself. 'These things I write unto you (saith our apostle) that you sin not; therein expressing the end of the whole gospel, which is not only to cover sin by spreading the purple robe of Christ's death and

---

[1] *The Works of Ralph Cudworth*, 1829, vol. iv., *Sermon* I.
[2] Bunyan, *Grace Abounding to the Chief of Sinners*.

sufferings over it, while it still remaineth in us with all its filth and noisomeness unremoved; but also to convey a powerful and mighty spirit of holiness to cleanse and free us from it. . . . Christ came not into the world only to cast a mantle over us, and hide all our filthy sins from God's avenging eye; but he came likewise to be a chirurgeon and physician of souls. . . . The gospel is a true Bethesda, a pool of grace, where such poor, lame, infirm creatures as we are, upon the moving of God's Spirit in it, may descend down not only to wash our skin and outside, but also to be cured of our diseases within. And whatever the world thinks there is a powerful spirit that moves upon these waters, the waters of the gospel, spreading its gentle healing, quickening wings over our souls. The gospel is not like Abana and Pharpar, those common rivers of Damascus, that could only cleanse the outside, but is a true Jordan in which such leprous Naamans as we all are may wash and be clean.'

God is not a tyrant thinking only of revenge and penalties, who 'to exercise his absolute authority, his uncontrollable dominion, delights rather in plunging souls down into infernal night and everlasting darkness. What shall we then make the God of the whole world? Nothing but a cruel and dreadful Erinnys with curled, fiery snakes about his head and firebrands in his hands, thus governing the world? Surely this will make us either secretly to think that there is no God at all in the world, if he must needs be such; or else to wish heartily there were none.' For Cudworth the Platonist God *is* Goodness and nothing else. 'Nay, I may be bold to add, that God is therefore God because he is the highest and most perfect good; and good is not therefore good because God out of an arbitrary will of his would have it so. . . . Virtue and holiness in creatures, as Plato well discourseth in his *Euthyphro*, are not therefore good, because God loveth them, and will have them be accounted such; but rather God therefore loveth them because they are in themselves simply good. Some of our authors go a little further yet, and tell us that God doth not fondly love himself because he is himself, but therefore he loveth himself because he is the highest and most absolute goodness; so that if there could be anything in the world better than God, God would love that better than himself; but because he is essentially the most perfect good therefore he cannot but love his own goodness infinitely above all other things. And it is another mistake which sometimes we have of God, by shaping him according to the model of ourselves, when we make him nothing but a blind, dark, impetuous self-will running through the world; such as we ourselves are furiously acted with, that have not the ballast of absolute goodness to poise and settle us.'

Cudworth's sermon is the most eloquent expression of the reaction against the fierce fanaticism of the century of a spirit of reasonableness, reasonable and spiritual religion developed under the auspices of that attempt at a *via media* between Roman and Genevan infallibilities along which Elizabeth for political reasons, the greater Anglican divines by the appeal to history, had endeavoured to guide the Church of England. But the number of people to whom a philosophic interpretation of their faith will appeal must always be few. One can understand how Cudworth's philosophic interpretation of God's relation to his own goodness would appear to Bunyan. Fanaticism had to run its course until the inevitable exhaustion and reaction set in, and then reason itself would appear in a bolder and more dogmatic statement. Cudworth and the Cambridge Platonists were aware that there was another foe to be encountered besides the spirit of religious fanaticism, that Hobbes and the new philosophy were in the field and required a more thorough-going examination and restatement of the faith that seemed to them so reasonable. But before we go on to consider the effect of the war on religious thought and its reaction in the secular literature of the later century, we must take up a fuller examination of the mind and poetry of Milton. The great Puritan poet he has been reckoned. We may find that it is only the temper of Milton's poem which is Puritan, for the theme of the poem in which he sets out his justification of God's ways to men is not quite the theme of Puritan sermons and treatises. It comes rather from the Humanist side of Milton's mind. His subject is not the Eternal and inscrutable Decrees of God, and the salvation of man through the Imputed Righteousness of Christ. It is the warfare of Reason and Passion in Man whom God has created free; the forfeiture of freedom through man's surrender to passion, Adam's too great love for his tempted and erring wife; the restoration of that freedom through the victory over temptation of the perfect Man, the Son of God, but not himself God. But it may be also that we shall find that both the Humanist and the Puritan in Milton suffered from the demoralising experience of the two perhaps greatest of social and moral disturbers, civil war and political revolution.

CHAPTER VII

JOHN MILTON: THE MAN AND THE POET

John Milton, the Man and the Poet—His early training and poems—His éducation sentimentale—The meeting of the Long Parliament and Milton's dreams and experience—Paradise Lost—The later poems.

THE life of John Ruskin, as he has described it in that delightful work *Præterita*, and the life of John Milton as we can gather it from the autobiographical digressions in his prose works English and Latin, and indeed from the whole tenor of his work, might well be taken as examples of the dangers as well as the advantages which beset a too careful, a too ideal education under parental supervision and control, of the truth that, in education as in the government of colonies, there is much to be said for a policy of 'wise and salutary neglect'. Each was in the eyes of his parents a dedicated being, and received the most careful education, secular and religious, which the parents were able to secure for him, the religious in each case predominating. 'I was born', says the latter, 'in London, of honourable parentage, a father of the utmost integrity, a mother of the most approved goodness, specially known for her charities throughout the neighbourhood. My father destined me from a boy to the classical studies (*humaniorum litterarum studiis*); in which I laboured with such avidity that from my twelfth year onwards I scarcely ever forsook my studies for bed before midnight;

which was the first thing that ruined my eyes; to whose natural weakness was added frequent headaches; but as all these could not retard my eager pursuit of learning my father had me daily instructed in the Grammar School and under other masters at home; so that he sent me to Cambridge, one of our two universities, proficient in more than one language and with no slight apprehension of the sweets of philosophy. Here I passed seven years in the usual course of instruction and study—with no stain on my character but with the approbation of all good men until I obtained *cum laude* the degree of master as it is called. Thereafter I did *not* flee into Italy as that vile fellow lyingly declares, but of my own will returned home, accompanied by the regrets of most of the fellows of my college, by whom I had been shown no small attention and courtesy. In my father's country seat, whither he had retired to pass the days of his old age, in a period of uninterrupted leisure I gave myself to the perusal of the Greek and Latin writers, not but that I exchanged the country at times for the city, either for the sake of purchasing books, or to learn something new in mathematics or in music, studies in which I at that time delighted. After five years spent in this manner, my mother having died, I set out, having prevailed upon my father, eager to see foreign lands and especially Italy;'[1] and he proceeds to recount the history of his experiences in France and Italy, his return by way of Venice and Geneva, and the history of his first essays in theological and political controversy, on behalf of liberty, ecclesiastical, domestic, and civil. Seven years at the university, five of learned leisure at Horton, and one of foreign travel

[1] *Defensio Secunda Pro Populo Anglicano Contra Infamem Libellum Anonymum*, 1654.

—these were Milton's preparation for his work as a reformer and a poet. He had not wanted admonitions, from within and from without, that he was 'long choosing and beginning late'. At the age of twenty-three he wrote the well-known sonnet:

> How soon hath Time, the subtle thief of youth,
> Stol'n on his wing my three and twenti'th year!
> My hasting days fly on with full career,
> But my late spring no bud or blossom shew'th.
> Perhaps my semblance might deceive the truth,
> That I to manhood am arriv'd so near,
> And inward ripeness doth much less appear
> That some more timely happy spirits endu'th.

But he proceeds at once to justify himself.

> Yet be it less or more, or soon or slow,
>   It shall be still in strictest measure ev'n,
>   To that same lot, however mean, or high,
> Toward which Time leads me, and the will of Heav'n;
>   All is, if I have grace to use it so,
>   As ever in my great Task-Master's eye.

And, probably a few months later, a friend (perhaps Carlo Diodati) seems to have reproached him with dilatoriness; and his reply, in which he transcribes this sonnet, is that he is biding his time, that he is one who 'does not press forward as soon as may be to undergo, but keeps off with a sacred reverence and religious advisement how *best* to undergo, not taking thought of being late, so it give advantage to be more fit, for those that were latest lost nothing when the master of the vineyard came to give each one his hire'.[1] Milton's early life was, as Mark Pattison has emphasised, a long preparation for some great task that

---

[1] *Facsimile of the MS. of Milton's Minor Poems . . . in the Library of Trinity College, Cambridge*, edited by W. Aldis Wright, 1899.

he felt was laid upon him, the exact nature of which it was not given to him at once to descry, though his natural aptitudes and inborn tastes pointed to a literary work, a great poem which should be an act of service to God and to his country, poetry 'doctrinal to a nation'. 'I began thus far to consent both to them' (his Italian friends) 'and divers of my friends here at home; and not less to an inward prompting which grew daily upon me, that by labour and intent study (which I take to be my portion in this life) join'd with the strong propensity of nature, I might perhaps leave something so written to aftertimes as they should not willingly let it die.'[1] So he wrote in 1641 when at last it seemed to him that he stood on the threshold of his great undertaking; but more than twenty years were to elapse before the fruit of that high enterprise was to see the light, and of these years at least eighteen were to be given to quite other tasks.

That the careful training which Milton's parents, like Ruskin's, provided for him, that the years of preparation and apparent inaction which his father allowed him, and he justified himself for accepting, were not wasted, we have his great poem to prove. But equally certainly such a training, such an indulgence of a young man's confidence in himself and his mission, were not without detriment to him as a man. Milton and Ruskin were fine instruments cunningly prepared for the special task they were to perform, but thereby to some extent unfitted for the contact into which they were to be brought with a rough and ready world, and suffering from the contact when it came in a way which has left a deep impress upon their work:

---

[1] *The Reason of Church Government*, Book II. Introduction.

JOHN MILTON: THE MAN & THE POET

>   Yet half a beast is the great god Pan
>   To laugh as he sits by the river,
>   Making a poet out of a man:
>   The true Gods sigh for the cost and the pain—
>   For the reed which grows never more again
>   As a reed with the reeds in the river.

For each it intensified the egotism which is probably inseparable from genius, though perhaps in Shakespeare it is less obvious than in any other writer of even approximate greatness. Milton's confidence in the high worth of his poetic endowment was not belied by the work that he achieved, yet perhaps a touch of modesty might have given it more of the indefinable quality of appeal. Never in Milton's poetry does one hear the note of some of Shakespeare's sonnets, even if it be difficult to believe that the note can be the expression of more than a passing mood, the humility of love rather than of conscious inferiority:

>   O how I faint when I of you do write,
>   Knowing a better spirit doth use your name,
>   And in the praise thereof spends all his might
>   To make me tongue-tied speaking of your fame,

or

>   When in disgrace with Fortune and men's eyes
>   I all alone beweep my outcast state,
>   And trouble deaf heaven with my bootless cries,
>   And look upon myself and curse my fate;
>
>   Wishing me like to one more rich in hope,
>   Featur'd like him, like him with friends possess'd,
>   Desiring this man's art, and that man's scope,
>   With what I most enjoy contented least. . . .

But granting Milton's right, with Shakespeare in other moods, to be confident of leaving 'something so written to aftertime, as they should not willingly let it die':

> And yet to times in hope my verse shall stand,
> Praising thy worth, despite his cruel hand,

it is not equally certain that he had the right to believe in the impeccability of his own judgement as he moved from one position in ecclesiastical and civil politics to another. No one was ever, in one way, more susceptible to experience than Milton. His views on almost every question to be discussed were determined by the accidents of his own career. For an experience to affect Milton it had to be *personal*—his unhappy marriage, the presbyterian condemnation of his pamphlets on divorce. No one, except perhaps Shelley, was more impenetrable by what one may call the general teaching of experience. All the bitter disillusionments which succeeded one another between 1640 and the Restoration never made him for a moment doubt of the absolute soundness of the abstract republican dogmas and the anti-clerical ecclesiastical tenets to which his own personal experiences and prejudices had led him. He came to doubt of human nature, to which at first he had been disposed to attribute something of his own high virtues; he never doubted the infallibility of John Milton.

But Milton's egotism was identical with his idealism. If he was moved by personal motives, they were always sublimated to take the aspect of high ideals. The cause for which he fought was always in his own eyes the cause of humanity, the great cause of liberty. 'This', he says, speaking of the episcopal controversy which followed the meeting of the Long Parliament, 'awakened all my attention and my zeal—I saw that a way was opened for the establishment of real liberty; that the foundation was laying for the deliverance of man from the yoke of slavery and superstition; that the principles of religion, which were the first objects of our care, would exert a salutary influence on the manners and constitution of the republic; and as I had from my youth studied the distinction between religious and civil rights, I perceived that if I ever wished to be of use, I ought at least not to be wanting to my country and to the church and to so many of my fellow-Christians in a crisis of so much danger; I therefore determined to relinquish the other pursuits in which I was engaged, and to transfer the whole force of my talents and my industry to this one important object. . . . When, therefore, I perceived that there were three species of liberty which are essential to the happiness of social life—religious, domestic, and civil, and as I had already written concerning the first, and the magistrates were strenuously active in achieving the third, I determined to turn my attention to the second or the domestic species;'[1] and so he wrote on the *Doctrine and Discipline of Divorce*. Such is Milton's lofty affirmation of his ideal ends. But it is just this idealism, subtly ministered to by an arrogant egotism, which is the most obvious result of an education like that which Milton and Ruskin received. Made for years the centre of life to those around him, trained in a definite moral and religious discipline, and a creed which admits of no qualification but is presented as the way by which alone happiness is to be sought and obtained, whether by individual or nation; for Protestantism had returned to the Old Testament view that righteousness is the guarantee of prosperity even here on earth; set free for years to

[1] *Defensio Secunda*.

contemplate the ideal aspect of things, to meditate what men ought to be—for such a one the contact when it comes is bound to bring shock and pain and disillusionment. To Milton, as to the Jews after the return from captivity, it seemed that God was almost pledged to give those who serve him aright victory over their enemies. 'O perfect and accomplish thy glorious acts,' he prays in 1641, 'for *men* may leave their works unfinished, but *Thou* art a God, thy nature is perfection; should'st *Thou* bring us thus far onwards from Egypt to destroy us in the wilderness, though *we* deserve; yet thy great name would suffer in the rejoicing of thine enemies, and the deluded hope of all thy servants.'[1] There is an almost outrageous daring in such a protest. 'Moreover the Lord answered Job and said: "Shall he that contendeth with the Almighty instruct him? he that reproveth God let him answer it."' Milton was to live to see all his confident hopes disappointed, 'the deluded hope of thy servants'; but God has many servants, and they are not all on the same side in human controversies:

> All is best though we oft doubt
> What the unsearchable dispose
> Of highest wisdom brings about,
> And ever best found in the close.

But all this is in the future. We have to consider first the reflection of Milton's character and training in his earlier, shorter poems. Setting aside one or two childish or mistaken experiments, are the first works of any poet at once so fresh in inspiration, so perfect in form? They have the freshness and perfection of

[1] *Animadversions upon the Remonstrant's Defence against Smectymnuus,* 1641, Sect. iv.

the newly created heavenly bodies as Satan beheld them:

> From Eastern Point
> Of Libra to the fleecy star that bears
> Andromeda far off Atlantic Seas
> Beyond th'Horizon: then from Pole to Pole.

There are poems whose spiritual quality is deeper, that come nearer the heart, the best of Shakespeare's sonnets for example, but their art is less sustained and perfect: the poems of Gray and Tennyson have something of the same perfection of technique, but their poetic inspiration is of less depth and spontaneity. Keats's fine odes are what I should feel tempted to place beside them to form an inner garden of English poetic art. And already these poems are entirely Miltonic. The young man takes his own way confident and accomplished. 'Our Late Fantastics' with their metaphysical wit have no charms for him. Milton's earliest poems are not devoid of conceit, but such as there are—leaving aside jests in which he does *not* excel—belong to the older Petrarchan, Spenserian, Sidneian tradition to which the Scottish poet William Drummond remained also faithful against all the counter-attractions of Donne and his followers:

> Nature in awe to him
> Had doff't her gawdy trim,
>   With her great Master so to sympathize ...
> It was no season then for her
> To wanton with the Sun her lusty paramour.

> Only with speeches fair
> She woo's the gentle Air
>   To hide her guilty front with innocent snow,
> And on her naked shame,
> Pollute with sinful blame,
>   The saintly Vail of Maiden white to throw,

Confounded that her Maker's eyes
Should look so neer upon her foul deformities.

The Stars with deep amaze
Stand fixt in stedfast gaze,
   Bending one way their pretious influence,
And will not take their flight,
For all the morning light,
   Or Lucifer that often warn'd them thence;
But in their glimmering Orbs did glow,
Untill their Lord himself bespake, and bid them go.[1]

Or less happily in the verses *The Passion*, a poem to be abandoned as 'above the years he had' when he wrote it:

Befriend me night, best Patroness of grief,
Over the Pole thy thickest mantle throw,
And work my flatter'd fancy to belief,
That Heav'n and Earth are colour'd with my wo;
My sorrows are too dark for day to know:
   The leaves should all be black whereon I write,
And letters where my tears have washt, a wannish white.

That was not to be Milton's maturer style. But these conceits are not those of Donne and Cowley. They are those of Marino and Southwell and Crashaw. And it was not only the conceits of the 'Metaphysicals' which had no attraction for the young poet trained in a classical and Italian school, it was also their carelessness in respect of form, their indifference to harsh concatenations of vowel and consonant, the

       I teach each hollow grove

efforts at which he sneers in Bishop Hall's satires. But not this alone. Even what has been, and may be, fairly reckoned for meritorious in the followers

---

[1] *On the Morning of Christ's Nativity. The Hymn*, stanzas i., ii. and vi.

of Jonson and Donne, the purity and naturalness of their diction and idiom, was not to Milton's taste. He told Dryden that Spenser had been his model. Mr. Bridges casts doubt on this; but surely, apart from all question of mere imitation (Milton is never a mere imitator), Milton is of the same caste as Spenser and Dante and Virgil and the Greek tragedians, the poets who are not content to confine themselves too rigidly to a 'language such as men do use' but claim for the poet the liberty to build for himself a statelier speech, to move in brocaded garments, to levy tribute on all the possible resources of a nation's speech, from archaic words to words of his own coinage.

But if these poems are Milton's in the perfection of their elaborate, decorative art, their finely builded verse, they are also, may we say it, Miltonic in their limitations, the rather self-centred nature of the emotions of which they are the beautiful expression. A kind of fastidious Puritan Epicureanism is the tone of these poems. The cheerful man is as solitary as the thoughtful. He is the scholarly, fastidious onlooker rather than the sympathetic sharer in the pleasures he describes. Nor has this young poet been taken out of himself by any strong passion for another. The love poems, whether Latin or Italian, are but sports of sentiment and fancy. Will Milton ever write, an onlooker might ask himself in reading these poems in MS. and not yet knowing what was to come, like Donne in the *Anniversary*?

> All kings and all their favourites,
> All glories of honours, beauties, wits,
> The sun itself which makes times as they pass
> Is elder by a year now than it was
> When thou and I first one another saw:
> All other things to their destruction draw,

> Only our love hath no decay;
> This no to-morrow hath nor yesterday,
> Running it never runs from us away,
> But truly keeps his first, last, everlasting day.

Will he ever be able to say with Shakespeare:

> Let me not to the marriage of true minds
> Admit impediments. Love is not love
> Which alters when it alteration finds,
> Or bends with the remover to remove.

King was only a college fellow-student; Charles Diodati was an intimate friend, Milton's closest friend in youth; and in the Latin elegy for his death, *Epitaphium Damonis*, there is more of a sense of personal loss:

> We only, an obdurate kind, rejoice,
> Scorning all others, in a single choice.
> We scarce in thousands meet one kindred mind,
> And if the long-sought good at last we find,
> When least we fear it, Death our treasure steals,
> And gives the heart a wound that nothing heals.[1]

Yet what a cold medium in which to express a personal sorrow is a Latin elegy; and even so the chief burden of Milton's poem is his journey to Italy, the compliments he has there received, and the great poem which he is meditating. Would Milton ever know the power of a self-forgetting passion, a love that worships as Dante loved and worshipped Beatrice? And so reflecting, an observer who knew nothing as yet of what the years were to bring forth might have doubts. Even in the poems of friendship he would think the egotistic stop is a very resonant one. Johnson's criticism of *Lycidas*, that wonderful

---

[1] Cowper's translation.

symphonic poem, is not altogether unjust. Deep sorrow does, even in poetry, speak a simpler language. Compare with *Lycidas* Vondel's poem on his little daughter. When *Lycidas* grows passionate, it is of himself and his own fortunes Milton is thinking. He too is a poet, and may be cut off before he has achieved the fame he knows he might gain:

> Comes the blind Fury with th'abhorred shears,
> And slits the thin-spun life. But not the Fame,
> Phoebus replied, and touch'd my trembling ears, etc.

He too has been 'church-outed by the Prelates', and of him too might St. Peter say:

> How well could I have spar'd for thee, young swain,
> Enow of such as for their belly's sake
> Creep and intrude and climb into the fold.

And if such an onlooker shifted his survey from *Lycidas* to *Comus*, the *pièce-de-résistance* of his early volume, the first attempt at a statement of the young poet's ideals, he might still feel a little uncertain. '*Comus*', says Professor Herford, 'is a Puritan hymn to Chastity,' but Professor Herford goes on to point out an essential difference between Milton's celebration of that high virtue in *Comus* and Dante's in the *Vita Nuova*. Beatrice in the latter inspires purity because she kindles in the hearts of her beholders a love that casts out baseness. Purity is the aura which surrounds the burning flame of love. It is not by the love which she awakens that Milton's Lady in *Comus* repels impurity. 'Milton's Chastity, sublime and exalted as it is, is at bottom a *self-regarding* virtue; his warrior maiden is concerned to disable her foes, not to ennoble them; and if a momentary suggestion of the creative and transforming glance of Beatrice has come into Milton's picture, if the Gorgon shield of her rigid look does not only freeze base thoughts, but awakens wonder and reverence, the change is important, not because her enemy is a "nobil cosa", but because he is no longer formidable. . . . Great and noble as both are, Dante's spirit is the richer and more human for it knows not only purity but love, a purity that is rooted in love, a love that is rooted in purity; whereas Milton describes a virtue which with all its dazzling and soaring splendour only repels and repudiates the humanity below it.'[1] 'A self-regarding virtue'—that is what all Puritan virtues are apt to prove. But to be fair to Milton, remember that *Comus* was written before he had known love as a serious, transforming experience; and in every young man at that stage purity will be to some extent—it may have also a religious sanction—a self-regarding virtue, a protection of the citadel of a man's soul against

> The expense of spirit in a waste of shame,

a guarding of the soul for an experience that is yet to come. Moreover, Milton and his Puritan friends set a higher value on marriage as the final sanction of love than perhaps Dante himself did, for whom the love of Beatrice and his marriage with Gemma were of a different order of things:

> Hail wedded Love, etc.[2]

To such an onlooker as I have been imagining it would, I think, have been clear that much for this man, young, passionate, pure, would depend on the woman with whom he first fell seriously in love, and whom he should make his wife. That experience came

---

[1] Herford, *Dante and Milton*, The John Rylands Library Publications.
[2] See earlier, p. 159.

to Milton simultaneously with the challenge that summoned him to leave the enchanted garden of culture and meditation, to take up his rôle in the world of action. The hour was come in 1640 of which Goethe speaks in *Tasso*:

> Ruhm und Tadel
> Muss er ertragen lernen. Sich und andre
> Wird er gezwungen recht zu kennen. Ihn
> Wiegt nicht die Einsamkeit mehr schmeichelnd ein.
> Es will der Feind—es darf der Freund nicht schonen;
> Dann übt der Jungling streitend seine Kräfte,
> Fühlt was er ist, und fühlt sich bald ein Mann;
> Es bildet ein Talent sich in der Stille,
> Sich ein Charakter in dem Strom der Welt.

That is true; and yet if the years of culture and retirement are unduly prolonged the character may have grown less ready to accept with equanimity the buffets of fortune and an unsympathetic world, may find it difficult to be just to men of coarser calibre and less culture, to be tolerant of difference of opinion even if one be a champion of toleration in the abstract.

Milton felt himself that the years of preparation were over when he returned from Italy in 1639. But his conception of what was to be his task remained academic. He had made up his mind that he was to write a great national poem such as Virgil and Tasso had each created in the *Aeneid* and the *Gerusalemme Liberata*. The subject was to be Arthur; and in the *Epitaphium Damonis* he records his first attempts to make a beginning and his failure.

Then came for Milton the *great awakening*. The Long Parliament met in November 1640, the impeachment of Strafford was at once set in motion, and as Clarendon says: 'All possible licence was exercised in preaching and printing any old scandalous

THE AWAKENING

pamphlets and adding new to them against the Church.' The effect of these events and the awakened spirit of the nation upon Milton was as great as that of the outbreak of the French Revolution and the destruction of the Bastille upon Wordsworth and Coleridge a century and a half later, or more exalted and intense as the temper of the Puritan was a deeper, a more religious temper than that of the philosophic Jacobins:

> Bliss was it in that dawn to be alive,
> But to be young was very heaven.

There is an exultant note in the pamphlets of 1641 which is never heard again in Milton's prose and poetry. To the young man of thirty-three it seemed that a new age was beginning for the English people and the Christian Church; a purified Church would bring with it an emancipated country; it might even be a Second Coming, Christ Himself was on the threshold, the hour is at hand 'When thou the Eternal and shortly expected King shalt open the clouds to judge the several kingdoms of the world, and distributing national Honours and Rewards to Religious and Just Commonwealths, shalt put an end to all earthly tyrannies, proclaiming thy universal and mild Monarchy through Heaven and Earth'.[1] And of this revolution Milton will be the poet. That is the temper in which Milton's great poem was at first dimly conceived, and it might, like Wordsworth's *Prelude*, have in a measure been written. It was not to be. That was written in 1641. In 1642 was penned the sonnet:

> Captain or Colonel or Knight in Arms
> Whose chance on these defenceless doors may seize.

---

[1] *Of Reformation in England*, at the end.

And then in the early summer of 1643 he made his sudden journey into the country, 'nobody about him certainly knowing the reason, or that it was any more than a journey of recreation', and returned with Mary Powell as his wife. Of what led up to the marriage we know nothing and can only assume with Mark Pattison and M. Saurat that the susceptibility to passion of which his Latin poems give evidence, which his high ideals of purity and love, his religious temper and training, had kept in check took revenge upon him, and made him too hastily discover the 'well-beloved' in a young girl of seventeen. The consequences were almost as disastrous for him as the very different marriage of Byron was for a very different poet. This first and fatal shock to a finely tempered and carefully nurtured and sheltered personality, on its very first encounter with the actualities of life and human nature, this first clash with the laws of existence or the conventions of society, call it which you will—it is a law of life that society will protect itself by conventions—coloured everything that he thought and wrote to the end of his life:

> There in a moment we may plunge our years
> In fatal penitence, and in the blight
> Of our own Soul turn all our blood to tears,
> And colour things to come with hues of Night;
> The race of life becomes a hopeless flight
> To those that walk in darkness; on the sea
> The boldest steer but where their ports invite—
> But there are wanderers o'er Eternity,
> Whose bark drives on and on, and anchored ne'er shall be.

But Milton had not sinned against his own soul as Byron had, nor was he the man to let his bark be driven at random across the sea of life. The harder the storm might blow, the more determinedly would he shape his own course and steer by the star-light of his own ideals:

> Because man's soul is man's God still,
> What wind soever waft his will
>   Across the waves of day and night
>   To port or shipwreck, left or right,
> By shores and shoals of good and ill;
>   And still its flame at midmost height
> Through the rent air that foam-flakes fill
>   Sustains the indomitable light
> Whence only man hath strength to steer,
> Or helm to handle without fear.
>
> Save his own soul's light overhead,
> None leads him; and none ever led,
>   Across birth's hidden harbour bar,
>   Past youth where shoreward shallows are,
> Towards age that drives on toward the red
>   Vast void of sunset hailed from far,
> To the equal waters of the dead;
>   Save his own soul he hath no star,
> And sinks, except his own soul guide,
> Helmless in middle turn of tide.

Milton was not even disposed to accept some disasters as irreparable. If his marriage had gone wrong, then the laws of marriage must be reconsidered, and by August 1643 Milton had published *The Doctrine and Discipline of Divorce, Restored to the Good of Both Sexes*, etc. But one storm begot another. If divorce is to be defended, there must be complete freedom of speech, so *Areopagitica* (that in some ways overrated pamphlet). But among the most censorious critics of the doctrine of divorce are the Presbyterians and they are the censors of the press. So Milton parts from his old friends, those whom he had defended against Bishop Hall. From 1645 onwards he never writes anything in which he does not pour contempt on the Presbyterian party, the new Forcers of Conscience, those who went all lengths against the King, and at the last turned tail, 'our dancing divines' who would fain be made 'classic and provincial lords, while pluralities greased them thick and deep'.[1] By 1649 Milton had identified himself in the closest way with the extreme republican party, and made himself the champion of regicide at home and abroad. Not on the question of marriage and toleration alone, but on the more theoretical dogmas of theology, was he growing more heretical. In politics, too, he will think for himself. Cromwell is our 'chief of men' (1652) and the *Defensio Secunda* (1654) includes a glowing eulogy of the character and achievements of him who 'had either extinguished or learned to subdue the whole host of vain hopes, fears and passions which infest the soul'. But Milton of all men was 'nullius in verba iurare addictus', and the eulogy closes with an appeal to Cromwell to seek no other title than that of Protector, 'a title most like to that of the Father of your country', nor to separate himself from the counsels of his companions in arms—Fleetwood, Lambert, Desborough, Whalley, Overton, Whitelocke, Pickering, Strickland, Sydenham, Sydney, Montague, Lawrence. And when the Protectorate ended and the Rump reassembled, he speaks of Cromwell's rule as 'a short but scandalous night of interruption'. Even Cromwell had failed him, for had not Cromwell supported a paid ministry and ruled alone? It remained for Milton himself to point out to Parliament the right way to a free government; but in vain. The Restoration brought the final ruin of his hopes.

[1] *The Tenure of Kings and Magistrates.*

THE LONGER POEMS

It is not my intention to trace the development of Milton's thought under the pressure of these successive happenings, hopes, and disappointments. I attempted once to sketch this in outline for Hastings' *Dictionary*. It has been done better and more fully by M. Denis Saurat. What I wish to consider is the final effect upon his poetry. A great poem is not simply the expression in verse of a poet's articulate thought. It is something much more complex. It is the reflection, the embodiment in a form adequate to communicate it with delight to himself and to his audience, of the interaction of thought and feeling, the whole complex web of a personality. *Paradise Lost*, *Paradise Regained*, and *Samson Agonistes* are not like the three *Kritiken* of Kant. They are the expression of the mood in which the long battle for freedom as Milton understood freedom, and the disillusionments of family and public life, had left a man, a great poet, whose indomitable will refused to succumb.

There have, pretty nearly always, in this country and among English-speaking peoples, been two views of *Paradise Lost*. The first is what we may call the orthodox, the 'accepted' view, which begins probably with Addison, and was acquiesced in by Johnson, who, however severe on Milton the man, has nothing but praise for the piety of *Paradise Lost*.

In Milton every line breathes sanctity of thought, and purity of manners, except when the train of the narrative requires the introduction of the rebellious spirits; and even they are compelled to acknowledge their subjection to God in such a manner as excites reverence, and confirms piety.[1]

Paradise Lost in this tradition is—with its sequel—

[1] Johnson: *Lives of the Poets, Milton*.

our great Protestant and Evangelical poem, a poem that might lie beside the Bible on Sunday, that might be studied with a minimum of Bowdlerisation at young ladies' academies. The Evangelical John Foster, in his interesting and strange essay *On the Aversion of Men of Taste to Evangelical Religion*, after surveying classical and our own religion comes to the melancholy conclusion that the spirit of polite literature, ancient and modern, has always been essentially *not* Christian, *not* Evangelical. From the general condemnation he cannot entirely exempt even Dr. Johnson, but he does except Milton: 'Milton's consecrated genius might harmoniously have mingled with the angels that announced the Messiah to come, or that, on the spot, and at the moment of his departure, predicted his coming again; might have shamed to silence the muses of paganism, or softened the pains of a Christian martyr.' 'Part of the poetical works of Young, those of Watts, and of Cowper, have placed them among the permanent benefactors of mankind.' That is an extreme expression of the view that is held, with interesting qualification, by Frederick Denison Maurice, and that dominated Masson's great Life. But Masson surveyed the field so widely, and supplies so much information about Milton's thought as well as life, that his work corrects a great deal which was inadequate in the traditional view. Masson well knew that Milton was *not* theologically an orthodox Protestant, a Puritan in quite the same sense as Cromwell, Bunyan, or Baxter. Apart from his theological heresies he lacked, indeed rejected, the Protestant doctrine of the entire worthlessness of human nature and, what flowed from that, *e.g.* the passionate devotion to the Divine Saviour, the doctrine of imputed righteousness. Of the inner wrestling of the spirit which is so characteristic of the Puritan, there is no evidence in Milton, nothing like Cromwell's message to his daughter, Fleetwood's wife: 'Salute your dear wife from me. Bid her beware of a bondage spirit. Fear is the natural issue of such a spirit—the antidote is Love. The voice of Fear is: If I had done this; if I had avoided that, how well it had been with me! I know this hath been her vain reasoning. Love argueth in this wise: What a Christ have I; what a Father in and through Him! What a name hath my Father: Merciful, gracious, long-suffering, abundant in goodness and truth; forgiving iniquity, transgression, and sin. What a Nature hath my Father: He is Love-free in it, unchangeable, infinite! What a covenant between Him, and Christ—for all the seed, for everyone; wherein he undertakes *all* and the poor soul *nothing*. The New Covenant is Grace—to, or upon the soul: to which it is passive and receptive; I'll do away their sins; I'll write my Law, etc.; I'll put it into their hearts; they shall never depart from me.'[1] That is the authentic Puritan and Calvinist note. Milton in the third book of *Paradise Lost* is at least a Semi-Pelagian. But the revelation of Milton's unorthodox view made by the publication of the *De Doctrina Christiana* in 1825 had no serious effect on the accepted tradition. Even his notoriously heterodox views on marriage and divorce counted for little against him, and no one studied the *De Doctrina*. In fact, apart from the *Areopagitica*, Milton's English prose works have been very little read, despite Macaulay's eloquent eulogy. And though in *Paradise Lost* a skilled theologian may easily detect Arianism

---

[1] Carlyle: *Oliver Cromwell's Letters and Speeches*, To Lieutenant-General Fleetwood, 1652.

and Semi-Pelagianism, these make little impression upon the average pious reader. For there are all the great traditional articles of his faith—the Eternal Decrees of Justice and Mercy, Man's Fall and Christ's Redemption, the Grace of God bringing out of Evil a greater Good. 'Christ won more wealth for God than Adam ever lost,' says Wyclif, and so Milton:

> O goodness infinite, goodness immense!
> That all this good of evil shall produce,
> And evil turn to good; more wonderful
> Than that by which creation first brought forth.
> Light out of darkness! full of doubt I stand
> Whether I should repent me now of sin
> By mee done and occasion'd, or rejoice
> Much more, that much more good thereof shall spring,
> To God more glory, more good-will to Men
> From God, and over wrauth grace shall abound.[1]

Personally I believe that Milton held these central tenets of Christianity to the last, however unorthodox he may have been on more purely speculative topics, however wanting his temper may seem to us in some of the more essential Christian graces—humility, forgiveness, charity.

But there has always been another view of *Paradise Lost* and Milton, held in different ways by two very different classes of critics. There have been, and there are, serious antagonists to the claim that Milton is a great religious poet. Those who have still reverence or affection for the Catholic tradition have recognised in Milton a thorough-going and undisguised enemy. Newman selected Milton and Gibbon as two great English writers both inspired by a bitter hostility to the Catholic Church and its

[1] *Paradise Lost*, Book XII. ll. 469-478.

teaching. But a distaste for Milton's thought, his theology as opposed to his art, has been expressed from what Newman would have called the Liberal side in religion—Landor, Pattison, Richard Garnett, the late Sir Walter Raleigh. All these in one way or another have endorsed Landor's words: 'After I have been reading *Paradise Lost* I can take up no other poet with satisfaction. I seem to have left the music of Handel for the music of the streets, or at best for drums and fifes. . . . Averse as I am to anything relating to theology, and especially to the view of it thrown open by this poem, I recur to it incessantly as the noblest specimen in the world of eloquence, harmony and genius.'[1] And if others have admired not only the art, the architectonic power, the majesty and freshness of the diction, the amazing splendour and variety of the harmonies, but also the spirit of the poem, the final ethical and religious impression which remains when it has been read aright, that has been because they believed they had found in the poem something which Milton had breathed into it unconsciously, not a justification of the ways of God to Men as Orthodoxy understands, but an arraignment of Orthodox conceptions of God and the Devil, a complete reversal of the apparent values of the poem.[2]

---

[1] 'We may feel great repugnance to Milton and Gibbon as men; we may most seriously protest against the spirit which ever lives, and the tendency which ever operates, in every page of their writings; but there they are, an integral portion of English literature; we cannot extinguish them; we cannot deny their power; we cannot write a new Milton or a new Gibbon; we cannot expurgate what needs to be exorcised. They are great English authors, each breathing hatred to the Catholic Church in his own way, each a proud rebellious creature of God, each gifted with incomparable gifts. We must take things as they are if we take them at all.'—NEWMAN: *English Catholic Literature.*

[2] *Imaginary Conversations, Southey and Landor.*

Milton, Dryden declared, would have been the greatest of epic poets after Homer and Virgil 'if the devil had not been his hero instead of Adam; if the giant had not foiled the knight and driven him out of his stronghold to wander through the world with his lady errant'.[1] What Dryden thus indicated, thinking of the poem as an heroic poem, and without reference to the theology, later critics have accepted as theologically true also. 'The reason', says Blake, 'Milton wrote in fetters when he wrote of Angels and of God, and at liberty when of Devils and Hell, is because he was a true poet, and of the Devil's party without knowing it.'[2] The Devil, Blake thought, was Desire, man's passionate, imaginative daring soul, and the God who overcomes and casts him out is cold reason, and the victory is a delusion. 'In Milton; the Father is Destiny, the Son a Ratio of the Five Senses, and the Holy Ghost vacuum!'[3] Shelley came to much the same conclusion. 'Milton's poem contains within itself a philosophical refutation of that system of which, by a strange and natural antithesis, it has been a chief popular support. Nothing can exceed the energy and magnificence of the character of Satan as expressed in *Paradise Lost*. It is a mistake to suppose that he could ever have been intended for the popular personification of evil. Implacable hate, patient cunning, and a sleepless refinement of device to inflict the extremest anguish on an enemy, these things are evil; and although venial in a slave, are not to be forgiven in a tyrant; although redeemed by much that ennobles his defect in one subdued, are marked by all that dishonours his conquest in the victor. Milton's

---

[1] Dryden: *Dedication of the Aeneis*.
[2] *The Marriage of Heaven and Hell*.
[3] *Ibid*.

devil as a moral being is as much superior to his God as one who perseveres in some purpose, which he has conceived to be excellent, in spite of adversity and torture, is to one who in the cold security of undoubted triumph inflicts the most horrible revenge upon his enemy, not from any mistaken notion of inducing him to repent of a perseverance in enmity, but with the alleged design of exasperating him to deserve new torments.'[1] Mr. Visiak, who in his condensed and difficult study approaches Milton in the light of modern psychology, seems to hold the same view with a difference. *Paradise Lost* is a product of 'inverted power', the expression as in a dream—for poetry and dreaming are closely akin—of Milton's thwarted purpose when all his high hopes for the Commonwealth were defeated, a cry of rage, 'his genius was inverted, so that what objectively appears evil in the demonic verse of *Paradise Lost* is subjectively good'. It is in the devils that Milton expresses his deepest feelings.[2]

Such is the strange confused condition of criticism of Milton as a great poet justifying the ways of God to men. The old orthodox view took Milton at his apparent valuation and made him a great poetic interpreter of the Bible story of the Fall and the Evangelical doctrine of salvation through Christ. For others,

---

[1] Shelley: *A Defence of Poetry*.
[2] 'In the *camera obscura* of the psychical transformation,' says the last of these critics, 'the protagonist, the subjugated yet indomitable Prometheus appears as Satan and the other fiends who, as Chateaubriand told the French Academy, represent Milton and his political associates. They alone of the characters are real; and they react so powerfully to the intolerable afflictions of their Nemesis, the implacable "Wrath and Might", that not only are they not miserable, since "to be weak is miserable", but they are so inspiring to the imagination that the old objection to *Paradise Lost* as making evil attractive would be justified if the evil were not, in fact, a form of ultimate value.'—E. H. VISIAK: *Milton Agonistes*, 1922.

such as Hurrell Froude, Newman, Professor Taylor, he is a great, bad man, an enemy of the Catholic Faith, almost blasphemous in the freedom with which he allows himself to speak of sacred persons and of our first parents. To yet another he is a Samson bringing down the pillars which he claims to be supporting on the whole orthodox system of beliefs, inverting all its values.

Of the phenomenon to explain which these theories have taken their rise, no one is likely now to raise any question. There is no doubt that Satan is Milton's greatest creation, and that the opening books where he is the chief figure far surpass in interest all that follows. There is nothing greater in poetry than these tremendous scenes—Satan and Beelzebub in converse in Hell while the fallen angels lie scattered around; Satan rallying his host, when comes perhaps the most sublime 'stroke' in the poem:

> He now prepar'd
> To speak; whereat thir doubl'd Ranks they bend
> From Wing to Wing, and half enclose him round
> With all his Peers; attention held them mute.
> Thrice he essay'd, and thrice in spite of scorn
> Tears such as Angels weep burst forth: at last
> Words interwove with sighs found out thir way.[1]

Satan's encounter with Death: the great invocation to the Sun; wherever he appears, Satan soars above every rival. And yet it is equally certain and obvious that neither consciously nor unconsciously does Milton identify himself with Satan, is on the side of Satan. He has never put into Satan's mouth any such speech of self-justification as Aeschylus puts

[1] *Paradise Lost*, Book I. ll. 615-621.

into the mouth of Prometheus, who is far more akin to Milton's Satan than to Shelley's lover of Asia and flowery caves:

> Ye see me prisoned here, a god ill-starred,
> Of Zeus the enemy, hated of all
> That tread the courts of his omnipotence,
> Because of my exceeding love for men.
>
> . . . . .
>
> Compassionating mortals in my heart,
> Myself refused compassion, to the shame
> Of Him in heaven I stand corrected here.
> Rescuing mankind I plung'd myself in woe.[1]

Satan never advances any convincing justification of his action. When he speaks before others, his pleas are obviously sophistical, and when he speaks to himself he acknowledges the justice of his lot:

> Hadst thou the same free Will and Power to stand?
> Thou hadst; whom hast thou then or what to accuse,
> But Heav'n's free Love dealt equally to all?
> Be then his love accurst, since love or hate,
> To me alike, it deals eternal woe.
> Nay curs'd be thou; since against his thy will
> Chose freely what it now so justly rues.
> Me miserable! which way shall I fly
> Infinite wrath and infinite despair?
> Which way I fly is Hell; myself am Hell;
> And in the lowest deep a lower deep
> Still threat'ning to devour me opens wide,
> To which the Hell I suffer seems a Heav'n.[2]

As M. Saurat has well brought out, the great protagonist of Satan is Milton himself. 'Milton throws himself personally into the struggle against

---

[1] *Prometheus Vinctus*, ll. 119-124, 239-241, Lewis Campbell's translation.
[2] *Paradise Lost*, Book IV. ll. 66-78.

Satan, and from the reading of *Paradise Lost* one derives two inevitable impressions: the greatness of Satan and the greatness of Milton. . . . He it is and not God, or the Son that overcomes Satan.'[1] Take a single instance. When Satan and Abdiel re-encounter one another after the latter's defiance:

> Among the faithless, faithfull only he,

it is Satan who captures our imagination as in the encounter with Death, and the meeting with Gabriel in Eden. There is the same splendid fearlessness and haughty assertion of liberty:

> But well thou com'st
> Before thy fellows, ambitious to win
> From me some Plume, that thy success may show
> Destruction to the rest; this pause between
> (Unanswer'd lest thou boast) to let thee know:
> At first I thought that Liberty and Heav'n
> To heav'nly Souls had bin all one;[2] but now
> I see that most through sloth would rather serve,
> Minist'ring Spirits, train'd up in Feast and Song;
> Such has thou arm'd, the Minstrelsy of Heav'n,
> Servility with freedom to contend,
> As both thir deeds compar'd this day shall prove.[3]

But if Satan's speech fires the imagination and the heart, Abdiel has the best of the argument, and that argument is the central theme of *Paradise Lost* and of all that Milton wrote, the supremacy of reason, the identification of true freedom with obedience to reason or conscience. He has already been commended for his care:

> To stand approv'd in sight of God, though Worlds
> Judg'd thee perverse; the easier conquest now

---
[1] Denis Saurat: *La Pensée de Milton*, Paris, 1920, p. 304.
[2] So had Milton thought in 1640.
[3] *Paradise Lost*, Book VI. ll. 159-170.

> Remains thee, aided by this host of friends,
> Back on thy foes more glorious to return
> Than scorn'd thou didst depart, and to subdue
> By force, who reason for thir Law refuse,
> Right reason for thir Law, and for thir King
> Messiah, who by right of merit Reigns.[1]

Abdiel's reply to Satan is of the same tenour:

> Apostat, still thou err'st, nor end wilt find
> Of erring, from the path of truth remote:
> Unjustly thou deprav'st it with the name
> Of Servitude to serve whom God ordains,
> Or Nature; God and Nature bid the same,
> When he who rules is worthiest, and excels
> Them whom he governs. This is servitude,
> To serve th'unwise, or him who hath rebell'd
> Against his worthier, as thine now serve thee.[2]

The same contrast meets us throughout the poem—Satan and the imagination carry us in one direction, Milton and his impassioned reasoning in another. So that I cannot agree with M. Saurat when he declares that it is Milton's greatest originality—and a very rare one—to have constructed a coherent system of philosophy and to have at the same time transposed this system into an artistic work of the first order. That is, I think, what he has failed to do. But I cannot, on the other hand, accept the view of Blake, Shelley, and Mr. Visiak that what he has done is just the opposite of what he set out to do, that he has unconsciously vindicated the rebellion of Satan or passion against God or reason, though he has certainly gone dangerously near it at moments. For Milton's confidence in his own arguments is stronger than those arguments sometimes appear to a dis-

---
[1] *Paradise Lost*, Book VI. ll. 36-43.
[2] *Ibid.* Book VI. ll. 172-180.

interested reader. My explanation is a rather simpler one. It is that in Milton the creative imagination and the critical intellect did not work in such harmony with one another as they have in some other poets, Virgil perhaps, certainly Dante. Milton is most a poet when his imagination, his creative power, works in most entire freedom from preconceived purpose:

> To justify the ways of God to men,

or Biblical or ecclesiastical tradition. Professor Gilbert Murray in an interesting essay has distinguished between poetry as *mimesis* or creation and poetry as criticism of life, and considered how these elements have been combined in different poets: 'Among the Ancients, Aeschylus and Euripides are both magical creators and earnest critics,' 'Virgil is a great and profound critic.' But of Milton he says, 'a copious and somewhat opinionated critic. But my own feeling is that, in the main, his imagined world is almost nothing to him but a place of beauty, a sanctuary of escape.'[1] The last words are a little too suggestive of Spenser or Morris, but essentially they are, I think, true. The poet, the creative poet, in Milton is one thing; the opinionated thinker, bent on justifying the ways of God to men, is another. The poem does *not* justify God's ways to our heart and imagination— rather the opposite—it is only in Milton's passionate reasoning about reason and free-will that God is vindicated. And this is why Satan holds the stage with such complete success. Here, in the early books of which Satan is the hero, Milton's imagination works in complete emancipation, unfettered by ecclesiastical tradition or Scriptural story. It is not the task of *Paradise Lost* to justify the ways of God to

[1] Gilbert Murray: *Poesis and Mimesis* in *Essays and Addresses*, 1921.

THE SON OF GOD

Satan, but to men. Satan was a part of the story he accepted as the starting-point of his poem. In the drama as originally planned Satan was to have played quite a subordinate part, appearing only once, though we hear of him through others. From tradition Milton only knew that Satan fell *through pride*. He was free like the old Miracle Playwrights or the Dutch poet Vondel to interpret and present that act of pride as he chose. In accordance with the rationalistic Arianism to which he had drifted, he chose to make the occasion the proclamation of the Son as God's Vicegerent:

> This day have I begot whom I declare
> My only Son.[1]

[1] I do not think that this can, as Dr. Saurat takes it (Engl. Trans. p. 119), refer to the creation of the Son, who would thus be younger than the Angels good and evil, whereas Abdiel later speaks of the Son as him

> by whom
> As by his Word the mighty Father made
> All things, ev'n thee and all the spirits of Heav'n
> By him created in thir bright degrees,
> Crown'd them with glory, and to thir Glory nam'd
> Thrones, Dominations, Princedoms, Virtues, Powers,

a doctrine which Satan disputes, claiming to be

> self-begot, Self rais'd
> By our own quick'ning power;

but he does not claim that the Son is a later-begotten being. Milton in the *De Doctrina* carefully distinguishes between two senses of the word 'generation' or 'begot' (genuisse) as used by the Father of the Son, the one proper, the other metaphorical, 'nempe vel producendo, vel exaltando', which 'theologians have confounded'. Of the Creation of the Son, he declares, the Scriptures tell us only that it was 'ante mundum conditum', not that it was eternal. 'The other passages', he continues, 'which are cited refer only to the metaphorical generation, *i.e.*, his resurrection from the dead or his anointing to the functions of a Mediator.' He refers again to Heb. i. 5, 'For to which of the Angels said he ever, Thou art my Son, this day have I begotten thee', where Milton says, 'de exaltatione supra Angelos'. He goes on to give examples of its use in reference to the Priesthood of Christ and to the Kingship of Christ. It is in this metaphorical sense, I think, that we must take the lines:

> Hear all ye Angels, Progeny of Light,
> Thrones, Dominations, Princedoms, Virtues, Powers,
> Hear my Decree, which unrevok't shall stand.

But this part of the story is theologically very difficult, and I believe that if pressed Milton could have said no more than that Satan, in some way we cannot trace, knowing the Will of God, refused deliberately to obey, and that that is the essence of sin. God is the absolute ruler of the creatures he has made, not the arbitrary ruler (to adopt Burke's distinction), because his ends are good: even out of evil he will bring good. But it is not in the story of Satan that the chief lesson of *Paradise Lost* is to be found; that is the story of Adam and Eve, and especially of Adam's surrender to Eve, the conquest of reason by romantic love:

> However, I with thee have fixt my lot,
> Certain to undergo like doom, if Death
> Consort with thee, Death is to mee as Life;
> So forcible within my heart I feel
> The Bond of Nature draw me to my own,
> My own in thee, for what thou art is mine;
> Our state cannot be sever'd, we are one,
> One Flesh; to lose thee were to lose myself.[1]

That is the language of romantic love, but for Milton, the first, the primal sin

> whose mortal taste
> Brought Death into the world and all our woe.

But, after the first four books, shades of the prison-

> This day have I begot whom I declare
> My only Son, and on this holy Hill
> Him have anointed, whom ye now behold
> At my right hand; your Head I him appoint;
> And by myself have sworn to him shall bow
> All knees in Heav'n, and shall confess him Lord, etc.

The words are obscure, probably designedly so. Milton is using the language of the Psalms and the Epistle to the Hebrews, but it is inconceivable that the reference should be to the Creation of the Son, and not to his Exaltation. It is against *that* Satan rebels.

[1] *Paradise Lost*, Book IX. ll. 952-959.

house begin to close on Milton's poem as it comes under the control of the Biblical narrative, the orthodox tradition. The story of Adam is never so interesting as these first scenes in the career of Satan.

In Milton, then, the story is everything, the argument which the poem is to establish is nothing. If we shut our eyes and recall what dwells in our mind after reading *Paradise Lost*, is it any criticism of life or theology made vivid in a symbolism of amazing variety and felicity? No. It is two stories knit to one another. The first is full of great Homeric figures—splendid scenery, Odyssean voyages and adventures, battle and overthrow, in all of which Satan is the dominant personality, a greater than Achilles or Diomede, with even in one scene a touch of the generosity of Hector. The second opens in the bowery, flowery loveliness of Eden and gives us the history of a pair of mortals, of whom the man is hardly sympathetic to a modern reader yet has his moments of dignity, and the woman betrays even in the hands of her somewhat harsh creator that she is drawn by one who felt even too intensely for his own peace of mind the charm of her sex:

> yet when I approach
> Her loveliness, so absolute she seems
> And in herself complete, so well to know
> Her own, that what she wills to do or say,
> Seems wisest, virtuousest, discreetest, best.[1]

And what is the moral of *Paradise Lost* if we thus read it just as a story? Is there any thought which seems to come so directly from the heart of the story and of the poet as this, that a man must learn to keep

[1] *Paradise Lost*, Book VIII. ll. 546-550.

his wife in her proper place, which is the moral of *Samson Agonistes*:

> Therefore God's universal Law
> Gave to the Man despotic power
> Over his female in due awe,
> Nor from that right to part an hour,
> Smile she or lour:
> So shall he least confusion draw
> On his whole life, not sway'd
> By female usurpation, nor dismay'd.[1]

How bitter and how enduring were the consequences of that hasty journey to the country in 1643, unknown to his friends, from which Milton returned with Mary Powell on his arm! No more than Byron could Milton for a moment forget his wife, his first wife:

> There are shades which will not vanish,
> There are thoughts thou canst not banish.

That is one side of *Paradise Lost*—the story, the characters, the scenes. The other is Milton's thought, theological, cosmical, ethical. It is no part of my thesis to deny the interest, the courage, the freshness of Milton's thought—I have read the *De Doctrina* with great interest—nor yet to deny the eloquence of passages in which Milton sets forth his strongly held opinions about predestination and freedom, God's justice and God's mercy, love and marriage. But it is a detachable element even more than Spenser's allegory. The justification of God's ways to men begins and ends in the arguments put into God's mouth in Book III.—viz., Adam's entire freedom. The scene comes somewhat as an anti-climax to the great preceding scenes in Hell. Yet it is a dignified, if

[1] *Samson Agonistes*, ll. 1052-1060.

severe and Puritan statement of the Protestant and Christian conception of Divine Justice and Divine Mercy—for to the Puritan mind Justice and Mercy are correlative. Milton, as I have said, accepted the scheme as here set forth—Freedom, Sin, Atonement, Redemption. Where he differed from his fellow-Puritans, from Cromwell, was in the stress he laid upon the freedom of the human will to accept or to reject the grace of God—he was a Pelagian, they Calvinists. He has the Humanist's conception of the supremacy of reason; the Quaker's belief that God's free grace is offered to all men. But he has not the large and generous conception of man's nature of the greatest of the Humanists; he has not the ardent love of God and his fellow-men which inspired Fox or Barclay.

There is much interest in Milton's thought, and occasionally it found adequate utterance. But generally it is more interesting in the *De Doctrina* than in *Paradise Lost,* for Milton failed completely to penetrate with his thought the characters and events of the story he tells. What as epic and dramatic story is most admirable is when regarded in its theological significance either meaningless or even shocking. Milton's Deity is, one gathers from the *De Doctrina* or M. Saurat's exposition of that work, a more transcendent being even than Dante's, for Catholic theology has always held that human reason can attain to *some* knowledge of God, though not, without the aid of revelation, to a saving knowledge. Milton's God is, as M. Saurat says, more like the Absolute of Hegelian philosophy—Uncreated, Infinite, Unknowable. We can think of him neither as creator nor saviour—these are functions delegated to the Son. 'Deus prout in se est humanam cogitationem, nedum sensus, longe superat.' He is 'brightness invisible'. Yet this Incomprehensible and Inaccessible appears in the poem as almost too accessible and comprehensible, expounding and justifying himself; pouring scorn upon the rebel angels in language of irony untouched with pity; giving orders and directions like a drill-sergeant. I gather from the *De Doctrina* that Milton's defence would be that in so doing he is simply following the language and example of Scripture. It is so that God delineates and depicts Himself in the sacred writings, lowering Himself to our level, and we must speak of Him in His own words. That may be, but the poetic effect falls infinitely short of that achieved by Dante, who leaves the exposition of philosophy to Virgil, and the high truths of theology to be learned from the lips of Beatrice, the Saints, the Doctors, and the Apostles, and gives us of the Divine only that vision which

> Was not for words to speak, nor memory's self
> To stand against such outrage on her skill.

. . . . .

> In that abyss
> Of radiance clear and lofty, seem'd methought
> Three orbs of triple hue clipt in one bound:
> And from another one reflected seem'd,
> As rainbow is from rainbow; and the third
> Seem'd fire breathed equally from both. O speech!
> How feeble and how faint art thou to give
> Conception birth. Yet this to what I saw
> Is less than little. O eternal Light!
> Sole in thyself that dwell'st, and of thyself
> Sole understood, past, present, and to come.

. . . . .

> Here vigour fail'd the towering fantasy:
> But yet the will roll'd onward like a wheel

In even motion, by the love impell'd
That moves the sun in heaven and all the stars.[1]

Even in this supreme vision of a moment what is it that Dante beholds?—It is the Catholic doctrine of the Trinity, no longer an abstract intellectual conception—even as such Milton rejected it—but for a moment visibly beheld. It is to the abstract tenets of Catholic theology that Dante gives poetic, symbolic expression. Whenever, on the other hand, Milton's peculiar doctrines obtrude themselves, the effect is almost invariably to lower the temperature of the poem; at the best, to substitute poetic declamation for poetic creation. Milton held, to close with a lower instance, that matter and spirit are ultimately one, and that both are included in the being of God—a noble and philosophic thought—but is there anything worse in the poem than Raphael's discourse on this theme and its corollary, the nature of Angelic digestion?

It may, I think, have been a realisation of what he had done, of how far his creative and vivid imagination had disturbed the balance of his thought, that led him to compose *Paradise Regained* in so different a tone and manner. A less great poem than its predecessor, it is a more harmonious poem. The tone is not that of Milton the poet, the creator, but of Milton the thinker, grave, restrained, austere. The *Book of Job* is the model, and like that poem it is a series of dialogues and monologues with beautiful descriptive connecting links. It has never been a general favourite, though it has appealed strongly to some readers, a select audience; and seen in a proper perspective it seems to me a noble and intriguing poem, pre-eminently

---

[1] *Paradiso*, XXXIII. ll. 115 *et seq.* (Cary's translation).

the poem of Miltonic Puritanism, which is not quite the Puritanism of Cromwell or Bunyan: the poem of the restrictive virtues—contempt of pleasure and wealth and glory, the submission of the will to God and to God only, the temper of the men who broke the yoke of Philip in the Low Countries and brought our attractive but impossible Charles to the scaffold. What Milton failed to apprehend, what his character and upbringing, his great disappointment in love, his years of political warfare made him incapable of fully apprehending, is that the restrictive virtues in themselves are somewhat cold and negative. They too must have their root in a passionate love of God and our fellow-men. 'The treasuries of Heaven are not negations of passion, but realities of intellect from which all the passions emanate uncurbed in their eternal glory.'[1] We miss in Milton's Christ the note of passionate, self-forgetting love. He is too serene and forbidding, if noble and imperturbable.

In *Samson Agonistes* Milton is again the creator, the mimetic poet, finding relief for his suppressed passion of disappointment, indignation, devotion to the good cause which has apparently gone under, in a dream, a 'wish-fulfilment', an imaginative creation; but he is also the critic, the thinker: and as before the two aspects of the work are imperfectly harmonised. As an expression of his thought about life, about sin as the failure to make reason supreme over passion, *Samson Agonistes* completed the series begun with *Paradise Lost*—disobedience, obedience, repentance. But as a work of art, as a drama vivid and moving, is *Samson Agonistes* really concerned deeply with the motive of repentance? Remorseful and repentant Samson certainly is; but surely the dominant note is

[1] Blake.

that of revenge rather than repentance, or at least of the vindication of the good cause, the cause of God, against the enemies who seem for the moment triumphant. God's ways are mysterious and past finding out:

> God of our Fathers, what is man!
> That thou towards him with hand so various,
>   Or might I say contrarious,
> Temper'st thy providence through his short course,
>   Not evenly, as thou rul'st
> The Angelic orders and inferior creatures mute,
>   Irrational and brute.

Yet surely God will vindicate his own cause, and cast down the mighty,

> While their hearts were jocund and sublime,
> Drunk with Idolatry, drunk with wine.

And in the end he does; and so Milton believes will it be with him, or at least the great cause for which he has spent his life and poured out his poetic genius. In Samson, Milton contemplates himself, blind and 'fallen on evil days':

> Eyeless, in Gaza, at the Mill, with slaves;

he too had wedded a wife from among the Philistines and she had betrayed his fondest hopes, cheated him of the hope for which he had garner'd up his heart; he too had driven from the field of battle a boasting Harapha in the person of Salmasius, and for him too would come a day of vindication. But Milton is never merely concerned with himself. His true self is his ideals, the good cause, and the English people. The English people had passed through the fire to perish in the smoke because they had not understood in what true liberty consists: 'For instead of fretting with vexation of thinking that you can lay the blame on anyone but yourselves, know that to be free is the same thing as to be pious, to be wise, to be temperate, to be just, to be frugal and abstinent, and lastly to be magnanimous and brave; so to be the opposite of all these is the same as to be a slave.'[1] The English people had chosen to be a slave, despite all that had been done for it, to put on the chains of prelacy, and lay down its head in the lap of harlots—Nell Gwynns, etc.:

> in the lascivious lap
> Of a deceitful Conçubine, who shore me
> Like a tame Wether, all my precious fleece,
> Then turn'd me out ridiculous, despoil'd,
> Shav'n, and disarm'd among my enemies.[2]

But the locks of England will grow again, the spirit of the Commonwealth will reawaken. And it is not amiss to remember that Milton composed *Samson Agonistes* in the year in which the guns of the Dutch were roaring in the Medway, and that twenty-one years later the Stewarts did finally depart, the shorn locks of England had grown again, and she took up, however clumsily and far from the ideal and pious manner in which Milton and the Puritans dreamed, the conduct of her own destiny. No one is likely to subscribe again to the view that Milton was a supremely wise and great man whose judgement on political and religious questions was always, as he believed, just. Yet he was a great man if purity and temperance, high ideals and dauntless courage, faithful service and great gifts well used are elements of greatness; and there he sits at the end of his life, 'his head is bloody but unbowed'. He has

[1] *Defensio Secunda.*   [2] *Samson Agonistes*, ll. 536-540.

moved far from his early faith and hope, but he has steered ever by the light of his own soul. If he had been less unyielding, if his early education had not perhaps over-nourished and strengthened his confidence in himself, he might have learned one lesson which he never did, the lesson which Cromwell besought the Kirk of Scotland to learn: 'I beseech you in the bowels of Christ, think it possible you may be mistaken.' And through all the years of conflict and disappointment, Milton's poetry, his art, was, one feels, his great escape. It is difficult to believe that he laid aside poetry in 1640–41 and, except for a few sonnets, never took it up again till 1658. Rather, I think, his mind dwelt ever, amid all tumults and conflicts, in the great poem that was to be, and he matured the science of his art. For the art of *Paradise Lost* marks a great advance in conscious technique on *Comus* and *Lycidas*. Milton had thought out everything—how he would spell certain words to avoid 'committing short and long'; what elisions he would allow himself; how he would build his verse paragraphs, varying the pauses, 'the sense variously drawn out from one verse into another'. He had stored his mind with classical, Biblical, and romantic images and allusions. His life and work are one sustained triumph of the will. It is no wonder that he found in man's freedom the source of his troubles and the only hope of his regeneration.

CHAPTER VIII

COMMONWEALTH AND RESTORATION

The Significance of Milton—The Spirit and Literature of the Commonwealth and the Restoration.

IT is in Milton's work, considered historically and in its entirety, that one can contemplate the tremendous character of the forces at work in this troubled age when, simultaneously with, and in part as a consequence of, the reawakening of the mind of man to a full consciousness of his rights to freedom of thought and freedom of imagination, came a requickening of the spirit of Christianity as an other-world religion making fresh demands on him for a rigid and meticulous orthodoxy, an ever stricter and closer walk with God. To the Puritan like Baxter or Bunyan as to the greater spirits of the Counter-Reformation, Ignatius Loyola and Francis Xavier, the world and all it has to offer, science and the arts as much as wealth and honour, are intrinsically vanities, this world has significance only as a field of battle and of discipline (*askesis*) in the great cause of the salvation of a man's soul. But Catholicism had inherited a tradition which allowed a certain subordinate place to the natural life and its needs, had made a clearer distinction between the duties demanded of the average man and of the saint. One of the chief tasks of the Jesuits was to accommodate the requirements of Christianity to the life of the man of the world, in discharging which they brought down upon themselves—not altogether justly—the anger and brilliant irony of Pascal.

SIGNIFICANCE OF MILTON

The Puritans, like the Jansenists, were less accommodating. They demanded of Everyman that he should, if he were to gain Heaven, become a spiritual hero. 'The highest aim of Puritan literature was the exaltation of the strong at the expense of the weak—of the pre-eminently good at the expense of the more moderately virtuous. It was not Milton's personal misogyny resulting in the substitution of Eve or Dalila for Juliet or Rosalind; it was the habit of looking for more than was to be achieved by human nature, till the search for ideal beauty and goodness led to contemptuous blindness to the beauty and goodness inherent in our mingled nature.'[1] These words of Gardiner's sum up the impression which such a survey as I have attempted leaves at least on my own mind. If ever there was a fully conscious child at once of the classical Renaissance and the Puritan Reformation it was John Milton. No poet ever moved more deliberately and determinedly to a preconceived goal, or at first sight arrived there so deserving of the victor's wreath. The man who, at the age of nineteen, had aspired to be the singer of some lofty theme:

> Such where the deep transported mind may soar
> Above the wheeling poles,

did live to write of

> Things unattempted yet in prose or rhyme.

And yet one doubts if the goal was quite that at which the poet dreamed of arriving when he first meditated an elaborate song to generations. It became at the last not a song of victory but of defeat, if defeat accepted in an indomitable spirit of no

[1] Chambers's *Cyclopædia of English Literature*, vol. i., 1901, p. 546.

surrender and confident hope. But on two of the main sources of his early inspiration he finally passes judgement in express words or by contemptuous silence. The philosophers and poets of Greece from whose works he had drunk so deep in youth, whose art to the end was the shaping influence in his own, are arraigned and condemned by Christ in *Paradise Regained*:

> Alas! what can they teach, and not mislead;
> Ignorant of themselves, of God much more,
> And how the world began, and how man fell,
> Degraded by himself, on grace depending?
>
> . . . . .
>
> Or if I would delight my private hours
> With Music or with Poem, where so soon
> As in our native Language can I find
> That solace? All our Law and Story strew'd
> With Hymns, our Psalms with artful terms inscrib'd,
> Our Hebrew Songs and Harps, in Babylon,
> That pleas'd so well our Victor's ear, declare
> That rather Greece from us these Arts deriv'd;
> Ill imitated, while they loudest sing
> The vices of thir Deities, and thir own,
> In Fable, Hymn, or Song, so personating
> Thir Gods ridiculous, and themselves past shame.
> Remove their swelling Epithetes thick laid
> As varnish on a Harlot's cheek, the rest
> Thin sown with aught of profit or delight,
> Will far be found unworthy to compare
> With Sion's songs, to all true tastes excelling,
> Where God is prais'd aright, and Godlike men,
> The Holiest of Holies, and his Saints.[1]

The speech is dramatic, one may say, but the speaker is Christ. One cannot but think that if the larger, more generous spirit in which Michael Angelo

[1] *Paradise Regained*, Book IV. ll. 309-312, 331-349.

painted the roof of the Sistine Chapel and Raphael the Camera della Segnatura had prevailed, Milton also might have given sanction and utterance to the thought that 'not only Judaism but also Graeco-Roman Paganism is an ante-chamber to Christianity; this antique culture gave not merely a negative but also a positive preparation for Christ... that there was a positive relationship between classical Antiquity and Christianity.... The four pictures of the Camera represent the aspiration of the soul of man in each of its faculties, the striving of all humanity towards God by means of aesthetic perception (Parnassus), the exercise of reason in philosophical inquiry and scientific research (School of Athens), order in Church and State (Gift of Laws Ecclesiastical and Social), and finally theology.... The principle elsewhere laid down is here affirmed, that the reception of a true Renaissance into the circle of ecclesiastical thought points to a widening of the limited mediaeval conception into universality, a transition to entire and actual Catholicity, like the great step taken by St. Paul when he turned to the Gentiles and released the community from the limits of Judaistic teaching.'[1] It was a beautiful dream that mutual war and persecution dissipated, but just such a dream as Milton might or must have entertained when he consecrated himself to the composition of a great

[1] *The Cambridge Modern History, The Reformation.* Chapter I. Medicean Rome. The late Professor F. X. Kraus, Munich; and compare: 'The religious, universalist Theism of the Italian Humanists.... By this I understand that the Godhead has been alike active in the different religions and philosophies, and is still in our day active. In the modern religious consciousness of every noble-spirited man the Godhead speaks. A statement in which the idea of a universal activity of the Godhead throughout the whole of nature and in the higher consciousness of man has its full expression' (Dillthey, *Auffassung und Analyse des Menschen im 15 und 16ten Jahrhundert*).

Christian poem, the central idea of which is, after all, more Humanist than Puritan, a poem doctrinal to a nation.

For Milton had tasted the sweets of the Renaissance poetry of Italy and England, and he accepted and maintained the Renaissance ideal of a complete development of human personality as the end of education and life. Witness his early Latin Elegies and those two ever delightful poems, *L'Allegro* and *Il Penseroso*. My friend Professor Hanford will have it that these poems were written at an earlier date than I should be disposed to assign to them, because 'we may assume that after a year or so of aesthetic leisure on his father's estate he would have felt the need of a return to more serious and purposeful endeavour'. I would not thus divide Milton. Two or more years given to 'aesthetic leisure' alone, and deliberately, would have been a demoralising experience. But I do not myself feel that such poems, full of exquisite but innocent delight in nature and art and life and study, are a whit less deserving of the labour and appreciation of a serious mind than the didactic *Comus* or the angry *Lycidas*, beautiful as both these are. If Milton thought so, that was the error of his age and party. The body and the secular have their full rights as well as the spiritual. The devil who is the mischievous person is as capable of taking a spiritual as a fleshly guise. Milton was perhaps a better man when he awoke like Wordsworth

> To hear the lark begin his flight,
> And singing startle the dull night,

and to spend his days

> In unreproved pleasures free,

MILTON & DRAMA

than when he was denouncing the Anglican bishops, gloating over the fate awaiting them in another world, describing country pastors like George Herbert as

> Blind mouths that scarce themselves know how
> To hold a sheephook,

or joining in the chorus that clamoured for war and blood:

> But that two-handed engine at the door
> Stands ready to smite once and smite no more.

Milton could not share Prynne's contempt for Aeschylus and Sophocles. He knew what a powerful ally a well-inspired drama might be in the elevation of a nation's character. In the hour of his highest hopes and exultation over the coming age of liberty and righteousness, he celebrates the power of poetry in all her forms, and summons the magistrates to take into their care, 'not only the deciding of our contentious law-cases and brawls, but the managing of our public sports and festival pastimes'—pastimes, a word which filled Baxter and Prynne with horror, for is it not written that Jesus wept, never that he laughed.[1]

[1] But both Milton and the Puritans were too ready to recall the laughter of God described in the second Psalm:

> he who in heaven doth dwell
> Shall laugh, the Lord shall scoff them, then severe
> Speak to them in his wrath, and in his fell
> And fierce ire trouble them.

Baxter tells how when 'Goring's army fled to Bridgewater . . . I happened to be next to Major Harrison as soon as the flight began, and heard him with a loud voice break forth into the praises of God with fluent expressions as if he had been in a rapture'. Cromwell and his generals were a little too ready to assume God's approval of battles and massacres if done by the right people: 'I believe', says Cromwell, reporting the storm of Tredah, 'all their friars were knocked on the head promiscuously but two; the one of which was Father Pete Taaf, brother to the

Milton had loved and valued the poetry and the drama of the ancients, and he had read Plato and learned from him a high doctrine of love; and one might have hoped for a finer union in his great poem of the humanist temper of the Greeks with the spirituality of the Hebrew prophets. Perhaps had things gone otherwise at home and in the state, it might have been effected. Politics and war made it impossible, and into poems, classical in form as no others ever written, he breathed a spirit of the intensest, almost a fierce, Hebraism, qualified by a spirit which is rather that of the dogmatic rationalism of the *Aufklärung* than the sweeter, humbler, more reverent reasonableness of the Cambridge Platonists. Unfortunately the Cambridge Platonists who essayed to write poetry had none of Milton's art. Joseph Beaumont's *Psyche* and Henry More's *Antipsychopannychia* are amongst the worst poems ever written.

But if in the end Milton had wandered far from the ideal of the finest minds of the Renaissance, of those who would have Christianised the philosophy of Greece and Rome, given the world the philosophy of Christ, had he not wandered equally far from his

---

Lord Taaf, whom the soldiers took the next day and made an end of. The other was taken in the Round Tower, under the repute of a lieutenant, and when he understood the officers in that tower had no quarter, he confessed he was a friar; but that did not save him.' . . . 'And now give me leave to say how it comes to pass that this work was wrought. It was set upon some of our hearts, that a great thing should be done, not by the power or might but by the spirit of God. And is it not so clearly? . . . it is good that God alone have all the glory.'—CARLYLE: *Oliver Cromwell's Letters and Speeches*, Part V. Letter cv. Carlyle derives much solemn satisfaction from these despatches: 'An armed Soldier, solemnly conscious to himself that he is a Soldier of God the Just,—a consciousness which it well beseems all soldiers and all men to have;—armed Soldier, terrible as Death, relentless as Doom; doing God's Judgments on the Enemies of God! . . . then, art thou worthy to love such a thing; worthy to do other than hate it, and shriek over it.'

first enthusiasm for the Reformation? When the Long Parliament met in 1640, Milton was turned almost giddy by the thought that a new age was beginning, 'the reforming of reformation itself'. When, twenty or more years later, he put into the mouth of Michael a *résumé* of the history of the Christian Church, its progressive corruption, he passes over the Reformation without a word. He foresees no check to the downward progress till Christ shall come again:

> so shall the world go on,
> To good malignant, to bad men benign,
> Under her own weight groaning, till the day
> Appear of reparation to the just,
> And vengeance to the wicked, at return
> Of him so lately promised to thy aid,
> The woman's seed, obscurely then foretold,
> Now ampler known thy Saviour and thy Lord.[1]

No one stood so much alone as Milton. He had no Church connection, as we say in Scotland, was not 'a jined member o' ony recognised releegious body'. The Quakers made a certain appeal to him—they, like him, did not believe in ministers and churches. He was nearer than he suspected to the Jesuits. His ideal is that of Ignatius Loyola—the perfect freedom of the will, a complete self-control manifested in a perfect obedience to the will of God. But Milton could admit of no human superior authorised to tell him what is God's will. For that he will hearken only to his own reason, his own interpretation of the text of the Bible. His theology is fully set forth, buttressed by texts, in the *De Doctrina Christiana*. A certain native arrogance, intensified by domestic disappointment and political warfare, would

[1] I owe to Professor Saurat my first realisation of the significance of this omission.

not let him listen *also* to the voice of his heart, the voice of the spirit as the Quakers termed it, so that, consciously or unconsciously, he spoke in the tone of the *Aufklärung*, the age of reason. Toland felt in Milton a kindred spirit, and was one of his first editors, biographers, and champions. But rationalism of the eighteenth century type and the spirit of religion cannot live together.

But Milton's achievement and Milton's failure—if one may use that word of poems so wonderful in their execution—mark a definite period in a movement, the origin of which lies far back in history. The work of many recent scholars,[1] starting in general from Burckhardt, has taught us to look for the common source of Renaissance and Reformation in a feeling, an expectation in men's hearts, which is traceable back to the New Testament, and beyond it to the Psalms and Prophetic books of the Old Testament, the idea of a rebirth, renewal, reformation (*renascentia, renovatio, reformatio*) at once in the spirit of the individual and in the world. The Christian Faith, and all the expectations of the Second Coming and end of the world in which the first generation of Christians had lived, were the first great manifestation of that hope. Then the expectation had died down, and the Church had become the greatest organism in the instituted life of Europe, and thoughts of a renewed world had grown remote. But when the Church had fallen on evil days, the hope which had never quite died was renewed and quickened by the teaching of Joachim of Flores concerning the three ages—of law, of wisdom, and of full knowledge and

---

[1] Burdach: *Reformation, Renaissance, Humanism*, 1926; Troeltsch: *Renaissance und Reformation*, 1913; P. Wernle: *Renaissance und Reformation*; J. Huizinga: *Het Problem der Renaissance*; *De Gids*, 1920, and in *Tien Studien*, 1926.

understanding, the ages of the Father, the Son, and the Holy Spirit. St. Francis, and perhaps even more the Franciscan Spirituals, had taken over and preached widely the idea of a coming 'renovatio vitae', but primarily a spiritual renewal. So it passed to Dante—the name of whose *Vita Nuova* is, Burdach points out, only intelligible if one recalls the significance and prevalence of the idea—and for Dante, with his political as well as spiritual interest, his deep sense of the dire need of Italy and Europe of good government and peace, the thought took a wider significance, became the dream of a restoration of the *Pax Romana* and of the spirit of Christianity, a renewal of the right relation of the two brains of the world, the Pope and the Emperor, the spiritual and the secular. 'The symbol of the world sighing for renewal and enfranchisement is, for Dante and Petrarch, Rome in mourning. What is fruitful in this symbol was that it represented Rome on every side: as the head of Italy oppressed by violence and the strife of parties; as the centre of the Church needing purification in head and members; as the stage of ancient citizen virtue and ancient culture, "Roma che il buon mondo feo". On whatever side regarded, the foremost conception is that of a return to the old as the source of healing' (Huizinga: *Tien Studien*, p. 329 ff.). And so for the early Humanists and Reformers alike, the restoration of classical learning connected itself with a renewal of life religious and secular. Huizinga quotes from Melanchthon: 'O nos felices si recta studia deum favore renascantur,' 'Nunc probitas, honestas, justitia, immo Evangelium, quod diu sub latebris latuit, reflorescit; renascuntur bonae literae.' 'Sperandum sit', writes Zwingli, 'veterum quandoque innocentiam renatum iri quemadmodum eruditionem videmus'; and Erasmus, writing to Leo X., speaks of all the three sides of the expected reform: 'Saeculo huic nostro quod prorsus aureum fore spes est, si quod unquam aureum fuit, ut in quo, tuis felicissimis auspiciis, tuisque sanctissimis consiliis, tria quaedam praecipua generis humani bona restitutum iri videam: pietatem illam vere Christianam multis modis collapsam; optimas litteras partim neglectas hactenus, partim corruptas, et publicam ac perpetuam orbis Christiani concordiam, pietatis et eruditionis fontem parentemque.'[1] Even the revived study and portrayal of the nude in art, Burdach considers, had its spiritual aspect as a desire for a return to nature as God had made it.[2]

By the seventeenth century much water had flowed under the bridge. The Renaissance and the Reformation had quickly fallen out of step. The emancipated spirit of man had found in the classics other philosophies of life besides the Platonism or Neo-Platonism which it had been possible to Christianise—Epicureanism, Scepticism; and in Italy, owing to its political condition and the character of its rulers, the emancipation had often proved the freedom to throw the reins upon the neck of animal passion unrestrained by religious or moral scruples. And the Reformation, partly in reaction from these excesses, had revived the spirit of early Christianity in its attitude towards secular literature and worldly pastimes, including

[1] This our age, which promises truly to be a golden age, if there ever has been a golden age, as that wherein, under your fortunate auspices, and by your most holy guidance, three of the chief blessings of the human race I may see restored: that true Christian piety in many ways decayed; the best literature hitherto neglected and in part corrupted; the public and perpetual unity of the world which is the true fountainhead and parent of piety and learning.

[2] 'Adamians go naked because man did so in Paradise.'—BURTON: *Anatomy of Melancholy.*

music and art, and nowhere more than in England. There is something heroic, whatever we may think of the wisdom and the effects, in the thorough-going fashion in which the English Puritans asserted the other-worldly character of Christianity, while, in distinction from Catholicism, they also spurned all thought of a retreat from the world, affirmed that the world itself is the arena of the spiritual *askesis* and warfare which prepares the soul of man for the world to come.[1] Cotton Mather tells us that one reason for

[1] 'The sphere of the operations of faith is the society of the world and its ordering.' With this sentence is pronounced the complete emancipation from every thought of Church activities. In it is completed the strenuous conflict of Luther against 'Official-buben', against the pomp, the might and the multiplication of good works, against 'holy garments'. In it appears one of the greatest organising thoughts which ever any man in history has conceived. Alas! that Luther did not succeed in realising it to the full. The mediaeval doctrine of the two Kingdoms, the secular and the spiritual, now encounters the sentence of the Reformation: 'Christ has not two bodies or a body of two kinds, the one secular, the other spiritual. There is one Head and he has one Body. The secular power is baptised along with us, it also is exercised by Christian persons, it also belongs to the spiritual order.'— DILTHEY: *Luthers Von den christlichen Standes Besserung*.

This, like much that is written on the Reformation, sounds rather magnificent. It may be doubted, however, if the attempt of Protestantism to break down the barrier between the sacred and the secular has really been fruitful. The Catholic recognition of the subordinate place allowed to the secular was not perhaps strictly logical—few things that work well are—but it did by allowing a fairly wide range to 'indifferent actions' secure a fair amount of freedom for the spirit of man. Science, art, sport, pastime of all sorts are innocent, or if the individual is led astray, the Church has means to bring him back to the fold, and can, if it has sufficient authority and the support of the state, check excesses. This has doubtless led to abuses, hypocrisy, and the undue restraint of freedom of speculation, but some restraint of speculation or the rash airing of speculation is no bad thing. With a popular press disseminating every latest guess of Presidents of the British Association, or the latest indecencies of Psychologists, the mind of the average man is a complete chaos. The Protestant attempt to break down the barrier has resulted either in a too great strictness, the condemnation and prohibition of pastime, the theatre, racing, cards, etc., and an often unwholesome strain on sensitive minds trying to live at impossible heights of unrelieved seriousness. Carlyle's doctrine was one of seriousness for its own sake. It produced the doctrine of the sacredness of work and the making of money, for with this inclusion of the

the resolution to which the Pilgrim Fathers came of seeking a home beyond the Atlantic was that not even in Protestant Holland could they 'with ten years endeavour bring their neighbours particularly to any suitable observation of the Lord's Day; without which they knew that all practical Religion must wither miserably'. There speaks the English Puritan. To our own day almost, the test of a man's religion in

secular came back, acknowledged or unacknowledged, something of the Jewish belief that worldly prosperity was a sign of God's approval of the fortunate person's conduct, person's or nation's: 'And it shall come to pass if thou shalt hearken diligently unto the voice of the Lord thy God, to observe to do all his commandments which I command thee this day, that the Lord thy God will set thee on high above all the nations of the earth.... Blessed shalt thou be in the city and blessed shalt thou be in the field. Blessed shall be the fruit of thy body, and the fruit of thy ground, and the fruit of thy cattle, the increase of thy kine, and the young of thy flock, etc.' The Catholic thought, if I may take Dante for guide, had been otherwise, that wealth is no reward but a trial: 'Master, I said to him, now tell me also: this Fortune of which thou hintest to me; what is she, that has the good things of the world thus within her clutches? And he said to me: O foolish creatures, how great is this ignorance which falls upon ye. Now I wish thee to receive my judgement of her. He whose wisdom is transcendent over all made the heavens and gave them guides so that every part may shine to every part equally distributing the light. In like manner, for worldly splendours, he ordained a general minister and guide to change betimes the vain possessions from people to people, and from one kindred to another, beyond the hindrance of human wisdom. Hence one people commands, another languishes; obeying her sentence, which is hidden like the serpent in the grass. Your knowledge cannot withstand her. She provides, judges, and maintains her kingdom, as the other gods do theirs. Her permutations have no truce. Necessity makes her be swift; so often come things requiring change. This is she who is so much reviled. But she in bliss hears it not. With the other Primal Creatures joyful she wheels her sphere and tastes her blessedness.' I seem to remember a time when our commercial prosperity was ascribed by some people to our stricter observance of the Sabbath than has ever been customary in the continent. A Scot in Italy has told me how it puzzled him at first to find young Catholics ready to give the whole of Sunday to a picnic, having been to Mass at an early hour of the morning. On the other hand, when this strictness breaks down, as it has done to an amazing extent with the advent of the bicycle, the motor-car, and the war, the consequence is a secularity of a thorough-going character, a spiritual vacancy which is liable to be invaded by an irruption of all sorts and descriptions of eccentric creeds and practices.

Evangelical and Nonconformist England and in the whole of Scotland has been his observance of Sunday, Sabbath, the Lord's Day.

Classical learning which had furnished the key with which the early Reformers unlocked the gate of the giant's castle became suspect. Fox and others distrusted Universities. You remember Addison's story of the young man who, during the Commonwealth, went up to the University 'with a good cargo of Latin and Greek', and found when he appeared before the 'famous Independent minister' then head of the College that 'his Latin and Greek stood him in little stead; he was to give an account only of the state of his soul; whether he was of the number of the elect; what was the occasion of his conversion; upon what day of the month, and what hour of the day it happened; how it was carried on and when completed. The whole examination was summed up with one short question, namely, whether he was prepared for death?'[1]

But Humanism was not dead. For Sidney, for Ben Jonson, for Milton, learning and virtue had a close connection. Each of them judged it impossible for any man 'to be a good poet without being first a good man'. In this spirit Milton composed his earlier as well as his later poems. And Milton, like Dante, had looked for a Renaissance, a Reformation at once in Letters, in the State, and in the Church. For him the meeting of the Long Parliament had been what the entry of Henry VII. into Italy had been for Dante. It was to inaugurate a 'reformation of reformation' in Church and State. Each was to be allotted its due place. He could not forgive even Cromwell that he granted tithes to the clergy. His own idea was a well-

[1] *The Spectator*, No. 494.

ordered community, free of Kings and governed by the best, by a spiritual aristocracy; a rightly-ordered scheme of education which should include a right ordering of drama, poetry, music, and other pastimes; within the state a free Church unsupported by the State, dependent only on the freewill offerings of the faithful, exercising no discipline that went beyond admonition, reproof, and in the last resort excommunication, with the door ever open to repentance—something like this, but including that freedom within the family which implies that mutual love shall be the only bond, freedom of divorce being in the power of husband and wife—such was Milton's dream of the renewal of all things to which he looked forward. He never, I think, abandoned it; but, when he sat down in the hour of defeat to compose the great poem that was to celebrate it, Puritanism and politics had embittered his mind. He had to be Scriptural. He had to concentrate on the all-absorbing theme of the Fall and the Atonement; and could not bring into his poem, as Dante had done, all the content of his thought about Church and State. That was scattered through polemical pamphlets or dry theological statements. His justification of the ways of God to men was an almost abstract statement of the doctrine of free will, made concrete in a story the actors in which, with the exception of the great Adversary, were hardly adequate to the fateful part they had to play. Neither the main thought nor the art of his poem suffered by his disillusionment, but the spirit, Joy, and even to some extent love, went out of his work. And with him the direct influence of the Renaissance and Reformation in literature ends. Milton's poetry is classical, in the sense of the Humanists, poetry modelled upon the work of the Ancients, as not even French tragedy was, far less the poetry of our own Augustans. A new spirit was moving upon the waters of men's minds, the spirit of science and rationalism.

For the tide of reaction against Puritanism was in full force when Milton was busy with the poem he had conceived twenty years earlier. In that interval England had been ruled and disciplined by the Saints, the Godly. The Church, that with all its faults had appealed to the heart and imagination of a large section of the people in the manner described by clerics like Herbert, by laymen like Izaak Walton and Sir Thomas Browne and Evelyn, had been trodden under foot, its pastors displaced as scandalous, which doubtless some of them were, though their judges were far from impartial, the *Book of Common Prayer* suppressed, the Churches stripped and desecrated. In 1644 Parliament issued an order 'for the speedy demolishing of all organs, images, and all matters of superstitious ornaments in all Cathedrals, etc., throughout the Kingdom of England and Dominion of Wales; the better to accomplish the blessed reformation so happily begun and to remove all offences and things illegal in the worship of God'. The organs were transferred to taverns. Singing men and boys, swept out of the churches, became soldiers, or gathered at certain centres, as Oxford. Anthony à Wood[1] has an interesting account of the gathering of displaced 'Music Masters' and their 'weekly meetings in the house of Will Ellis, late organist of St. John's College. . . . Among them was Proctor the mirror and wonder of his age for music, excellent for the Lyraviola and Division Viola, good at the Treble Violin,

[1] *The Life of Anthony à Wood* . . . written by himself, and published by Mr. T. Hearne, etc., 1772.

and all comprehended in a man of three or four and twenty years of age.' 'The gentlemen in private meetings, which A. W. frequented, play'd three, four and five parts with Viols, as Treble Viol, Tenor, Counter Tenor and Bass with an Organ, Virginal, or Harpsicon: and they esteemed a Violin to be an Instrument only belonging to a common fiddler and could not endure that it should come among them for fear of making their meetings to be vain and fiddling. But before the Restoration, and especially after, Viols began to be out of fashion and only Violins used, as Treble Violin, Tenor and Bass Violin; and the King according to the French Mode would have twenty-four Violins playing before him while he was at meals as being more brisk and airy than Viols.' The airy and brisk violin was perhaps too characteristic of the restored Court and its influence. But had the Puritans been wise to drive music out of religion, consign organs to taverns, and violins to the accompaniment of those precursors of opera with which, even before the Restoration, Davenant was beginning to herald the coming era? It had surely been better with Plato, somewhat of a Puritan as regards the arts, to cultivate those modes at least which were appropriate to the mood they wished to evoke. It is not through the intellect and its dogmas alone that the spirit of man is raised to communion with the divine. One Puritan knew that when he wrote:

Blest pair of Sirens,

and Milton's scheme of education was to include both poetry and the drama and, in the intervals of gymnastics, 'the solemn and divine harmonies of music heard or learned; either while the skilful organist plies his grave and fancied descant in lofty fugues,

MUSIC

or the whole symphony with artful and unimaginable touches adorn and grace the well-studied chords of some choice composer; sometimes the lute or soft organ stop waiting on elegant voices, either to religious, martial, or civil ditties; which, if wise men and prophets be not extremely out, have a great power over the dispositions and manners to smooth and make them gentle from rustic harshness and distempered passions'.[1]

It was not, of course, hatred of music that expelled organs and choirs from Churches—other Puritans beside Milton loved music. Pepys was a Puritan in his youth and retained some Puritan traits of speech and thought to the end. It was the passionate, fanatical determination to rid 'the worship of our Lord Jesus Christ' of 'all humane inventions and additions', as Cotton Mather puts it, to have the sanction of Scripture for every usage. But music to flourish must have the support of an organised system of supply and demand, some institution which promises employment and support to those who make it the study of their lifetime, that and an educated public taste. The Lutheran service gave Bach his opportunity and determined to a large extent the character of his work. There can be no doubt that the English people has suffered from the neglect of music by the Puritans and, for long, by their descendants the Nonconformists. A few Cathedrals and College Chapels will hardly suffice to make religious music a national force. In Scotland the result has been deplorable, for we as a people have need of every influence which could 'smooth and make gentle' our 'rustic harshness'.

If Puritanism in the Commonwealth dealt harshly with Church organs and choirs, it dealt not less

[1] *Of Education.*

harshly with popular festivals, so far as it was able, for the English people is not easily coerced.[1] Maypoles, seasonal festivals, wakes, and Church Ales were forbidden and, as far as might be, suppressed. The first exploit of Hudibras is an effort to stop bear-baiting, and Ralpho expresses the spirit in which they went to work:

> To this quoth Ralpho, verily
> The point seems very plain to me.
> It is an Antichristian game,
> Unlawful both in thing and name;
> First, for the name; the word Bear-baiting
> Is carnal, and of man's creating:
> For certainly there's no such word
> In all the Scripture on record,
> Therefore unlawful, and a sin.
> And so is (secondly) the thing.
> A vile assembly 'tis, that can
> No more be proved by Scripture than
> Provincial, Classick, National;
> Mere human creature-cobwebs all.

[1] 'But even after the first panic was over, race-meetings, cock-fights, and bear-baitings were prohibited, partly on political grounds, as likely to be made the scene of seditious meetings, and partly for the moral welfare of the community. Unnecessary public-houses were suppressed in large numbers. Rogues and jolly companies; wandering minstrels, bear-wards, and Tom Goodfellows; tipsy loquacious veterans, babbling of Rupert and Goring; and the broken regiment of stage-players whose occupation was now gone; all the nondescript population that lived on society in olden times and repayed it in full by making it merry England, were swept up before the military censors, and if they failed to show their respectability and means of livelihood, were sent to prison or banishment. These proceedings were not only unjust but illegal. Thus the rule of the Saints in its latest stage was not a clerical but a military and magisterial inquisition, conducted partly to "discourage and discountenance all profaneness and ungodliness", but partly also "for the preservation of the peace of the Commonwealth", breaking the designs of the enemies thereof.'—TREVELYAN: *England under the Stuarts*, p. 308.

It was because of the treatment meted out first by Parliament and then by the Protector to the general body of rural Cavaliers that Puritanism was allowed no religious or civil status in England at the Restoration.—TREVELYAN: *op. cit.* p. 309.

POPULAR PASTIMES

> Thirdly, it is idolatrous:
> For when men run a-whoring thus
> With their Inventions, whatsoe'er
> The thing be, whether Dog or Bear,
> It is Idolatrous and Pagan,
> No less than worshipping of Dagon.[1]

Possibly bear-baiting and other popular sports were pagan in origin, but even so, and admitting the element of revelry and debauchery which popular amusements are generally invested with, they were in many aspects innocent enough, and it might have been better, one thinks, to purify than to destroy or suppress. Some innocent gaiety went out of life with these old customs and festivals, as Corbet laments:

> At morning and at evening both
>   You merry were and glad,
> So little care of sleep or sloth
>   These pretty ladies had;
> When Tom came home from labour,
>   Or Cis to milking rose,
> Then merrily went the tabour,
>   And nimbly went their toes.
>
> Witness those rings and roundelays
>   Of theirs, which yet remain,
> Were footed in Queen Mary's days
>   On many a grassy plain;
> But since of late, Elizabeth,
>   And later, James came in,
> They never danced on any heath
>   As when the time hath been.
>
> By which wee note the Fairies
>   Were of the old profession;
> Their songs were Ave Maries,
>   Their dances were procession;

[1] *Hudibras*, Part I. Canto 1. ll. 801-820.

> But now, alas! they all are dead,
>   Or gone beyond the seas;
> Or farther for religion fled,
>   Or else they take their ease.[1]

To suppress popular pastimes may operate in two ways. It drives those whom the Puritan would call carnally-minded to coarser pursuits. Puritan countries like Scotland have not been notable for sobriety and chastity. When allied with the stimulation of religious excitement suppression makes for hysteria; witness the record of revival campaigns in Wales and other countries. No student of the religious history of the Commonwealth—the doings of Ranters, and Seekers and Quakers—making full admission of the sincere spirituality of many of them, the real value of the work of the Quakers—to say nothing of Anabaptists and Fifth Monarchy men, with their ravings and incitements to murder and massacre, or the horrible excesses at Tredah and Drogheda—no student can deny that there was an hysterical spirit abroad, if some men used religious enthusiasm as a cloak for native cruelty and greed. And as for immorality, we have heard and read so much of the licence and immorality in Courtly circles after the Restoration that it is only fair to recall that there are many evidences of a general lowering of morality in the later years of the Commonwealth. Barebones' Parliament met in 1653 for the great task, Carlyle tells us, of 'the introducing of the Christian Religion into real practice in the social affairs of this nation. Christian Religion, Scriptures of the Old and New Testament: such for many hundred years has been the universal

---

[1] *A Proper New Ballad, intituled The Faeryes Farewell; or, God-a-mercy Will*, vv. 3-5.

solemnly recognised Theory of all men's affairs: theory sent down out of Heaven itself: but the question is now that of reducing it to practice in said affairs; a most noble surely and most necessary attempt which should not have been put off so long in this Nation! We have conquered the enemies of Christ; let us now in real practical earnest set about doing the Commandments of Christ, now that there is free room for us.'[1] Well, one of the few actions of this Christian Parliament was the institution of civil marriage, a promise before a Justice of the Peace, no other marriage to be valid,[2] which to the mass of people of that day was equivalent to the abolition of marriage; and a recent writer points out that the murder of bastard children by their mothers had become so frequent that in 1655 the 'Lord Mayor ordered a precept on the subject to be read in all the Churches of London on Sunday February 11, together with the Statute of Child Murder of 21 James I.' In 1658 'a writer seriously proposed to Cromwell that he should introduce polygamy as a remedy', adding as an inducement, 'you shall want no other ram to batter the walls of Rome'. 'On January 22, 1658, Cromwell ordered a Committee to consider of the book concerning polygamy and to report.' Milton, you will remember, would have had polygamy sanctioned. The kind of sermon which

[1] Carlyle, *Oliver Cromwell's Letters and Speeches*, Letters clxxxix.-cxci.

[2] 'I know not how I stumbled upon a new's book this week and for want of something else to doe read it. . . . I met with something else in it that may concerne any body that has a minde to marry, 'tis a new form for it, that surely will fright the Country people Extreamly, for they aprehend nothing like goeing befor a Justice; they say noe other Marriage shall stand good in Law; in conscience I beleeve the olde is the better, and for my part I am resolved to stay till that com's in fashion againe.'—DOROTHY OSBORNE: Letter 34 (Moore Smith), 1928.

Evelyn describes (November 2, 1650) was not such as would stay this or other social evils. 'There was nothing now preached practical or that pressed reformation of life, but high and speculative points and strains that few understood, which left people very ignorant, and of no steady principles, the source of all our sects and divisions, for there was much envy and uncharity in the world. God of his mercy amend it! Now indeed that I went at all to Church while these usurpers possessed the pulpits, was that I might not be suspected for a Papist, and that, though the minister was presbyterianly inclined, he yet was, as I understood, duly ordained, and preached sound doctrine after their way, and was besides an humble, harmless, and peaceable man.' For Communion he went to some private assembly of those who used the banned and anti-Christian Book of Common Prayer. '20 December I went to London to receive the Blessed Communion this holy festival at Mr. Wild's lodgings, where I rejoiced to find so full an assembly of devout and sober Christians.' On one such occasion 'the chapel was surrounded with soldiers, and all the communicants and assembly surprised and kept prisoners by them. . . . In the afternoon came Colonel Whalley, Goffe and others to examine us one by one. When I came before them they took my name and abode, examined me why, contrary to the ordinance made that none should any longer observe the superstitious time of the Nativity (so esteemed by them) I durst offend, and particularly be at Common Prayers which they told me was but the Mass in English, and particularly pray for Charles Stuart for which we had no Scripture. . . . These were men of high flight and above ordinances, and spoke spiteful things of our

Lord's Nativity. As we went up to receive the Sacrament the miscreants held their muskets against us as if they would have shot at the altar.' A little later he notes: 'There was now a collection for persecuted Ministers of the Church of England whereof divers are in prison. A sad day! The Church now in dens and caves of the earth.'

With Cromwell's death the restraining power of the Army and the Saints began to disintegrate. As Baxter and his Presbyterian colleagues passed through the streets of London to congratulate Monk on his policy they felt that the spirit of licence and debauch was abroad. Of the rejoicings on the night when Monk had declared for a free Parliament and the doom of the Rump was pronounced, Pepys says 'indeed it was past imagination both the greatness and the suddenness of it. . . . All along burning and roasting and drinking for rumps. . . . Bowbells and all the bells in all the Churches were a-ringing.' Of the details of what followed it is not my business to speak at length. Anglican and Presbyterian had combined to bring home the King, weary of the excesses of soldiers, sectarians, and fanatics; but all efforts at conciliation and compromise failed with consequences of far-reaching effect for the history of the English people at home and in America. History has placed the blame, and not without considerable justification, on the Bishops and the exasperated spirit of an oppressed and insulted Church suddenly restored to power. But a candid reader of Baxter's elaborate statements will, I think, feel that what the Presbyterians demanded came to a fairly complete surrender of the whole position for which the Anglican Church stood as a reformed but still Catholic and historic church; and would also, as Arnold maintained, have imposed upon her just those doctrines of Predestination and Justification by the Imputed Righteousness of Christ, from which the finest Puritan spirits in the Cambridge Platonists had revolted. Whatever its faults and its errors of policy, for which it had paid and was to pay dearly, the Church of England was even at the Savoy Conference defending the more liberal, the more Humanist, interpretation of the Christian creed and spirit. 'For the Church of England,' says Chillingworth, 'I am persuaded that the constant doctrine of it is so pure and orthodox, that whosoever believes it and lives according to it, undoubtedly he shall be saved; and that there is no error in it which may necessitate or warrant any man to disturb the peace or renounce the communion of it. This in my opinion, is all that is intended by subscription.' The misfortune is that the Bishops could not trust sufficiently to the attractive power of a humane creed and a beautiful ritual, and grant that toleration outside the Church to which they were to be driven later when feeling was embittered and prejudice hardened. But toleration no one understood. Even Baxter, when asked by Charles 'that others also' beside Anglicans and Presbyterians 'be permitted to meet for religious worship, so be they do not go to the disturbance of the peace; and that no Justice of Peace or Officer shall disturb them': in a word, that toleration be extended to Roman Catholics and other orderly worshippers—even Baxter said 'no'. 'As we humbly thank your Majesty for your indulgence to ourselves, so we distinguish the tolerable parties from the intolerable. For the former we humbly crave great lenity and favour; but for the latter, such as Papists and Socinians, for our part we cannot make their toleration our request.' So Baxter gave away the cause of toleration. Even Milton, who had maintained 'that it is not lawful for any power on earth to compel in matters of religion', excepts Catholicism from toleration—at first on the grounds, political rather than religious, that 'their religion the more considered the less can be acknowledged a religion, but a Roman principality rather endeavouring to keep up her old universal dominion under a new name and mere shadow of Catholic religion' (1659); but later, when Charles's policy was making 'all Protestant hearts to tremble', he places the refusal on religious grounds also: 'toleration is either public or private, and the exercise of their religion, as far as it is idolatrous, can be tolerated neither way' (1672). Whatever disgust there may have been with Puritan tyranny, there was no English movement towards Rome. The memories of Queen Mary's reign and the fear bred by Jesuit policy abroad were too potent factors, as Charles's failure to secure the support of even the Nonconformists for a toleration which included Catholics was to show.

But the conflict of the Churches was already beginning to take a subordinate place, becoming political in character rather than religious. The full tide of fervour and fanaticism had spent itself. For all Protestants toleration was soon to come, if limited in scope and leaving the Nonconformists subject to galling disabilities, for which the Anglican Church has had to pay a heavy penalty. A change had come over the whole spirit of the age. The last and greatest consequence of the revival of learning and the Renaissance, the recovery of the scientific mind of the Greeks, was in evidence. The Royal Society was founded and Descartes and Locke were formulating the philosophy of rationalism, of the *Aufklärung*. It remains to ask what was the effect on the mind of Englishmen, as expressed in literature, of the attempt at suppression of its secular interests, the compelled preoccupation with the things of the spirit. If the spirit refuse to allow the flesh its due, if other-worldly interests are to obscure altogether our interests in this world, the effects are evil for both. The spirit, the world, the flesh, each has its legitimate claims; the devil is the spirit of separation, which would tempt each to claim self-sufficiency, or even absolute dominion. This, if anything, is the lesson of the literature of the years following the Restoration.

During the twenty years of the Commonwealth, polite secular literature may be described as marking time. Through the pages of the *Stationers' Register* flows a dense, turbid stream of theological treatises, sermons, and collections of sermons, with some religious poetry by the Puritan Wither or Anglicans such as Benlowes, Beaumont, and Henry Vaughan. But secular literature is in evidence also. The theatres were closed, and booksellers took the opportunity of printing plays, no longer restrained by the interests of the players, and reprinting those which had already appeared: for if one might not see, one might read—plays were not the Book of Common Prayer. Poems too, by young courtiers, were collected and published—Lovelace, Suckling, Carew, Herrick—poems which had circulated in manuscript. Witty anthologies continued to be issued, their contents drawn mainly from earlier Jacobean and Caroline poets. There is no savour of Puritanism in these, even when the authors are the nephews and pupils of John Milton, John and Edward Philips. The wit is of the old cut and the humour of a coarseness, at times a filthiness, which goes some way to justify Mrs. Hutchinson's description of the taste of the Court of James I., from which a good deal of it dates. The Court had gone under, but the old fashions were still in vogue. New refinements and extravagances of wit and compliment are the ideals of a young Cambridge poet like the author of *Amanda* (1653). Poetry went its own way, in lyrics or would-be Heroic poems, showing the influence of the Greek romances, no longer of the mediaeval chivalrous and courtly romance that had still delighted Ariosto, Tasso, and Spenser. The sacred and the secular are kept in different compartments: in the poems, for example, of such a light-hearted and charming poet as Herrick, the greatest of the later 'Sons of Ben', or the more trivial yet not valueless verses of Patrick Cary. There was no attempt at such an interpenetration of the secular and sacred as Spenser had dreamed of, and which, whatever we may think of Spenser's success or failure, is the index of a movement in which religion promises to give fresh colour and enrichment to the whole range of experience.

The best of the poets, as of those who used the other harmony, like Sir Thomas Browne and Izaak Walton and Jeremy Taylor and Fuller, were Royalists—with always the great exception of Milton, and he had laid aside poetry to fight in the forefront of religious freedom and republican government. They were either abroad with Charles, as were Crashaw, Denham, Davenant (captured and imprisoned in 1650, when *Gondibert* had already appeared), Waller (who returned to England in 1651), Cowley; or they stood aside, lookers-on, with sympathies drawn one way or another, but all, except Milton, hating the sectarian turmoil, and desiring the return of the King, or, if that were hopeless, inclined to acquiesce in the rule of Cromwell as the best guarantee of peace. It is clear from Baxter that, the moment war actually broke out, many, whatever their sympathies, drew back, and would fain have remained at least neutral; that others were driven over to the Parliamentary cause only by the excesses of Prince Rupert's undisciplined troopers.[1] It is a little difficult for us, with our recent experience of the omnivorous demands and all-absorbing interest of war, to understand how Evelyn, after war had actually broken out, could calmly procure 'a licence of his Majesty, dated at Oxford, and signed by the King, to travel again', and spend the years of warfare travelling as a virtuoso. In such circumstances, one would have imagined that the King would have gently suggested that 'those who are not with me are against me'. But when Evelyn returned in 1647 from his elegant tour, and found the King in prison, he merely remarks: 'I came on the tenth to Hampton Court, where I had the honour to kiss his Majesty's hand and give him an account of several things I had in charge, he being now in the power of those execrable villains who not long after murdered him.' It may be that Evelyn had been charged with secret missions abroad. Marvell, too, was self-exiled during the years of active warfare.

If Denham, Davenant, and Waller seemed to Dryden, looking back, the poets who prepared the way for a new fashion in wit and verse, the poets who best maintained through this troubled period the Jacobean and Caroline tradition in wit and feeling are Marvell and Cowley. They both, with Browne and, in a simpler way, Walton, and, among the clergy, Taylor and Fuller, represent the combination

[1] An excess deplored as much by Chillingworth as by Baxter. See the *Works of William Chillingworth*, Oxford, 1838, vol. iii. *Sermon I.*

of culture and seriousness, a love of literature and a sober piety, to which the Anglican *via media* conduced. Marvell is the most Puritan, but, though he rallied more whole-heartedly to Cromwell, he was throughout a Royalist and an Anglican. His few religious poems, *The Resolved Soul and Created Pleasure, On a Drop of Dew, A Dialogue between the Soul and the Body*, are to my mind the finest Puritan poems written in the century, after Milton's early *At a Solemn Music, To Time*, and the best things in *Comus*: not so bitter as Milton's later poetry; concerned, like his, with the perennial conflict of soul and sense, the assertion of spiritual and ethical values; unhampered by doctrines of the eternal decrees and imputed righteousness, or extravagances of emotional conversion, and the inner sense of sin and salvation—poems, perhaps, more ethical than religious, if the two must be distinguished. In his secular poems, written in the delightful security of Appleton House, where he was tutor to the niece of Fairfax, whom the execution of Charles had driven into retirement, Marvell is, like Cowley, a virtuoso enjoying the play of wit which was the fashion, but not taking either that, or the love of which they both sing, too seriously. Marvell is the author of one of the best of the 'metaphysical' love-poems, *To his Coy Mistress*, but the mistress is imaginary. 'On ne badine pas avec l'amour' in this fashion, if the passion is a real one. Marvell's heart was not here. Where it was when he wrote these earlier poems is clear enough—in Nature, retirement, and the innocence and beauty of childhood. If Marvell has, less than the mystic Vaughan, the inclination to read into Nature his own spiritual intuitions and aspirations, he shows in *The Garden* something of Shelley's desire to escape from the complexities and exactions of humanity into the simpler, freer life of natural things:

> Here at the Fountain's sliding foot,
> Or at some fruit-tree's mossy root,
> Casting the Body's Vest aside,
> My soul into the boughs does glide:
> There like a bird it sits and sings,
> Then whets and combs its silver wings;
> And till prepared for longer flight,
> Waves in its plumes the various Light.

It is the same simplicity and innocence which delights him in children, of whom he writes without any of the religious implications of Vaughan, but with an exquisite sense of the beauty of the closed bud from which the woman will unfold in all her power:

> See with what simplicity
> This Nimph begins her golden daies!
> In the green Grass she loves to lie,
> And there with her fair Aspect tames
> The Wilder Flow'rs and gives them names:
> But only with the Roses playes;
>   And them does tell
> What Colour best becomes them, and what Smell.
>
> Who can foretell for what high cause
> This Darling of the Gods was born!
> Yet this is She whose chaster Laws
> The wanton Love shall one day fear,
> And, under her command severe,
> See his Bow broke and Ensigns torn.
>   Happy, who can
> Appease this virtuous Enemy of Man![1]

Lord Falkland was not the only man who in those evil days went about 'ingeminating peace'. The same

[1] *The Picture of Little T. C. in a Prospect of Flowers*, vv. 1 and 2.

longing was in the heart of Baxter and Vaughan, Marvell and Cowley, Benlowes and Walton:

> Peace! Home of Pilgrims, first song at Christ's birth;
> Peace, his last legacy on earth;
> Peace, gen'ral preface to all good; Peace,
> Saints' true mirth.[1]

It was this longing for peace which, as the Royal cause seemed to be utterly defeated, drew men's eyes to Cromwell as the only likely deliverer from the anarchy of jarring sects. Marvell's *Horatian Ode* is a nobler, because a more clear-sighted and just, expression than Milton's sonnet of the impression made, on minds that could rise above prejudice, by the sheer capacity and greatness of 'the War's and Fortune's Son'. If not, like Milton, a theoretical republican, Marvell had perhaps more of the best republican temper, the sense of worth, of the need of virtue to preserve the State. He would not, after eulogising Cromwell as 'our chief of men', have deserted him on the single issue of an endowed clergy, and described his rule as 'a scandalous night of usurpation'.

Cowley was a more ambitious virtuoso than Marvell. From the time he read Spenser as a boy, Cowley's chief interest was in poetry as an art:

> When in the Cradle, Innocent I lay,
> Thou, wicked Spirit, stolest me away,
>   And my abused Soul didst bear,
> Into thy new-found World, I know not where,
>   Thy Golden Indies in the Air;
> And ever since I strive in vain
> My ravisht freedom to regain;
> Still I Rebel, still thou dost Reign,
> Lo, still in verse against thee I complain.[2]

[1] Benlowes: *Theophila's Love-Sacrifice.*
[2] *The Complaint.*

He passed from one experiment to another—verse tales, anacreontics, 'metaphysical' love-poems, Pindaric odes, religious epic, essays and verse intermingled. To appreciate Cowley one must resist the temptation to compare him with Donne on the one hand and Dryden on the other, and admire the real virtuosity of his witty poems and the varied rhetoric of his odes and addresses, and even of his tedious epic paraphrase of Old Testament history. But Cowley's temper is more attractive than his art, and that finds its best expression in personal and occasional poems: the temper of a humanist spirit in an age of fanaticism and conflict, enamoured of peace and leisure (Cowley and Marvell are both garden-lovers), turning to the new science, even the lucid if limited philosophy of Hobbes, as to an escape from fanaticism and wire-drawn theology, and withal a pious Christian.

The Restoration was at its outset a restoration of the old order in wit and poetry and drama. The stage opened with plays by Shakespeare, and Jonson, and Beaumont and Fletcher, and Webster, and Middleton, to confine oneself to those which Pepys records; and the greatest poet is Cowley, who, Clarendon tells us, 'had made a flight beyond all men, with that modesty yet to ascribe much of this to the example and learning of Ben Jonson'. But it was soon evident that this revival was a passing phase. Three things become clear as one studies the history and literature of the years after 1660. The first is the new force and savageness which satire had acquired since the days of Hall and Donne and Marston. The conquered and mulcted Cavaliers had avenged themselves on Pym and Parliament, Cromwell and the saints, Presbyterians and Anabaptists by a constant succession of satiric songs and verses, which culminated in the savage outburst of scorn and glee which hailed the advent, inglorious history, and final defeat, by Monk, of the Rump. The spirit of these poems passed into Butler's *Hudibras* (1663, 1664, 1678), a remarkable poem, though not to be fully appreciated without some careful study of the history and temper of the time. 'A new book of drollery', Pepys calls it, indicating its relation to the songs and satires with which they were familiar. Butler, one feels, was a bigger man than his poem: a grave, sardonic spirit into whom the iron of rule by saints and hypocrites had entered deeply, but who must like others have been soon disillusioned by the Court of the Restoration; very far (as his *Characters* and *Thoughts* show) from being a mere satirist or droller; a forerunner of Swift rather than a rival of Cleveland. But savage satire was not the monopoly of the Royal party. When the first enthusiasm was over and Pepys and his friends could speak of Cromwell as 'a brave fellow' and contrast the esteem which England had enjoyed under his rule with that to which it was fallen, Andrew Marvell and other satirists wrote as savagely as Butler, and far more brutally and coarsely, of Charles and James and their favourites and mistresses. Dryden was to raise satire to the level of great poetry.

The second fact that emerges is that the wit and fashions of the last age were not to the taste of the returned Court. 'I saw *Hamlet, Prince of Denmark*, played,' says Evelyn on the 16th of November 1662, 'but the old plays begin to disgust this refined age, since his Majesty's being so long abroad.' Pepys, always anxious to square his literary judgements to the fashion of the hour, notes: 'Up and to Deptford by water, reading *Othello, Moor of Venice*, which I ever heretofore esteemed a mighty good play, but having so lately read *The Adventures of Five Hours* it seems a mean thing.' Dryden with all his admiration of the Elizabethan dramatists is in 1667–68 convinced that their manner of writing is harsh and old-fashioned: 'If we yield to them in this one part of poesy' (the dramatic) 'we more surpass them in all the other; for in the epic or lyric way it will be hard for them to show us one such amongst them as we have many now living or who lately were. They can produce nothing so courtly writ, or which expresses so much the conversation of a gentleman, as Sir John Suckling; nothing so even, sweet, and flowing as Mr. Waller; nothing so majestic, so correct as Sir John Denham; nothing so elevated, so copious, and full of spirit as Mr. Cowley. . . . All of them were thus far of Eugenius' opinion that the sweetness of English verse was never understood or practised by our fathers; . . . everyone was willing to acknowledge how much our poesy is improved by the happiness of some writers yet living; who first taught us to mould our thoughts into easy and significant words, to retrench the superfluities of expression, and to make our rhyme so properly a part of the verse, that it should never mislead the sense, but itself be led and governed by it.'[1] Even some of the names here mentioned were too much in a fashion that was passing. Cowley's reputation was short-lived. 'Though he must always be thought a great poet, he is no longer esteemed a good writer,' was Dryden's later judgement. To all later criticism, to and including Sir Walter Scott, a new age of poetry begins with Dryden.

The third thing one feels in the new literature is the lowering of the spiritual temper. Pepys, that strange blend of piety, lechery, and worldliness in

[1] *Essay of Dramatic Poesy.*

SCEPTICISM & CYNICISM

the person of an efficient, honest (as honesty goes) bureaucrat, and an enlightened connoisseur, notes the change at once. 'I perceive my Lord is grown a man very indifferent in all matters of religion, and so makes nothing of these things'; 'at night my Lord came home, with whom I staid long and talked of many things . . . and talking of religion I found him to be a perfect Sceptic, and said that all things would not be well while there was so much preaching, and that it would be better if nothing but Homilies were to be read in the Churches.' The same observer notes with an amused irony how this or that friend goes to the theatre or drinks healths as he would not have done a few months earlier. Charles II.'s Court was not what his father's had been. 'At Court', Pepys notes early, 'things are in a very ill condition, there being so much emulation, poverty, and vices of drinking, swearing, and loose amours that I know not what will be the end of it but confusion. And the clergy so high that all people I meet with do protest against their practice.' But of courtly licence and irreligion it is easy to exaggerate the importance as a symptom of national demoralisation. The irreligion did not go very deep. The Earl of Rochester, the most profane and licentious of them all, died an edifying penitent. Charles and James were both at bottom religious, or superstitious, if licentious. But the religious spirit itself was a lower one. 'Catholicism', says Goldwin Smith, 'debased and in low hands was the religion of kings to whom it promised absolute rule over an unreasoning people, and of voluptuaries to whom it held out hope of salvation through magical rites and deathbed absolution.' The Anglican Church was too intent on securing its power and privileges. Nobody with a deep sense of its spiritual character would have consented to its most sacred and mysterious rite being made a test for office-holders. Nonconformists were scattered and dispirited and divided among themselves. The religious spirit of the English people was far indeed from being dead, as time was to show. Barclay's *Apology for True Christian Divinity* (1678) and Bunyan's *Pilgrim's Progress* (1681) are only two of the deeply religious works of the age. But in those courtly circles which still, if for the last time, were the arbiters of taste and gave its tone to polite literature the prevailing mood was disillusioned and cynical, and I wish to consider the effect, but not in the admittedly immoral work of the dramatists. It is easy to misjudge the Renaissance in Italy or the Restoration in England by concentrating attention on extreme but partial aspects. I would rather consider the work of the great poet of the period, the rightful successor to Spenser and Donne and Jonson and Milton; I mean John Dryden.

CHAPTER IX

JOHN DRYDEN

John Dryden, the Man and the Poet—Dryden and Milton—Puritan Reaction—Collier on the Drama—The Town—Summing up.

DRYDEN occupies a very peculiar position in the roll of English poets. If Spenser be the poets' poet, Dryden might be called the critics' poet, so great is the interest he has always excited in critical historians of our literature. Johnson's peroration to his biography is classical: 'What was said of Rome adorned by Augustus may be applied by an easy metaphor to English poetry embellished by Dryden, *lateritiam invenit, marmoream reliquit,* he found it brick and he left it marble.' In the *Progress of Poesy* Gray selects as the first of English poets Shakespeare, Milton, and Dryden. Sir Walter Scott subscribes to the same estimate: 'I have thus detailed the life of John Dryden . . . who, educated in a pedantic taste and a fanatical religion, was destined, if not to give laws to the stage of England, at least to defend its liberties; to improve burlesque into satire; to free translation from the fetters of verbal metaphrase, and exclude it from the licence of paraphrase; to teach posterity the powerful and varied poetical harmony of which this language is capable; to give examples of the lyric ode of unapproached excellence; and to leave to English literature a name second only to those of Milton and Shakespeare.' We think of Pope as the High Priest of the Eighteenth Century, but Gray and Johnson, the latter a zealous champion of Pope against the denigration of early romantics like the Wartons, are at one in deeming Dryden the greater poet. 'Of genius, that power which constitutes a poet—that quality without which judgement is cold and knowledge inert; that energy which collects, combines, amplifies, and animates, the superiority must, with some hesitation, be allowed to Dryden.' 'Works of imagination excell by their allurement and delight; by their power of attracting and detaining the attention. The book is good in vain which the reader throws away. He only is the master who keeps the mind in pleasing captivity; whose pages are perused with eagerness and in hope of new pleasure are perused again; and whose conclusion is perceived with an eye of sorrow, such as the traveller casts upon departing day. By his proportion of this predomination I will consent that Dryden should be tried; of this which, in opposition to reason, makes Ariosto the darling and the pride of Italy, continues Shakespeare the sovereign of the drama.' 'Remember Dryden and be blind to all his faults,' said Gray to Beattie, to whom he confessed 'that if there was any excellence in his own numbers he had learned it wholly from that great poet, and pressed him with earnestness to study him, as his choice of words and versification were singularly happy and harmonious.' The late Professor Verrall in 1912–13 leaned to the same verdict: 'New competitors have arisen in the nineteenth century. These have not yet been sifted; even if the two great Poet Laureates of last century, Wordsworth and Tennyson, obtain two hundred years—and perhaps they will not obtain more of permanent interest, their work can hardly be of higher value than that of Dryden.' Some of our younger critics and poets have rallied to the same allegiance: 'Homage to John Dryden' is the cry of critics, like Mr. Eliot and Mr. van Doren—to John Dryden even when his rival is John Milton.

If by interest we mean interest, not historical only (and that is great) but the spontaneous interest we take in the exhibition of great and various gifts, of a master in his craft; if the admiration with which another artist, or a connoisseur, or every admirer in some measure, regards brilliant achievement, is a factor in our aesthetic enjoyment of a work of art (as I myself tend to believe, though it has been denied by artists and critics and philosophers), then I admit to the full the great interest of Dryden's poetry. But if that is not all, or even the chief element, if there is something more vital in the vision in which the work of art has its origin, and which with greater or less fullness it conveys to the reader or contemplator or listener, then I for one cannot accept the verdict that Dryden is a great poet in quite the same sense of the word as Chaucer and Spenser and Shakespeare and Milton and Wordsworth and Keats. There is some deficiency in Dryden's poetry which Wordsworth and Arnold, both true poets, felt; and in such judgements on poetry I prefer the verdict of the poet to that of the critic, however cultivated.

But before I begin to develop my argument as in some measure the *advocatus diaboli*, from no ill-will to Dryden but in the quest of my theme, the reaction of the spiritual temper of an age on even a true poet, let me first delight myself by citing some examples of his high poetic merits, merits which I am prepared to admit even when passing to his work from that of Milton and Shakespeare. The merits of Dryden's diction and verse began soon to be evident. Even in the *Astraea Redux* and other of his early panegyrics are lines with the sweetness and elegance of Waller, and more not only of energy but of imagination, and a keener sense of the beauty of words and images and cadences:

> How shall I speak of that triumphant day
> When you renew'd the expiring pomp of May?
>
> . . . . .
>
> And now time's whiter series is begun
> Which in soft centuries shall smoothly run:
> Those clouds that overcast your morn shall fly,
> Dispell'd to farthest corners of the sky.

or from the *Panegyric on the Coronation*:

> Time seems not now beneath his years to stoop,
> Nor do his wings with sickly feathers droop:
> Soft western winds waft o'er the gaudy spring,
> And open'd scenes of flowers and blossoms bring
> To grace this happy day while you appear
> Not king of us alone but of the year.
>
> . . . . .
>
> Music herself is lost; in vain she brings
> Her choicest notes to praise the best of Kings:
> Her melting strains in you a tomb have found,
> And lie like bees in their own sweetness drown'd.
> He that brought peace, and discord could atone,
> His name is music of itself alone.

Even when compared with Milton's grand style so full of classical artifice, and Shakespeare's, pestered, as Dryden says somewhere, with metaphor and hyperbole, there is beauty in this writing, so idiomatic, so natural in phrase and order of words, and withal so dignified and musical.

But Dryden's style was to gain in vigour and variety, in conversational ease and oratorical elevation. To the question was Dryden a poet it is sufficient to quote from almost any work he produced. I will content myself with one or two passages, leaving the satirist for the moment aside: and first from his lines on the young poet Oldham, Virgilian in their dignity and beauty:

> Farewell, too little and too lately known,
> Whom I began to think and call my own:
> For sure our Souls were near alli'd, and thine
> Cast in the same poetic mold with mine.
> One common Note on either Lyre did strike
> And Knaves and Fools we both abhorr'd alike.
> To the same Goal did both our Studies drive:
> The last set out the soonest did arrive.
> Thus *Nisus* fell upon the slippery place,
> While his young Friend perform'd and won the Race.
> O early ripe! to thy abundant Store
> What could advancing Age have added more?
> It might (what Nature never gives the Young)
> Have taught the Numbers of thy Native Tongue.
> But Satire needs not those, and Wit will shine
> Through the harsh Cadence of a rugged Line.
> A noble Error, and but seldom made,
> When Poets are by too much force betray'd.
> Thy gen'rous Fruits, though gather'd ere their prime,
> Still show'd a Quickness; and maturing Time
> But mellows what we write to the dull Sweets of Rhyme.
> Once more, hail and farewell! farewell thou young,
> But ah! too short, Marcellus of thy Tongue!
> Thy Brows with Ivy and with Laurels bound;
> But Fate and gloomy Night encompass thee around.

If it is dramatic as well as poetic power one seeks, then read the speech of Sigismunda over the heart of her lover:

> Source of my Life and lord of my Desires,
> In Whom I liv'd, with whom my Soul expires!
> Poor Heart, no more the Spring of Vital Heat,
> Curs'd be the Hands that tore thee from thy Seat!

JOHN DRYDEN

The Course is finished which thy Fates decreed,
And thou from thy Corporeal Prison freed:
Soon has thou reached the Goal with mended Pace;
A World of Woes dispatch'd in little space:
Forced by thy Worth thy Foe, in Death become
Thy Friend, has lodged thee in a costly Tomb;
There yet remain'd thy Fun'ral Exequies,
The weeping Tribute of thy Widow's Eyes;
And those indulgent Heav'n has found the way
That I, before my Death, have leave to pay.
My Father even in Cruelty is kind,
Or heaven has turned the Malice of his Mind
To better uses than his Hate design'd:
And made th' Insult which in his Gift appears,
The Means to mourn thee with my pious Tears;
Which I will pay thee down, before I go,
And save myself the Pains to weep below,
If Souls can weep. Though once I meant to meet
My Fate with Face unmov'd, and Eyes unwet,
Yet since I have thee here in narrow Room,
My Tears shall set thee first afloat within thy Tomb;
Then (as I know thy Spirit hovers nigh)
Under thy friendly Conduct will I fly
To Regions unexplor'd, secure to share
Thy State; nor Hell shall Punishment appear;
And Heaven is double Heav'n if thou art there.[1]

That is splendid and passionate oratory, and yet I think a sensitive reader will feel the difference between it and dramatic and poetic writing that comes straight from the imagination if he will read the whole poem beside. I will not say Shakespeare's *Othello*, but the last Canto of Chaucer's *Troilus and Criseyde*. Nothing in the rather hard rhetoric with which Dryden's story is told has prepared you for, and so made dramatically convincing, this brilliant outburst. Chaucer has not more eloquent speeches, but he is sensitive to every turn in the story, every

[1] *The Fables*, Sigismunda and Guiscardo, 651-680.

movement of Troilus' anguished heart. The speeches seem to come from Troilus himself, not to be eloquent flights of the poet.

Lastly, to illustrate how near the sublime Dryden can come, let me cite his lines on the Roman Catholic Church:

> One in herself, not rent by Schism, but sound,
> Entire, one solid, shining Diamond,
> Not Sparkles shatter'd into Sects like you,
> One is the Church, and must be to be true:
> One central principle of Unity,
> As undivided, so from errors free,
> As one in Faith, so one in Sanctity:
>
> . . . . . .
>
> Thus one, thus pure, behold her largely spread
> Like the fair Ocean from her Mother-Bed;
> From East to West triumphantly she rides,
> All Shoars are water'd by her wealthy Tides.
> The Gospel sound diffus'd from Pole to Pole,
> Where winds can carry, and where waves can roll.
> The self same doctrine of the Sacred Page
> Convey'd to ev'ry clime in ev'ry age.[1]

If these are not the verses of a poet it would be hard to say what are; and to do full justice to Dryden one must emphasise his range—satire, argument, lyric, and ode. And yet, *some* want has made Dryden fall short of the greatest poetry, and that want is, I think, the want of his generation, at least of the audience for which he catered with such abundance and variety, the want of spiritual content. Dryden believes in nothing, is interested in nothing, except it be good verses:

> Trust to good verses then,
>   They only will aspire,
> When pyramids as men
>   Are lost i' the funeral fire.

[1] *The Hind and the Panther*, II. 526-532, 548-555.

JOHN DRYDEN

> And when all bodies meet
> In Lethe to be drown'd,
> Then only numbers sweet
> With endless life are crown'd.

So says Herrick and not without truth; but both he and Dryden are proofs that it is not quite all the truth, that technique is not everything, that there is also the content, the spirit of the work, what it does communicate, on the character of which will also depend a great deal of what is subtlest and finest in the workmanship. Dryden is preeminently the poet by whom to judge the doctrine of art for art.

Mr. van Doren, in his excellent study, has claimed that Dryden, like Spenser, is a poets' poet. In a sense that is true. Poets of the most diverse kinds have learned from Dryden, and admitted their debt—Pope, Gray, Churchill, Byron, Keats. Yet Dryden is not a poets' poet in the same way as Spenser. Lockhart was nearer the truth when he spoke of Dryden's enduring popularity with 'those who make literature the chief business or solace of their lives'. For Spenser owes the title, not even primarily, to his great influence on other poets, though that is greater than Dryden's or any other poet's, but to the remoteness of the imaginary world to which his poetry conveys us from the actual world in which we dwell. 'Of all poets', says Hazlitt, 'he is the most poetical. . . . If Ariosto transports us into the regions of romance, Spenser's poetry is all fairyland. In Ariosto we walk upon the ground in company gay, fantastic and adventurous enough. In Spenser we wander in another world, among ideal beings. The poet takes us and lays us in the lap of a lovelier nature, by the sound of softer streams, among greener hills and fairer valleys. He paints nature not as we find it; and fulfils the delightful promise of our youth.'[1] I do not know that I should put it just that way, if I had had the eloquence of Hazlitt. There is too little of the beauty of nature in Spenser; but the criticism does indicate the charm of Spenser's poetry when it comes closest to music and painting, and leaves morality and reality to look after themselves. And Hazlitt's words describe well what he and Lamb meant by calling Spenser 'a poets' poet'. Could you transfer the epithet in this sense to Dryden? Is one ever far from London and the Coffee Houses and the stream of life and politics in his poems of any kind? Can you read far in any of the most serious and heroically pitched without being reminded at every turn of the wit and the satirist? '*Absalom and Achitophel* is more than a satire, it is an heroic poem,' says the late Professor Verrall; 'the speeches are proper to epic or grave drama, such as we should expect in a heroic poem or play and not a satire. Occasional archaisms . . . point directly to the influences of the English epics, *The Faerie Queene* and *Paradise Lost*—the last just then coming, with Dryden's help, into fame and vogue.'[2] The influence of Milton indeed is unmistakable in the whole cast and texture of Dryden's poem, in the character of Achitophel and the Whig leaders, and in the temptation of Absalom. Yet one cannot read far in the mood evoked by the study of *Paradise Lost* without receiving a jar to that mood, without coming on a line which is characteristic of Dryden at his best but bespeaks the wit and the satirist:

---

[1] Hazlitt: *Lectures on the English Poets*, Lecture II., *On Chaucer and Spenser*.
[2] Verrall: *Lectures on Dryden*, 1914.

JOHN DRYDEN

They led their wild desires to woods and caves,
And thought that all but savages were slaves.
The Jewish Rabbins, though their enemies,
In this conclude them honest men and wise;
For 'twas their duty, all the learned think,
To espouse his cause, by whom they eat and drink.

. . . . . .

The Egyptian rites the Jebusites embrac'd,
Where Gods were recommended by their taste.

. . . . . .

And nobler is a limited command,
Given by the love of all your native land,
Than a successive title, long and dark,
Drawn from the mouldy rolls of Noah's ark.[1]

What *Absalom and Achitophel* reminds one of, quite as much as of *Paradise Lost*, is a political, platform speech, not of Burke, who in his greater passages is more Miltonic than Dryden, but, say, of Lord Beaconsfield. There is the same blend of dignity and elevation with passages of direct, incisive, effective satire; the same magnanimity (Pope and Gladstone were more intense and savage); and both in the higher flights and the satiric onslaughts the same touch of the conscious artist, as of one contemplating even as he speaks the admirable point of his own wit, the eloquent turn and cadence of his sentences. Indeed there is a good deal of resemblance between Disraeli and Dryden as men, if Disraeli were as much the nobler man as Dryden was the greater poet. They show the same strange blend of personal ambition and self-confidence with a superiority to personal sensitiveness and vindictiveness, the same absence of exalted principles and distrust of those who vaunted such lofty motives, whether politicians

[1] *Absalom and Achitophel*, l. 65-66, 104-107, 118-119, 299-302.

or priests. They neither of them loved Saints—
especially political Saints. They were both artists,
aware of what they were doing and enjoying their
own efficiency, more interested in the art, the game
of politics or literature than inspired by great aims,
though each had in his day dreamed of higher things,
an Heroic Poem, a nobler, a less mercantile England.
Dryden had never attempted to justify the ways of
God to men. Disraeli had not Burke's or Gladstone's
flaming zeal for the cause of justice and humanity,
or what they chose to regard as such, though he
sometimes proved himself a wiser man than either,
seeing more clearly than Gladstone what prudence
and justice alike demanded of England when feeling
was running high over the civil war in America or
after the mutiny in India.

Dryden's poetry is oratorical, splendid oratory,
argumentative, witty, satirical, weighty, felicitous.
But the difference between such oratory as that of
Dryden and Disraeli and poetry or prose which has
the quality of poetry, the prose of Plato or Pascal or
Donne or Browne, is just that which Matthew
Arnold indicated when he wrote: 'The difference
between genuine poetry and the poetry of Dryden,
Pope and all their school is briefly this: their poetry
is conceived and composed in their wits, genuine
poetry is conceived and composed in the soul.' This
has been criticised of late by champions of Pope, in
an age that is disposed to exalt once more wit and
cleverness at the expense of imagination and feeling,
as though it were a criticism of Pope's art, and
nothing is more easy than to exhibit and admire the
brilliance of Pope or the power of Dryden. But it is
not that, it is a criticism of the spirit, the imaginative
vision in which their art is rooted. Mr. van Doren,

indeed, declares that Arnold is judging Dryden's work by an implicit comparison of it with his own. Nothing is easier than such a *tu quoque*. The fact is that Mr. van Doren's own brilliant study is just Arnold's sentence 'writ larger'. For what are those false lights by which, he tells us, Dryden was for a time misled, but just the lights which beacon to great poets, the stars by which they sail—Imagination, Passion ('passionate utterance in drama and narrative'), Insight, Vividness of Description? None of these Mr. van Doren will allow to Dryden, nor the finer, inner music of the best poetry. 'Dryden was most at home', he tells us, 'when making statements. His poetry was the poetry of declaration. At his best he wrote without figures, without transforming passion.'[1] But is not this just to give chapter and verse to make good Arnold's criticism, his relegation of Dryden to another class of poets than Dante and Milton and Shakespeare?

With all his great gifts Dryden was not a great poet, because he believed in nothing. Whether it be eulogies or elegies, or heroic play or poem, or satire or religious apologies in verse, all is for him business or art—business inasmuch as he must live and these are the goods in demand, art inasmuch as he has a good craftsman's delight in the exercise of his craft. He never writes as one inspired by his subject in itself, which Dante declares is the secret of great poetry:

> To whom I thus: 'Count of me but as one
> Who am the scribe of love; that when he breathes
> Take up my pen and as he dictates write.'[2]

Dryden's wheels grow hot *with* driving. Once he has

[1] M. van Doren: *John Dryden*.
[2] Dante: *Purgatorio*, xxiv. 52-54.

begun, the pleasure of writing animates and delights him. His eulogies are splendid and outrageous. His willingness to praise has no relation to the worth of the object. He learned from Donne the transcendental style in eulogy, and elaborated it in his own less pedantic and metaphysical, more oratorical and effective fashion. 'He appears never to have impoverished his mint of flattery by his expenses, however lavish. He had all the forms of excellence, intellectual and moral, combined in his mind, with endless variation . . . and brings praise rather as a tribute than a gift, more delighted with the fertility of his invention than mortified by the prostitution of his judgement' (Johnson). Of the prose dedication of the *State of Innocence* to Mary of Modena, the same admirer and critic writes: 'It is written in a strain of flattery which disgraces genius, and which it is wonderful that any man that knew the meaning of his words could use without self-detestation. It is an attempt to mingle earth and heaven by praising human excellence in the language of religion.'

The Heroic Plays have been justly described as 'glorious nonsense'. It was in his dramas that Dryden learned both to reason acutely and to declaim eloquently in verse. But the declamations are so obviously rhodomontade, reveal so little of character or passion, that Fielding's parody in *Tom Thumb* is not more absurd. Dryden knew his Shakespeare well, and as a critic he justly and eloquently preferred him to Jonson and Fletcher; but of all the Elizabethans Fletcher is Dryden's true predecessor and affinity in the combination of swelling rhetoric and spiritual emptiness. In four different scenes, Mr. van Doren points out, Dryden has dramatised quarrels between men on the model of the famous scene in *Julius*

Caesar where Brutus and Cassius jar. Well, read that great scene, the generous humanity of which is emphasised by its immediate sequence to that in which the cold-blooded politicians prick down the names of those who are to be proscribed, and then turn to the quarrel between Hector and Troilus in Dryden's *Troilus and Cressida* (Act III. scene ii.) and enjoy an admirably written piece of fudge, for nothing in the character of either Hector or Troilus has prepared us for such a high-flown quarrel and sentimental reconciliation, or made us care a pin whether they quarrel or not. It is as an exercise in dramatic writing that we admire, as we admire his eulogies of Cromwell or of the 'best of Kings'. Or take Dryden at his very best, in *All for Love*, and compare it with *Antony and Cleopatra*. Dryden's play is well constructed and admirably written, but it rings false throughout. Shakespeare's play is not the work of a moralist. Critics have been rather hard put to it to extract lessons from this glorious romance. Yet the moral implications are left to speak for themselves. If the poet has set forth all the romantic appeal of a world well lost, he has not for a moment left us blinded to the waste and degradation in which Antony is involved, or to the true character of Cleopatra, the splendid strumpet who takes her life in magnificent fashion, not after all for love of Antony, or less for that than because she realises that the day of her conquests is over, that the thin-blooded Octavius is immune to her charms:

> Know, sir, that I
> Will not wait pinion'd at your master's Court;
> Nor once be chastis'd with the sober eye
> Of dull Octavia. Shall they hoist me up
> And show me to the shouting varletry

LYRICS & SATIRES

> Of censuring Rome? Rather a ditch in Egypt
> Be gentle grave unto me! rather on Nilus' mud
> Lay me stark nak'd, and let the water-flies
> Blow me into abhorring! rather make
> My country's high pyramides my gibbet,
> And hang me up in chains![1]

Dryden, as Johnson says, 'by admitting the romantic omnipotence of love has recommended as laudable that conduct which through all ages the good have censured as vicious, and the bad despised as foolish'. And after all Antony's love, as Dryden represents it, is but sentimental rhodomontade. Shakespeare has shown the working of a reckless passion in all its bearings, its splendour, and its waste.

Dryden's lyrics have been praised, and justly, for the variety of their harmony. Dryden and his fellows among Restoration song-writers are the last of a long tradition. And yet to my mind he is also the first writer of operatic songs, glittering rhetoric for musical elaboration. *Alexander's Feast* is a brilliant *tour de force*, the finest piece of noise in English poetry till we come to Mr. Vachel Lindsay, and there is more of true poetry in the *Chinese Nightingale* than in all Dryden's Odes, which are surely not great odes in the same sense as *Intimations of Immortality*, *Dejection*, or *The West Wind*, or the *Nightingale*.

Satire is admittedly Dryden's *forte*, and one may allow that Dryden was quite sincere in his defence of authority and contempt for the mob. Yet even as a satirist one feels that Dryden's art is greater than the temper that informs it. Butler, to say nothing of Swift, is inspired by a deeper earnestness of passion, a sincerer hatred of the hypocrisy he lashes. With Dryden it is all business, admirable in execution, like

[1] *Antony and Cleopatra*, Act v. sc. ii. ll. 52-62.

JOHN DRYDEN

Disraeli's attacks upon Sir Robert Peel. The same is true of his most serious poems, such as *The Hind and the Panther*, a poem full of beauties, but not a beautiful poem. The question has often been asked, was Dryden's conversion to Romanism sincere? That is a question between Dryden and his own conscience and God.[1] We have no right, I think, to dispute it. What we may ask is whether, in the light of his own career, Dryden had the right to constitute himself the critic and satirist of the English Church, the Presbyterians, or the Sects. Butler, one feels, had. He had suffered, and imbibed a deep and sincere hatred of those among whom Dryden was reared, precisians and fanatics; and he was a disillusioned man, a man of the temper of Jonathan Swift, but not irreligious. In *Hudibras* he says nothing scornful of religion as such. Dryden from the outset of his literary career

---

[1] From his earliest writings to his conversion he had pandered to Protestant prejudices or Catholic sympathies as was likely at the moment to be profitable. See Beljame, *Le Public et les hommes de lettres*, 2nd ed., 1897, p. 216 ff., whose summing up is difficult to answer. 'When a man who has been long a sceptic or indifferent, finds himself by a late and sudden illumination enlightened by faith, his new life is affected by the new condition of his soul. Catholic or Protestant religion, when strictly practised, commands respect for certain things, and these things Dryden had but little respected hitherto. To gratify the taste of his contemporaries he had flattered vice and made modesty blush. He felt so well himself what duties were imposed upon him by his conversion that he cried:

Good life be now my task.

One would expect then to see him repent of his errors and bid them adieu for ever. When Racine, in the fulness of his powers, after the success of *Phèdre*, felt himself called to the practice of religion, he abandoned never to return, with a rigour which letters must lament, the works that had won him glory. Dryden who had much more to reproach himself with than Racine remained what he had been. He brought on the stage the *Amphytrion* of Molière, enriching it with lascivious scenes, and in his translations was able to exceed the audacities of Juvenal, to change the daring strokes of Lucretius into revolting cruelties and to introduce indecencies into the Georgics.' 'It is true', the same writer adds in a note, 'that he made the *amende honorable* to Collier in 1700 for his drama. It is at that date I should place his conversion.'

'THE HIND & THE PANTHER'

had spoken of priests as such with unvaried hatred and contempt. 'Thus foolishly did Dryden write, rather than not show his malice to the parsons' (Johnson), a survival, perhaps, of his training as an Independent. He had written of religious topics when they came his way in a manner that to any religious person could appear hardly other than blasphemous:

> The Egyptian rites the Jebusites embrac'd
> Where gods were recommended by their taste,

such is his witty reference to the doctrine of the Real Presence. He had attacked the Catholics in the way of business in *The Spanish Friar*. Of all this he had doubtless on his conversion repented, but it would have become him better to be silent. But, now that he was a Catholic, his pen is at the service of the Catholic Court. At every turn of the poem he follows, he adapts his tone to, the shifting and shifty policy of the Court. To begin with, James had hoped that the Catholics might find shelter under the wing of the Church of England, and, accordingly, in the opening scenes the Catholic Hind is all politeness to the Anglican Panther:

> The Panther, sure the noblest, next the Hind,
> And fairest creature of the spotted kind.

When that policy failed, the endeavour of the Court became to unite Catholics and Nonconformists in a demand for toleration, and Dryden's satire accordingly is directed chiefly against the *via media* and the policy of the Anglican Bishops, especially Burnet. Only in the opening confession, and in the fine lines which I have quoted on the Catholic Church, is the poem touched with grave and sincere feeling. Thus Dryden's most serious and ambitious effort, a poem full of just sentiments and eloquent writing, abounding in art of a kind, is yet a poem written to order, wanting in conviction. Dryden would have better served his cause, in great measure a just cause, by less wit and adroitness, less of politics, and more of religious conviction. No English poet of anything like the same genius and talent has suffered so obviously from what I venture to call spiritual emptiness, by which I do not mean to complain that he did not write specifically religious poetry, but that he had no sense of the ideal, the poetical aspect of any subject on which he wrote—nature, character, politics, or religion. His only Dalilah was his art; but art, like happiness, is apt to elude us if we seek her too consciously for her own sake alone. She is the means by which we express and communicate our vision of the beauty, the value of life and love and nature, our loves and hates, our joys and sorrows. 'Poetry is the breath and finer spirit of all knowledge; it is the impassioned expression which is in the countenance of all science.' Dryden's poetry leaves us with no quickened sensibility, no deepened intuition of the theme on which he writes. 'The power that predominated in his intellectual operations was rather strong reason than quick sensibility. Upon all occasions that were presented he studied rather than felt, and produced sentiments not such as Nature enforces, but meditation supplies' (Johnson), and the meditations, powerfully elaborated and expressed, are of a uniformly mundane character. Neither his loves, nor his hates, rise from the deeper levels of the soul.

In Dryden's work, and in Milton's, we see in different ways the outcome of a long conflict. Milton had entered on the conflict with confidence, almost with exultation. He was to be the poet of a new earth and a new heaven, of a reformation in Church and State that would give to every instinct and faculty of human nature, secular and spiritual, full and free expression. 'When thou hast settled peace in the Church and righteous judgement in the Kingdom, then shall all the Saints address their voices in joy and triumph to thee, standing on the shore of that Red Sea into which our enemies had almost driven us. And he that now for haste snatches up a plain un-garnished present as a thank-offering to thee, which could not be deferred in regard of thy so many late deliverances wrought for us one upon another, may then perhaps take up a Harp and sing thee an elaborate Song to Generations. . . . Come forth out of thy royal chambers, O Prince of all the Kings of Earth, put on the visible Robes of thy imperial Majesty, take up that unlimited Sceptre which thy Almighty Father hath bequeath'd thee: for now the voice of the Bride calls thee, and all creatures sigh to be renew'd.'[1] That is the last great utterance of the longing for and expectation of a 'renovatio', 'renascentia', 'reformatio', which, first given voice to in the preaching of Joachim of Flores and St. Francis, was the beginning of the movement towards Renaissance and Reformation. That was over till a new hope and expectation was awakened by the French Revolution, and the young Wordsworth and others were fired with the belief that Democracy was to effect what the Saints had failed to:

> I with him believed
> That a benignant spirit was abroad
> Which might not be withstood, that poverty

[1] *Animadversions upon the Remonstrants' Defence*, etc.

JOHN DRYDEN

> Abject as this would in a little time
> Be found no more, that we should see the earth
> Unthwarted in her wish to recompense
> The meek, the lowly, patient child of toil,
> All institutes for ever blotted out
> That legalised exclusion, empty pomp
> Abolished, sensual state and cruel power,
> Whether by edict of the one or few.[1]

The hope of a great restoration which had inspired the Jewish prophets in the hour of foreign conquest and during the Captivity, of restoration for the Jewish people, had through Christianity become the hope of the race; and has excited passionate anticipations that have invariably ended in bloodshed and disillusionment, so that the bitterest drop of the cup that Shelley's Prometheus drinks is the consciousness that the would-be benefactors of mankind have brought on men their heaviest afflictions. For nearly twenty years after Milton wrote these words, England, conquered and held down, was governed by the Saints. Scotland and Ireland were subdued as they never had been in history; and the end of it was the outburst of joy and relief which Pepys witnessed in the streets of London, the bitter disillusionment of Milton, the savage satire of Butler, the dissolute Court of Charles and the drama of Wycherley, and the strange spiritual emptiness of the work of the greatest successor to the line of Chaucer, Spenser, Donne, and Milton. The poetry of Dryden wants not only the spiritual fervour of great religious poetry, but the spiritual values of secular poetry, such as Shakespeare's, Spenser's, Milton's—values which Puritan fanaticism had refused to recognise, with

---

[1] *The Prelude,* Book IX. ll. 518-528. The reference is to General Beaupuy (1755-1796), and his walks and talks with the poet at Blois in 1792.

disastrous consequences. The effect of the Puritan attempt to make a nation of saints by means of prohibition and repression is not unlike that described in the Gospel: 'When the unclean spirit is gone out of a man he walketh through dry places seeking rest and finding none. Then he saith I will return unto my house from whence he came out; and when he cometh he findeth it empty, swept and garnished. Then goeth he and taketh to himself seven other spirits more wicked than himself, and they enter in and dwell there; and the last state of that man is worse than the first.' The Puritan condemnation of Shakespeare had only led to giving the English stage Wycherley and Dryden.

But human nature, and not least English nature, abhors excess. Court life and drama and literature was only, after all, an agitation on the surface of the nation's life. Neither religion nor Puritanism was dead. The licentiousness of the stage only increased the number of those for whom the theatre was a forbidden amusement. As he gains in wealth and position Pepys grows very shy of being seen in this so favourite haunt. 'I was in mighty pain lest I should be seen by anyone to be at a play' (Dec. 7, 1666). The main stream of imaginative literature was gradually transferred from the drama to the essay and picaresque story, and so ultimately to the novel of sentimental analysis and contemporary manners.

The protest against licence was first clearly voiced by Jeremy Collier in *A Short View of the Immorality and Profaneness of the English Stage* (1698), a work that it is interesting to compare with Prynne's *Histriomastix* (1633). The first notable thing about it is that the attack does not come from a Puritan in the historical sense of the word but from a high-church-man, and 'high' in a later sense of the word also, as his version of the Communion Office shows, a Non-Juror outlawed for having absolved upon the scaffold two of the Jacobites who had been condemned for their part in a plot to assassinate William. His work, and later Law's *Absolute Unlawfulness of Stage Entertainment* (1716), bear out what I suggested in an earlier lecture, that in their condemnation of the theatre the Puritans were only extreme exponents of the feeling of stricter Christians. To the Christian Church the stage has always been somewhat of a problem. But it is also a proof of the fact that the Puritans were not the only guardians of morality as they boasted, and text-books have taught us. To Evelyn the Puritan preachers seemed to be more intent on high points of doctrine and small points of ritual than on conduct; the Anglican Church a better guardian of sober morality.

In almost every respect Collier's work is superior to Prynne's, especially in the opening parts. Collier allows, as Prynne would never have done, that the drama has, at least theoretically, a function to fulfil: 'The business of Plays is to recommend Virtue, and discountenance Vice; to show the uncertainty of Human Greatness, the sudden turns of Fate, the Unhappy Conclusions of Violence and Injustice. It is to expose the Singularities of Pride and Fancy, to make Folly and Falsehood contemptible, and to bring everything that is Ill under Infamy and Neglect.' This, whatever we may think of it, is the line of defence taken earlier by those who, such as Sidney, Heywood, Randolph, opposed the condemnation of Reynolds, Stubbes, and the rest. The pity is that Collier somewhat illogically seems at the end of his essay to retreat from this position and endorse

Prynne's absolute condemnation of the stage as such.

In the second place, Collier is not so sweeping in his condemnation as the impetuous and ill-informed Prynne. He does not consign Aeschylus, Sophocles, and every other great dramatist to the fire. He distinguishes. Indeed one part of his argument, which he elaborates in a rather pedantic fashion, following Rymer in his *Short View of Tragedy* (1692), is that the ancient drama was superior to the modern in its regard for morality and decency and in the respect shown to religion and the priesthood. Aristophanes he admits to be an exception, but Aristophanes is proved by *The Clouds* to be 'a downright atheist', and Collier, like Addison, is quite sure that 'A Scepticke has no notion of conscience, no Relish for Virtue, nor is under any moral restraint from Hope or Fear. Such a one has nothing to do but to consult his Ease, and gratify his Vanity, and fill his pocket.' Even for the poets of the last age, the objects of Prynne's invective, Collier has a good word to say when he compares them with those of his own day. Shakespeare he judges very severely, misled by Rymer, and shocked by the songs of Ophelia. But he quite approves of the condemnation and fate of Falstaff; and he repeatedly holds up Jonson and Fletcher as a contrast to the profligacy and profanity of the dramatists of the day. Ben Jonson, in the *Dedicatory Epistle of his Fox*, 'declaims with a great deal of zeal, spirit, and good sense against the Licentiousness of the Stage'.

Finally, Collier, unlike Prynne, has read the plays he condemns, and if he is no great critic, and to some extent, as Mr. Whibley says, confounds 'art with life', he has a shrewd wit of his own, and makes his case forcibly and with a generous indignation. Dryden's rhodomontade (which would often be blasphemous if it were to be taken seriously, but blasphemy and indecency with Dryden are business, ingredients necessary to make a play go) is amusingly exposed; and the licentiousness of comedy, which it is idle and impossible to defend on artistic grounds, is attacked by Collier with point and vehemence: 'To sum up the evidence, A fine Gentleman is a fine Whoring, Swearing, Smutty, Atheistical Man. These Qualifications, it seems, complete the Idea of Honour. They are the Top-Improvements of Fortune, and the distinguishing Glories of Birth and Breeding! This is the Stage-Test for Quality, and those that cant stand it ought to be Disclaim'd. The Restraints of Conscience are unbecoming a Cavalier. ... You have here a Man of Breeding and Figure that burlesques the Bible, Swears and talks Smut to Ladies, speaks ill of his Friend behind his Back and betrays his Interest. A Fine Gentleman that has neither Honesty, nor Honour, Conscience nor Manners, Good Nature nor Civill Hypocrisy. Fine only in the Insignificancy of Life, the Abuse of Religion, and the Scandals of Conversation,' etc.

Collier's plea for decency and reverence met with an immediate response from a nation which was far indeed from being either licentiously or irreligiously disposed at heart. In truth the day of the Court as a shaping influence in literature was over. The lyrical and dramatic poetry of the Restoration is the last chapter in the history of Courtly literature. The town took the place of the Court, and the taste of the town, as expressed in, say, *The Tatler* and *The Spectator*, was at least for decency and reverence, and was also affected by a temper which was neither enthusiastic nor licentious, but reasonable, tolerant, moderate.

Some of the most interesting chapters in the *Cambridge History of Literature* are those in which Mr. Routh has traced what he calls the advent of modern thought in our literature, the growth and diffusion of a spirit which reacted from Puritan fanaticism not towards licence but towards moderation, good sense, that spirit which the Anglican Church, as Hooker defined its position, should have stood for, and for which some of the best of its divines pleaded, but which, by its intolerant political attitude and revengeful spirit after the Restoration, the Church had hampered the growth of, stimulating Puritan fanaticism and impoverishing the culture that would have enlarged the mind of the Nonconformists. But the war had quickened this spirit, for 'when bloodshed once began the ordinary citizen realised that civil war was far worse than the victory of either party'. This was the spirit which gradually made impossible the burning of witches and similar superstitions and in the end secured religious toleration, if political, not religious, motives limited the scope of toleration for more than a century.

But this spirit of reasonableness, of distrust of 'enthusiasm', included, though it was not identical with, a more dogmatic spirit, that of philosophical rationalism, which before the end of the century was on the way to become a more formidable foe to Christian orthodoxy and feeling than the passing licence of Court life and literature. Hobbes was the ominous name on the lips of clerical antagonists and Courtly sympathisers, though it is probable that such outspoken and systematic rationalist materialism delayed rather than promoted the growth of the spirit of which it was an outcome. Hobbes had not with him the finest scientific minds of the century, such as Newton, though these were laying the foundations of modern rationalism. The age of the *Aufklärung* was beginning. The conflict between the secular and the religious, of the world and the flesh with the spirit, was shifting its terrain from literature and the arts to science and philosophy. 'The *Aufklärung*', says Troeltsch, 'is the beginning and the foundation of the modern period in European culture in opposition to the hitherto controlling theological and ecclesiastical culture against which, since the end of the Middle Ages, vigorous counter-currents had set in, but which, since the cleavage in the Church, had re-established itself with intensified strength.' The aim and endeavour of the new philosophy would be to shift the sanctions of moral and political life from supernatural and authoritative to natural and rational grounds. The philosophy of the *Aufklärung* represents the first comprehensive conflict with the traditions of the Church and of Antiquity, a conflict in which the protagonists were filled, to begin with, with a confidence in the power of reason to achieve a betterment of the world by an uninterrupted progress such as had never been dreamed of before except by the way of a supernatural interposition. Reason was to do what the Renaissance and Reformation had failed to effect. But this confident rationalism, we can now see, or are beginning to see, was not, as its champions claimed and its antagonists feared, 'the natural and normal form of human thought whenever it is left free to go its own way, but an historically determined product of definite circumstances and conditions. . . . Her methods are determined by the traditions of ancient thought and the new science . . . her proper work is confined to the annihilation of the supernatural element in tradition and the releasing of powers hitherto in chains' (Troeltsch). That is to say, the eighteenth century, an 'age of reason', philosophically of rationalism, would not prove to be an age of final unbelief and secularism; the conflict of the sixteenth and seventeenth centuries was not to end in the final victory of the secular. Rationalism would not prove able to supply humanity with a rounded and sufficient philosophy of life. The Romantic Revival would reassert unsatisfied cravings and needs; and, if romantic hopes were soon disappointed, we have lived to see the foundations of rationalistic materialism crumbling. To a candid student the eighteenth century is far from being the howling wilderness of barren scepticism which it seemed to Carlyle, that strange child of a marriage of Puritanism and rationalism. 'The Eighteenth Century was a Sceptical Century; in which little word there is a whole Pandora's box of miseries. Scepticism means not intellectual Doubt alone, but moral Doubt; all sorts of infidelity, insincerity, spiritual paralysis. . . . That was not an age of Faith—an age of Heroes! The very possibility of Heroism had been, as it were, formally abnegated in the minds of all. Heroism was gone for ever; Triviality, Formulism, and Commonplace were come for ever. . . . An effete world. In one word, a godless world.'[1] That is a sweeping judgement, not an entirely just one. If one must have heroes, I confess I would rather have Howard and Whitfield and Berkeley and Butler and Johnson and Burke and Wilberforce and Bishop Chaloner than Cartwright and Brown and Laud and Pym and Cromwell and

[1] Carlyle: *Heroes and Hero-Worship, The Hero as Man of Letters, Johnson.*

Fox! Yes, even than Milton except for his poetry, or Bunyan except for the *Pilgrim's Progress*. The eighteenth century was a century of great humanitarian movements and witnessed two religious awakenings, the Wesleyan and the Evangelical, precursors of the Catholic revival, Roman and Anglican.

What then is one to say, if one can say anything, on the significance of the conflict so often renewed, which set its mark so deep on the history and literature of the century that we have been considering? It is not a conflict, as it seemed to the religious champions, between good and evil, the battle of the spirit of man and the allurements of the world and the flesh, certainly not that alone. It is a conflict, rather, in which at times the best and sanest elements of man's nature seem to be arrayed against one another or at least to be incapable of logical harmonisation. Is it an ultimate and inexplicable conflict doomed for ever to be renewed, or can one detect any goal, or any point of intersection towards which the divergent curves on which the human spirit seems to move are yet converging?

The first view is well expressed by Ernst Troeltsch, from whom I have so often quoted, and I will translate his words: 'As regards the past, at all events, and the changes in the relation of the two great phenomena which this inquiry has investigated, we have learned to see in this opposition of German Reformation and Italian Renaissance at any rate something typical. It is the original opposition in European life which recurs in ever new forms and with every emergence of great new life-problems remains unbridged. It is the opposition latent in the dual origin of our European world, from the world of Prophetic and Christian religion, and from the spiritual culture of antiquity. It is not a thoroughgoing opposition. From the first intermingling there ran connecting threads from the one to the other; but the opposition is by far preponderant.... The Christian "Ascesis" builds ever anew her kingdom of the supersensible and ranks all natural beauty and personal power beneath a higher world of strength and earnestness to attain which all else must be sacrificed as for the pearl without price of the Gospel. On the other side, ever and again arise in self-assertion the needs and impulses of nature, the aesthetic feeling for the beauty of the world, the tradition of antiquity and the wide-ranging activity of thought which calls everything in question. Therefrom arise again the elements of an ethic more artistic than moral, and metaphysical Pantheisms of the most diverse kinds. But here again the soul can find no rest. Again "Ascesis" raises her head and directs her gaze sometimes in Christian, sometimes to-day in Indian fashion to the great beyond (*das grosse Jenseits der Natur*). A proof may be found in the statement of the investigator who has given us of to-day our controlling picture of the Renaissance, I mean Jacob Burckhardt, who in a more all-embracing view of the field of history closes a great chapter upon the Crises of History with these words: "This whole opposition can only come from the very inner constitution of man. Will the Optimism which has been impressed upon us as an inherited and potent thought last much longer? Or will there come, as the Pessimism of to-day seems to suggest, a general change in men's ways of thinking such as came about in the third and fourth centuries" —*i.e.* the centuries of "Ascesis", of Puritanism?'[1]

Perhaps I had better leave it at that. We have seen

[1] Troeltsch: *op. cit.*

in our literature since the seventeenth century not a few of the connecting threads of which Troeltsch speaks above. No student of the deeper thought and feeling of the English people could confine himself to the study of specifically religious poetry alone, the eighteenth-century hymn-writers or their successors Evangelical, Catholic, and Anglican. He must include the secular poetry and prose of great spirits like Johnson, Burke, Blake, Wordsworth, Shelley, Keats, and others, poets and novelists. But again the connection between secular literature and Christian has been broken. Meredith and Hardy led the way, and a great deal of the secular literature of to-day is definitely un-Christian or anti-Christian, some of it anti-religious; and correspondingly the religious spirit, as one sees in many young writers, is turning to definite Christian doctrine and 'Ascesis', to Thomas Aquinas and Thomas à Kempis. So much only seems to be clear, that both the secular and the spiritual have their imprescriptible rights, that if brought into too sharp opposition, both suffer. It is not by suppression that the spirit wins its victories, but by its power to transmute and transcend.

INDEX

Aeschylus, 97-8, 259
Allegory, value of, 46-7; in Spenser, 47-53; in Bunyan, 47-9, 201-2
Anglican Church, *via media* of the, 204-5; and the arts, 206; defence of reason and learning, 207-9; Anglican sermons, 211-14; Anglican poetry, 215-219; under the Commonwealth, 289, 295-7; after the Restoration, 297
Arnold, Matthew, on Nonconformists, 296

Barclay, R., *Inner Life of the Religious Societies of the Commonwealth*, 188
Barlaeus, Casper, on classical tragedy, 106
Bastard, Thomas, *Chrestoleros*, 169
Baxter, The Reverend Richard, 30, 32, 81, 185-95, 220, 297; and toleration, 298; *Reliquiae Baxterianae*, passim
Bellarmine, Robert, 19 *n.*, 33 *n.*, 272 *n.*
Blunden, Edmund, *On the Poems of Henry Vaughan*, 219
Bridges, Robert, on Shakespeare's audience, 173
Browne, Sir Thomas, 204
Bunyan, John, 47, 196-203, 228, 310

Cambridge Modern History, 131, 277

Carlyle, Thomas, 12, 253 *n.*, 280 *n.*, 295, 337
Cartwright, Thomas, and the Puritan movement, 40-41
Chambers, Sir Edmund, *The Elizabethan Stage*, Oxford, 1923, 69, 71
Chapman, George, 34, 93, 102, 126, 141
Chillingworth, William, 212-214
Christian Literature, Early, The exclusively religious character of, 5-6
Coleridge, S. T., 14, 15 *n.*, 92
Collier, Jeremy, *A Short View of . . . the English Stage*, 332-334
Commonwealth, Literature of the, 300-306
Constable, Henry, Religious imagery in love-poetry of, 137
Court, the, as a literary influence, 42-5, 166-71
Cowley, Abraham, 305-6
Crashaw, Richard, his religious poetry, 180-82
Crashaw, William, and Selden, 78
Cromwell, Oliver, 80, 185 *n.*, 228, 250, 297, 305
Cruttwell, Charles T., on the literature of early Christianity, 5
Cudworth, Ralph, his sermon before the House of Commons, 225-30

INDEX

Dante, 36-7, 52-3, 244-5
Doren, Mark van, *John Dryden*, 318-22
Drama, Elizabethan, 66-129; and Puritan protest, 69-81; Scriptural, 74-7; influence of Puritan disapproval on, 82; Jacobean and Caroline, 127-9
Dryden, John, on the Sects, 175-176, 182; the man and the poet, 311-28

Ford, John, 73, 105, 126, 164
Foster, John, *On the Aversion of Men of Taste to the Evangelical Religion*, 1-4, 29-30, 252

Guthrie, Anna M. B., on Milton as a lover, 155, 162

Herbert, George, 215-17
Herford, C. H., on Shakespeare and marriage, 147; on Milton and Dante as poets of purity, 245
Hobbes, Thomas, 91, 231, 335-336
Hooker, Richard, his defence of reason, 207-9
Huizinga, J., *The Waning of the Middle Ages*, 16; *Tien Studien*, 282 *n.*, 283
Hutchinson, Mrs., *Memoirs of ... Colonel Hutchinson*, 70

Johnson, Dr., on *Paradise Lost*, 252
Jonson, Ben, 34, 92-101, 126

Landor, Walter S., on *Paradise Lost*, 255
Love-poetry, Courtly and Petrarchan, 130-40; religious imagery in, 137-9; Platonic, 140-42; Naturalist, Donne, 142-6; popular in song and drama, 146-8; Puritan, Wither and Milton, 148-62; Restoration, 163-5

Marlowe, Christopher, 84, 85-6, 103
Marvell, Andrew, 303-4
Mary Magdalen, the cult of, in art and literature, 181 *n.*
Massinger, Philip, 100, 126
Middle Ages, cruelty of, 16; dualism of, 18
Middleton, Thomas, 104-5
Milton, John, 25, 59-60; development as a lover and critic of marriage and women, 155-162; on the Court, 170-71; his religious development, 195-196; his life and work, 232-273; early poems, 239-45; and Dante on purity, 244-5; and the meeting of the Long Parliament, 246-7; marriage and consequences, 248-50; and the Presbyterians, 250; *Paradise Lost*, divergent views of, 251-6; Satan, 258-61; the Son of God, 263; the moral of *Paradise Lost*, 265-6; compared with Dante, 268-9; *Paradise Regained*, its tone and thesis, 269-70; *Samson Agonistes*, 270-72; historical significance of Milton's career, 274; his repudiation of Classical Humanism and Protestant Reformation, 276-81; and Ignatius and the Quakers, 281-2; ideals of Society, the Church and Education, etc., 287-8

INDEX

Montaigne, the Humanist, 13-17
Murray, Gilbert, on poetry as *mimesis* and as criticism of life, 98

Neumann, Carl, *Rembrandt*, 177
Newman, Cardinal, on the spirit of secular literature, 4; on Milton, 255

Pascal, and Montaigne, 15; and the Jesuits, 274
Pastimes, popular, 80, 130-132
Plato, and the immoral elements in mythology, compared with the Hebrew prophets, 113
Platonists, the Cambridge, 221-230
Populace, the, their influence on literature and the drama, 172-174
Powicke, F. J., *The Cambridge Platonists*, 222
Praz, Mario, 178, 181-2
Predestination, 24, 182, 189-90; rejected by Milton and Vondel, 196-7; embraced by Bunyan, 197-8
Presbyterians, the spirit of their doctrine and discipline, 182-194; their attitude towards culture and the arts, 192 *n*.
Prynne's *Histriomastix*, 71-81
Puritanism, 23, 24, 40-41, 61; and the drama, 69-81, 118, 192-5, 274; its heroic 'all or nothing', 285-6; reaction against, 289-99

Quiller-Couch, Sir Arthur, on the *Merchant of Venice*, 87

Raleigh, Professor, 255
Reformation, the, 19-28; origin and history of, 282-4
Renaissance, the, 13-19; origin and history, 282-4; end of, 329
Renwick, Professor, on Spenser, 38-9
Restoration, the, spirit and literature of, 306-10
Robertson, J. M., on *Julius Caesar*, 94
Roman Catholic Church, her influence on literature and the arts, 176-82, 192 *n*.
Romance of the Rose, the, 58-9, 133-4

Saurat, Denis, *La Pensée de Milton*, 251, 259, 261, 263 *n*., 281
Schirmer, Walter F., *Antike, Renaissance und Puritanismus*, 23, 203
Secular and sacred, their complete opposition, 33
Selden, John, 78
Shakespeare, William, 13, 22; the moral standpoint of his comedies, 86-9; of the Histories, 89-90; of the Roman plays, 90-95; of the tragedies, 96-122; the moral and religious undertone, 119-26; sonnets, 136-7
Sidney, Sir Philip, *Astrophel and Stella*, 134-5
Smith, Preserved, on Erasmus, 25
Southwell, Robert, his censure of love-poetry, 137-8; his religious poetry, 178-180

INDEX

Spenser, Edmund, and Milton, 25-8; Life and Work, 35-65; *Shepheardes Calendar*, 41-2; *Faerie Queene*, 43-60; *Muiopotamos*, 60; *Amoretti*, 135-6; *Hymn in honour of Love*, 140-141; *Hymns of Heavenly Love and Beauty*, 142; *Colin Clout's Come Home Againe*, 153-4, 171

Te Winkel, Jan, on tragedy and religion, 96, 111
Tourneur, Cyril, 101, 104
Tragedy, the religious significance or implications of, 96-7; Greek, 97-8; Christian and Mediaeval, 99; Biblical, in Elizabethan age, 99-100; Senecan, 100-101; Elizabethan, 101-5; Shakespeare's, 105-122; the conflict of principles or of principle and passion in, 112-18; the conflict in Shakespeare's tragedy, 116-118

Trevelyan, G. M., *England under the Stuarts*, 292 n.
Troeltsch, Ernst, *Renaissance und Reformation*, 11, 189 n.

Vaughan, Henry, his censure of love-poetry, 138-9; his religious poetry, 217-19
Visiak, E. H., *Milton Agonistes*, 257 n.
Vondel, Joost van den, 53, 75, 100, 180, 190

Webster, John, 104
Wither, George, *Fair Virtue* and *Fidelia*, their significance, 149-151
Wolff, Max J., *Shakespeare*, 114, 117
Wood, Anthony à, on music under the Commonwealth, 289-90
Wordsworth, William, his hopes at the outbreak of the French Revolution and those of Milton in 1640, 247, 330

PRINTED IN GREAT BRITAIN BY THE REPLIKA PROCESS BY
LUND HUMPHRIES & CO. LTD. LONDON & BRADFORD